C. & J. KIMMANCE

IN
CHRIST
JESUS

By the same author

When The Spirit Comes
My Father Is The Gardener
Anything You Ask
Faith For The Future
Holy Fire
The Positive Kingdom
Receive Your Healing
Listen And Live
Personal Victory
My Dear Child
My Dear Son
Explaining Faith
Explaining Deception
The Truth That Sets You Free
From Mercy To Majesty
Friends Of Jesus

IN CHRIST JESUS

COLIN URQUHART

Kingdom Faith
HORSHAM, ENGLAND

British Library Cataloguing in Publication Data

Urquhart, Colin
    In Christ Jesus
    1. Theology, Doctrinal
    I. Title
    230   BT77.3

ISBN 1-900409-16-X

Copyright © 1981 by Colin Urquhart. First printed 1981. Ninth impression 1997. All rights reserved. No part of this publication may be reproduced or transmitted in any form or by any means, electronic or mechanical, including photocopying, recording or any information storage or retrieval system, without either prior permission in writing from the publisher or a licence permitting restricted copying. In the United Kingdom such licences are issued by the Copyright Licensing Agency, 33-34 Alfred Place, London WC1E 7DP.

Printed by Indeprint, Guildford for Kingdom Faith Ministries, Foundry Lane, Horsham, West Sussex RH13 5PX. Charity No. 278746. E-mail 106074.700@Compuserve.com.

Cover design by: Mark Oliver Design, 9 Newhouse Business Centre, Old Crawley Road, Horsham, West Sussex, RH12 4SA.

**In thanksgiving to my heavenly
Father for the Bethany Fellowship
and all those who share in the
Kingdom Faith ministry – those
with whom I live out my life
"in Christ Jesus".**

ACKNOWLEDGEMENTS

My thanks are freely given to all those who have helped in the preparation of this book, especially all the members of the Bethany Fellowship, the community in which I lived in Sussex, England. It was in living with the members of that community that I have had to live out the teaching of this book. So this is not spiritual theory. We discover that what God says in His word works when we live it.

I could name many who have been of particular help, but will mention only Vivienne, who did the major part of the typing, David and Charles for their continual encouragement, and Cathy, Marigold, Paul and Brian for their assistance at various stages. The illustrations were drawn by Jeremy, another member of the community.

I praise God for my wife, Caroline, and children, Claire, Clive and Andrea, who were very patient and understanding every time Dad disappeared to write his book.

Finally, my apologies to all those who waited (I hope patiently) for the publication of this book. For over two years I heard of it being on order in bookshops as far apart as Canada and Australia. At last I need have no further pangs of conscience when people ask me "Have you finished that book yet?"

The Bible references are from the New International Version, except where indicated.

CONTENTS

PART 1: WHAT GOD HAS DONE FOR YOU IN JESUS

1.	FREEDOM?	13
2.	THE KINGDOM OF GOD	16
3.	THE GOSPEL OF THE KINGDOM	21
4.	THE CROSS	29
5.	ETERNAL LIFE	36
6.	CONFLICT AND PEACE	43
7.	DEAD	49
8.	AND BURIED	57
9.	COUNT YOURSELF DEAD	64
10.	SPIRIT, SOUL AND BODY	69
11.	IN CHRIST	80

PART 2: YOUR NEW LIFE IN JESUS

| 12. | RECEIVING THE TRUTHS | 89 |
| 13. | SET FREE | 91 |

Alive with Christ; crucified with Christ; old self crucified; baptised into His death; hidden with Christ; dead to the world; dead to the law; no condemnation; free by grace; freedom maintained.

| 14. | WHAT JESUS HAS DONE | 98 |

God loves you; Christ died for you; the veil removed; victory over death; healed; Christ ascended for us; our great High Priest; Jesus the same for ever.

8 *In Christ Jesus*

15. THE RESULTS OF FAITH ... 103
    Righteousness by faith; found in Him; justified through faith; redemption; included in Christ; made alive with Christ; born of God; salvation of your souls.

16. CHOSEN TO BE IN GOD ... 108
    In God; 'In Christ'; the True Vine; a new creation; fulness in Christ; enriched in every way; every spiritual blessing; chosen; raised with Christ.

17. MADE HOLY ... 116
    The will of God; made perfect forever; perfect in Christ; washed, sanctified, justified; our righteousness, holiness, and redemption; sanctified; God's holy nation; God's building; one body.

18. FAITHFUL SONS ... 123
    Sons of God through faith; Heirs; love of the brethren; live as a son; quality of our life in Jesus; light in the Lord; put sin to death; forgiveness; no to temptation; help in temptation; no anxiety; set your hearts and minds on things above; dead to sin; do everything in the name of Jesus; with all your heart; equipped by God; living as Jesus did.

19. LIVING IN OBEDIENCE ... 139
    Continue in Him; purify yourself; living in obedience; loving obedience; abide in love; promise; warning; faith and love; knowledge and insight; continue in Him.

20. STAND FIRM IN VICTORY ... 147
    Weak, yet powerful; submit and resist; freedom; stand firm; strong in grace; be strong in the Lord; peace and victory; more than conquerors; led in triumph; your name in heaven; reign in life; victory.

Contents

21.	PROCLAIM THE VICTORY	158

Overcome the world; faith; the challenge of faith; the prayer of faith; ask 'in my name'; no anxiety; signs; boldness; given all things with Christ; every need met; Jesus – the fulfilment of all God's promises; agreeing together.

22.	YOUR INHERITANCE	168

Faith tested; 'With Him'; resurrection; the fruit of belonging; we shall be like Him; future glory; He will come again; your Kingdom come.

23.	AND SO . . .	176

Abiding; a great promise; God's presence; power over the enemy; forgive; Come to me; God's will for us.

24.	YOUR PORTRAIT IN JESUS	182

Called and chosen by God
Crucified with Christ
You have died
You have new life
You are set free
You are made right with God
You are made holy
What Jesus does for you
You are 'in Christ Jesus'
You live by faith
God lives in you by His Spirit
You live in God's grace
You are to be fruitful in Christ
You are in His love
You are a son of God
As a son you are to live in obedience to God
The importance of God's word for you
You are weak
You are to live in the victory of Jesus

>   You are part of the Body of Christ
>   God will answer your prayers
>   The promise God gives you
>   Your future hope in Jesus

| 25. | CONFESSING THE WORD | 192 |

PART 3: HOW YOU ARE TO LIVE IN JESUS

26.	APPLYING THE TRUTHS	207
27.	SONS AND BROTHERS	222
28.	CALLED TO BE HOLY	229
29.	CALLED TO OBEY	237
30.	OFFER YOURSELF	247
31.	GOD'S DIVIDING WORD	259
32.	FOR THE GLORY OF GOD	271
33.	IN CHRIST TOGETHER	278
34.	THE NEW AND LIVING WAY	287
35.	THE JOY THAT IS SET BEFORE US	298

PART 1

WHAT GOD HAS DONE FOR YOU IN JESUS

1

FREEDOM?

THE DILEMMA
"I'm a failure."

"I am no use to God; I can't think why He bothers with me."

"He wouldn't want to answer *my* prayers."

"I seem to come back to Him asking forgiveness for the same thing over and over again."

Wherever I travel I come across 'defeated' Christians. Should they have to resign themselves to such defeat? Is it possible to know victory over temptation, weakness, futility and spiritual inadequacy? If so, how?

Why do so many, who say they believe in Jesus, have needs that are apparently not met? Does faith in Him really enable us to live in freedom from fear, anxiety, depression, pain, sickness and a continual falling into sin? If so, how can I have that faith in my life?

Many Christians want to live by faith in Jesus in a world full of problems and dilemmas, but feel inadequate and powerless to do so.

AN ANSWER?
We want to be free; free from sin and guilt, pain and sickness, doubt and despair, fear and anxiety. We want freedom to love, to serve, to obey God in the way He desires. Jesus said: "The truth will set you free" (John 8:32). What is the truth to which He refers?

Many imagine that if they know the truth about their problems, they will be set free from them. There can be a ceaseless quest to understand why we are what we are, and why we do what we do. It is thought that, if we can delve deeply enough into the past or the dark recesses of the mind, then we can understand the nature of the problem and be set free from it.

Although modern psychological techniques have been a help to some, they cannot lead to the freedom of which Jesus speaks. The truth to which He refers is the truth of who God is, and what He has done for us. It is this truth that will not only set us free, but will also enable us to continue in freedom, in what Paul calls "the glorious liberty of the sons of God".

People from all over Britain, and from many other parts of the world, visit our community in Sussex. Often they come in desperation, having tried every technique of ministry available, in an endeavour to find a "break-through" in their lives. Often they have received so much ministry in the past that they come feeling defeated, hardly daring to believe that there could be an answer for them.

They are not offered new forms of healing or new prayer techniques; they are directed to the truth of Jesus Christ: what God has done for them through Him, and what He makes them because they believe in Him. Some have been Christians for many years and, although familiar with the scriptures, have never learned how to live in the power of these truths, or to be set free by them.

Within forty-eight hours these people appear different, because they are different; something has happened to them. The Holy Spirit of God has brought the truth of His word to their hearts. They have received the revelation that they needed to set them free and enable them to walk in freedom.

This is not an invitation to visit our community for help! We would be overwhelmed by the response. As you read these pages, pray that God will give you the revelation of His truth that will enable you to live in freedom from failure, fear and doubt. Let Jesus, the Living Word, work in you and set you free with His truth and show you how you can live in His life and power.

If you continue in my word, you are truly my disciples, and you will know the truth, and the truth will make you free. . . . So if the Son makes you free, you will be free indeed (John 8:31–32, 36 R.S.V.).

NEGATIVE ATTITUDES

Most people live by their feelings. God will teach you to live in the truth. Instead of seeing yourself through the mist of your fears and feelings, He will show you how *He* sees you Then you will be able to react positively in situations where before your reactions were negative: "Oh dear!" "How terrible!" "What next!" "I feared as much." "I told you so." "It never rains but it pours."

There is one clause of scripture that has gained universal acceptance: "In this world you will have trouble." However, Jesus continued by saying: "But take heart! I have overcome the world" (John 16:33). In the midst of all his suffering Job said: "What I feared has come upon me; what I dreaded has happened to me" (Job 3:25).

Living in a negative society does not encourage Christians to live by the truth. It is easy to be sucked down by the negative attitudes of those around us while, at the same time, having to fight the naturally negative reactions that go on within us. These truths that will set us free and enable us to continue in freedom will have to take root in our hearts, so that we become positive in our attitudes and able to combat the negativity around us.

We need *to know* not only the truth, but also how to live in *the power* of that truth.

Where does this sense of failure and defeat come from? Is it all the fault of the world in which we live, and the way in which we have been influenced by others? No, God's enemy, and ours, encourages us to be negative and to feel defeated failures. Jesus describes him as the thief who comes to steal, to destroy and kill. He encourages us to believe feelings rather than the words of God, because he knows the power and the truth of these words.

Can we lay all the blame for our negative attitudes on our spiritual adversary? No; we cannot shift the blame away from ourselves. We only react negatively because of the weakness of our human nature. It is this fact that defeats so many – unnecessarily.

It is easy to be aware of our futility before God, of our uselessness to Him; that we are powerless to obey all His commands and to live up to the high standards that He apparently demands. It seems that failure to please Him is inevitable, and that we must accept this fact with resignation.

This attitude denies what God has done for us in Jesus. It shows that we have little understanding of what He makes us, once we have accepted Him and put our faith in Him.

You need to understand these great revelations of the New Testament:

1. What God has done for you in Jesus;
2. The truths about the new life you have in Jesus;
3. How you are to live in Jesus.

Your words of faith: "YOU WILL KNOW THE TRUTH, AND THE TRUTH WILL MAKE YOU FREE."

At the end of each chapter, you will be given words of faith, one or more sentences from scripture that will speak God's truth to your heart. Meditate on these scriptures. Above all, sit down quietly and 'receive them'. Realise that God is speaking His words to you personally. Repeat them quietly over and over again. Allow them to sink deeply into your heart so that they become part of you.

2

THE KINGDOM OF GOD

You cannot forgive your own sin: Jesus has made forgiveness possible for you.

You cannot make yourself acceptable to God: Jesus has already done that.

You cannot make yourself holy: only Jesus can do that.

You cannot please God by your own efforts, no matter

The Kingdom of God

how hard you try: only through Jesus can you please Him.

Jesus is the heart of the Christian faith; without Him there would be no Christianity and we would not be able to know God as our Father. When He began His preaching ministry, His message was direct and to the point:

Repent, for the kingdom of heaven is near (Matt. 4:17).

Jesus is saying three things here:
1. He is speaking of the Kingdom of heaven or the Kingdom of God – both phrases are used in the Gospel accounts.
2. He says that this Kingdom is 'near' or 'at hand'.
3. He calls men to repentance.

1. THE KINGDOM OF GOD

Jesus is the Word that God spoke to bring creation into being. He was with God 'in the beginning' (John 1:2). He was not only with God: 'the Word was God' (John 1:1). With the birth of Jesus the Word of God comes in human flesh, the King of heaven comes to live among men.

The Kingdom of God is where Jesus Christ reigns. He did not attempt to make this world His Kingdom; He brought His reign *into* this world. When the King of heaven came, His Kingdom could be established on earth in a way that previously had not been possible.

2. 'AT HAND'

This Kingdom is, therefore, 'near' or 'at hand'. Heaven had previously seemed out of the reach of men, at least during this lifetime on earth. They hoped for peace and beauty beyond the grave, and some aspired to live lives worthy of attaining such a haven.

When Jesus says that the Kingdom of heaven is near, He is saying something revolutionary. Heaven is now within men's reach. They can enter the Kingdom *now*. More than that; Jesus is specific in teaching that, if a man does not enter the Kingdom now, he will not enter it at all.

3. 'REPENT'

To be part of God's Kingdom means that a man's life must be under His reign, His rule and sovereignty. Instead of living his own life in his own way for his own ends, that man will need to submit himself to the King of heaven to live His life in His way for His ends. That complete change of attitude is called repentance.

Without that repentance, men are unacceptable to God.

> I tell you the truth, unless a man is born again, he cannot see the kingdom of God (John 3:3).

> I tell you the truth, unless a man is born of water and the Spirit, he cannot enter the kingdom of God (John 3:5).

Jesus explains why this is the case:

> Flesh gives birth to flesh, but the Spirit gives birth to spirit. You should not be surprised at my saying, 'You must be born again' (John 3:6–7).

MAN

Jesus does not teach that "everyone will be all right in the end." He does not say that all will go to heaven and be part of His Kingdom.

Are not all men and women children of God? Is it not true that everybody is His from the moment of birth?

All men belong to God in the sense that all creation belongs to Him, for they are part of that creation. But that does not make them God's children. To be a child of God is to know Him, to live in union and fellowship with Him.

Every person born into this world is a sinner. Even the most beautiful and innocent-looking baby will inevitably sin – and it does not take too long to demonstrate the fact! It is not the first sinful action that makes that child a sinner. The child commits that sin because he is expressing the sinful nature with which he was born. He sins because of his sinful nature.

> Surely I have been a sinner from birth, sinful from the time my mother conceived me (Ps. 51:5).

The Kingdom of God

That natural life is sinful because it is centred upon 'self', rather than upon God. 'Self' is the centre of the child's desires and intentions. He is bent upon pleasing himself and having his wishes fulfilled.

We may want to jump to the child's defence and say, "He is only behaving naturally. What else could you expect?" That is the heart of the problem. It *is* natural to please ourselves. But when we act naturally, as a result of the selfish nature with which we were born, we inevitably sin and displease God.

> For all have sinned and fall short of the glory of God (Rom. 3:23).

That shows the destructive nature of sin. Not only does it displease God, it also separates the people He created from the glory that He intends for them. Sin divides men from God. Sinners are alienated from Him; they do not know Him, neither can they enjoy fellowship with Him.

From birth everyone is separated from God. If this was not the case, every man, woman and child would know God naturally. That obviously is not so.

He wants us to know Him, to know His will for us and, out of love for Him, be prepared to fulfil the purpose He has for us. He wants us to be part of His Kingdom and to become His children. First, our sins must be forgiven. Second, the sinful nature with which we were born must be put to death and we must be 'born again'. Then we shall have a new nature and be able to know God and enjoy fellowship with Him.

> It is for this reason that Jesus says: "You must be born again" (John 3:7).

NEW BIRTH

We all share the inheritance of a sinful nature at birth, our lives being centred upon ourselves. We are sinners, opposing God's purposes and in need of His forgiveness. We are unacceptable to Him in our natural, sinful condition, unholy, selfish and disobedient. Without a new birth and the new nature that God gives through that event, a man will continue in his sinful state and remain unacceptable to God. He will not be able to know Him or to please Him.

> I tell you the truth, unless a man is born again, he cannot see the kingdom of God (John 3:3).

Jesus used the phrase "I tell you the truth" to introduce statements about which He was absolutely emphatic and which He knew His disciples would find it difficult to believe. Here He is saying that unless a man is 'born again' he cannot even see the Kingdom of heaven, let alone be part of it. Jesus is emphatic about this. He said:

> The Spirit gives life; the flesh counts for nothing. The words I have spoken to you are Spirit and they are life (John 6:63).

New birth occurs when a man puts his faith in Jesus Christ, in what He has said and what He has done on the cross. It was there that God dealt with our sin and the sinful nature that produces that sin. At the moment of new birth, the believer is 'born of the Spirit'. God Himself comes to live in him. His human spirit is brought to life by God's Spirit.

> Flesh gives birth to flesh, but the Spirit gives birth to spirit. You should not be surprised at my saying, "You must be born again" (John 3:6–7).

If you are a Christian, God wants you to know that you are part of His Kingdom *now*. If you do not already know Him, He is telling you that His Kingdom is at hand: you can reach out and take hold of it. He wants you to be 'born again'. If you have already experienced that second birth, He wants to teach you how to live in the power of the new nature that He has given you.

Your words of faith: "REPENT, FOR THE KINGDOM OF HEAVEN IS NEAR." "YOU MUST BE BORN AGAIN."

3

THE GOSPEL OF THE KINGDOM

All the teaching of Jesus is, in one sense, teaching about the Kingdom of heaven, of God's rule and reign in the hearts and lives of those who love Him. The Gospel is the good news of the Kingdom of God.

There are many scriptures which speak of the Kingdom of God as coming in the future. These do not contradict all those that speak of the Kingdom as a present reality. It is God's purpose for His people to experience the new spiritual birth by which they are born into His Kingdom. He wants them to live out their lives in the power of that Kingdom life.

However, during our time on earth we only begin to taste the glory of God's reign. The Kingdom will come fully and finally when the King comes again, as He has promised. He comes in the weakness of a human body to secure our salvation; He will return in power and triumph and great glory. And those who belong to Him will reign with Him.

THE KINGDOM OF GOD

has come	comes	will come fully
with Jesus	in the lives of those who believe in Him	when Jesus comes again

It is not our purpose to discuss this future dimension of the coming of the Kingdom, but to discover what it means to enter that Kingdom now and to live in the power of Jesus the King.

PARABLES

One of the forms of teaching Jesus used was the parable, and many of the parables He told concerning the Kingdom are recorded in the first three gospel accounts.

> Jesus spoke all these things to the crowd in parables; he did not say anything to them without using a parable (Matt. 13:34).

However, the meaning of these parables was not self-evident.

> The disciples came to him and asked, "Why do you speak to the people in parables?" (Matt. 13:10).

The disciples could see clearly that not all the people were able to understand what Jesus was saying. Perhaps they were politely suggesting that He change His method of teaching. After all, a good teacher should surely teach in such a way that people are able to understand Him?

But Jesus makes it clear that He uses this method because it is not His intention that everyone who hears Him should understand this revelation of the Kingdom of heaven as a present reality.

> He replied, "The knowledge of the secrets of the kingdom of heaven has been given to you, but not to them" (Matt. 13:11).

The power and authority of this Kingdom is so dynamic that it is not for everyone, but only for those who respond in faith to the Lord Jesus, who follow Him as His disciples. The disciples had a hidden motive in asking this question of Jesus: they did not understand all the parables themselves! However, the Lord wanted them to understand, and so He would take them aside and explain the parables to them.

HIDDEN TREASURE

> The kingdom of heaven is like treasure hidden in a field. When a man found it, he hid it again, and then in his joy went and sold all he had and bought that field (Matt. 13:44).

The Kingdom is that hidden treasure. Jesus does not want us to stop short at knowing Him and His love for us. He wants us to know the life and power of His Kingdom, of His reign and rule in our lives now, and of His promise of His eternal glory.

The revelation that you are part of that Kingdom comes suddenly, as it does to that man digging in the field. The realisation that every spiritual blessing in heaven is yours breaks through to your heart like sunshine piercing through thick cloud.

Nothing could be more precious than that hidden treasure. Your heart wants to sing for joy and you desire nothing above praising your Lord and Saviour, who has made it possible for you to discover that Kingdom *now*, to know the life of that Kingdom *now*, to devote yourself to the spreading of that Kingdom *now*.

Your kingdom come,
Your will be done on earth as it is in heaven (Matt. 6:10).

THE SOWER

A farmer went out to sow his seed. As he was scattering the seed, some fell along the path, and the birds came and ate it up. Some fell on rocky places, where it did not have much soil. It sprang up quickly, because the soil was shallow. But when the sun came up, the plants were scorched, and they withered because they had no root. Other seed fell among thorns, which grew up and choked the plants. Still other seed fell on good soil, where it produced a crop – a hundred, sixty or thirty times what was sown. He who has ears, let him hear (Matt. 13:3–9).

The meaning was not evident to the disciples. Spiritual ears quickened by the revelation of God would be needed to understand what Jesus was saying. That is not surprising, because a man can only receive the revelation that he is part of God's Kingdom now, if he is given that revelation by God Himself. It is a work of the Holy Spirit bringing the word of life to the heart of the believer.

THE PATH

When Jesus explains the parable of the sower to the disciples, He says:

> Listen then to what the parable of the sower means: When anyone hears the message about the kingdom and does not understand it, the evil one comes and snatches away what was sown in his heart. This is the seed sown along the path (Matt. 13:18-19).

This is a parable about 'the message of the kingdom'. The seed of the word of that Kingdom is sometimes not received. Why? Because "the evil one comes and snatches away what was sown in his heart."

There is nothing that Satan desires more than to see the message of the Kingdom rejected. The reason for that is simple. Until a person receives this revelation that he is part of the Kingdom, and has all the privileges and inheritance of that Kingdom – "every spiritual blessing in the heavenly places" – Satan can and will inflict one spiritual defeat after another upon him. If that Christian has not received that revelation, the enemy will be able to persuade him of one or more of the following:

That his salvation is not assured.

He should be striving to earn his entrance into the Kingdom of heaven.

That he is under condemnation because of the guilt in his life.

That he is a spiritual failure, continually repeating the same sins.

That there is no good reason why he should expect any favours from God.

That God couldn't be expected to answer his prayers.

That all the difficult circumstances of his life raise serious questions as to whether God really loves him.

That he is unholy, unacceptable and unrighteous.

Jesus teaches us that Satan is the father of all lies, the deceiver of the brethren. He will do anything he can to prevent a person from believing that he is part of the Kingdom of heaven. Until that revelation becomes a reality he can inflict upon him one spiritual defeat after another. Once the revelation is received, the tables will be completely reversed, for the Christian is given the authority to overcome powers of darkness, and he receives the power to resist temptation and to stand firm against the devil.

So Satan has a vested interest in trying to encourage disbelief in the word of God. He will appeal to the intellect and will show how irrational it is to accept what the New Testament teaches. "God has given you a mind to think for yourself. You only have to accept what is intellectually sound and rational." Satan's constant plea to us is to reject the revelation of God's word and trust to our own understanding instead.

> You must no longer live as the Gentiles do, in the futility of their thinking. They are darkened in their understanding and separated from the life of God because of the ignorance that is in them due to the hardening of their hearts (Eph.4:17–18).

Satan wants us to disbelieve the words of the Kingdom, and he would also try to explain away the works of the Kingdom. In modern times he appeals to the minds of many believing Christians, trying to persuade them that the signs and miracles, which are the demonstration of the Spirit's power, are not for today. Such things passed away with the apostolic age. He would even encourage them to think that any demonstrations of miraculous power were the counterfeit manifestation of Satan himself. No wonder Jesus calls him "the deceiver of the brethren".

While it is true that he counterfeits much of the genuine works of God's grace, he is laughing all the way to hell when he manages to persuade Christians that the genuine works of the Spirit are really the works of God's enemy.

Should we not expect the Spirit of God to perform the same works today? For He is the same Spirit! Should we not expect to see the fulfilment of God's word today? For it is the same word! "Heaven and earth will pass away, but my words will not pass away."

Should we not expect to see the manifestations of God's Kingdom, for it is the same Kingdom of which Jesus spoke, and God gives that same Kingdom power and authority to those who believe Him?

Another ploy of Satan is to try to persuade the Christian that the Kingdom can only be a future hope rather than a present reality. He will do anything to dissuade the believer from believing! In particular he wants to prevent him from taking hold of that Kingdom life and authority now, of living in the victory of Jesus. He wants the Christian to think of himself as an unholy, unacceptable spiritual failure, no good in God's sight and totally unable to please Him in any way. Such things would be true apart from Jesus, but they are lies about any Christian, because of what Jesus has done for him.

Satan's desire is that we believe his lies. So he will try to snatch away whatever word of truth is sown in the heart. Part of the good news of what God has done in Jesus is that Satan is defeated by the cross. The enemy would even try to persuade us that this is not true!

ROCKY SOIL

Then Jesus explains the meaning of the seed falling on rocky soil:

> What was sown on rocky places is the man who hears the word and at once receives it with joy. But since he has no root, he lasts only a short time. When trouble or persecution comes because of the word, he quickly falls away (Matt. 13:20–21).

Receiving the revelation that you are part of the Kingdom of God is not enough. This man receives the revelation with joy when he hears it. "Hallelujah, I am part of God's Kingdom. He has forgiven me, accepted me and He loves me! Hallelujah!" He may continue to rejoice – for a while, but it is not long before the pressures begin to build up. Many difficulties arise during the course of our lives and each one prompts the question: "How can you be under God's reign if such things happen to you? How can He really love you?" This man will easily listen to his doubts and his feelings, and if anyone should challenge him as to what he believes about the Kingdom of God, he will soon be reduced to silence. He still does not know how to combat difficulties and opposition, because of his lack of knowledge and understanding of what it means to be part of the Kingdom.

The revelation is essential, otherwise the man will only have 'head-knowledge' about the Kingdom. But revelation is not enough. That man will need to turn constantly to the word of God to discover what his inheritance is as a child of the Kingdom. The revelation opens up a new threshold, but he will need to enter in and take possession of the house.

> If you continue in my word, you are truly my disciples, and you will know the truth, and the truth will make you free (John 8:31-32 R.S.V.).

It is only the truth of God's word that will give that man the liberty and freedom that he needs, especially in times of opposition. He will need to know how to use the scriptures to combat fear and doubts, and to deal with his negative feelings.

The seed of the word of the Kingdom has no depth or root in his life, Jesus says; so he quickly loses sight of the revelation when trouble arises, no matter how wonderful that revelation seemed to be at the time it was first received.

THORNS
What about the seed falling among the thorns?

> What was sown among the thorns is the man who hears the word, but worries of this life and the deceitfulness of wealth choke it, making it unfruitful (Matt. 13:22).

This is the man who has received the personal revelation of the Kingdom and hears the word of God concerning the nature of his inheritance as a child of the Kingdom. He is growing in Kingdom life.

But he is "a double-minded man, unstable in all he does" (James 1:8). His attention is not wholly upon God's Kingdom and will; he is easily drawn away by the temptations of the world around him. He gets frustrated and downhearted because he spends so much time contemplating his problems, rather than believing in the victory of the Kingdom.

He may want to live the life of the Kingdom on the one hand, but he also desires to satisfy his own fleshly desires on the other. He is a kind of spiritual schizophrenic. The life of the Kingdom is growing, but so are the weeds, the thorns. And Jesus warns that the weeds will throttle the good life, so that he cannot be fruitful in the way that God intends.

And God has brought us into His Kingdom that we may live for His glory and be fruitful.

> This is to my Father's glory, that you bear much fruit, showing yourselves to be my disciples (John 15:8).

FERTILE SOIL

For the seed of the word to be fruitful it needs to fall on fertile, weed-free soil.

> What was sown on good soil is the man who hears the word and understands it. He produces a crop, yielding a hundred, sixty or thirty times what was sown (Matt. 13:23).

If our lives are to be fruitful in the way that God intends, we need not only to hear the word, but also to understand it. If we are to learn what it means to be part of the Kingdom of God here on earth, then we shall need to understand what it means to live in the King Himself.

The remarkable revelation of the New Testament is that those who belong to God actually live 'in Christ Jesus'. To live in the Kingdom is to live in the King. To live in the King is to live in the Kingdom.

What does it mean to say that we live 'in Christ Jesus'? How can it be true to say that we live in God? And what makes such an amazing thing possible?

"It is because of him that you are in Christ Jesus" (1 Cor. 1:30). It is because of what God Himself has done that we can live in Christ. You need to understand from the word of God:

First: what He has done to make it possible for you to live in Christ.

Second: what you become because you are in Him.
Third: how you are to live because you are in Him.
Your words of faith: "THE KINGDOM OF HEAVEN IS LIKE TREASURE HIDDEN IN A FIELD."
"YOUR KINGDOM COME, YOUR WILL BE DONE ON EARTH AS IT IS IN HEAVEN."

4

THE CROSS

God demonstrates his own love for us in this: while we were still sinners, Christ died for us (Rom. 5:8).

For Christ's love compels us, because we are convinced that one died for all (2 Cor. 5:14).

God, in His love, had to send His own Son to die on the cross. That was the cost He had to pay to enable men to be forgiven, and to break the power of sin in their lives; to enable them to be restored to fellowship with Himself, become members of His heavenly Kingdom and be restored to His divine glory.

We deserve nothing from God, because of our sinfulness. His just and holy judgment upon sin is eternal death or separation from Him. Because of His great love for us, He does not want us to come under such judgment, but makes salvation possible for us, who naturally oppose Him and sin against Him.

Why should such a barbaric death be necessary to enable the almighty God to give forgiveness to His people? Could there not have been another way? Could He not simply say that He would forgive them? St Paul answers these questions for us:

God offered him, so that by his death he should become the means by which people's sins are forgiven through their faith in him. God did this in order to demonstrate that he is righteous. In the past he was patient and overlooked people's sins; but in the present time he deals with their sins, in order to demonstrate his righteousness. In this way God shows that he himself is righteous and that he puts right everyone who believes in Jesus (Rom. 3:25-26 G.N.B.).

"God is love" (1 John 4:16), and so He acts out of love for His people. But He is also righteous. Nothing can stand in His Presence that is not right, perfect and holy in His sight. That would seem to suggest that, because we sin we could stand no hope of ever being acceptable to Him. Without Jesus that would indeed be the case. It is for that reason that He said: "No one comes to the Father except through me" (John 14:6).

FOR THE FATHER FIRST
Jesus died on the cross, first for His Father, then for us. God's holiness and righteousness demanded that a sinless life be given for sinners, a perfect life for the imperfect, a holy life for the unholy, a righteous life for the unrighteous. God could not metaphorically shrug His shoulders and say: 'Their sin doesn't matter; I will forgive them.' It was sin that had alienated the whole of mankind from Him; it was sin that caused men to miss the glory for which they were created.

Sin is awful in God's sight; we cannot imagine how awful. Neither can we fully grasp the immensity of His love for us in making Jesus the atonement for our sins: through Him we can be once more at-one-with God.

The perfect sacrifice of Jesus on the cross totally satisfies the holiness and righteousness of God. He accepts the blood that Jesus shed as the payment for our sins.

Just as God could not shrug at our sin as if it was not grievous in His sight, so neither can we shrug our shoulders nonchalantly with the attitude "These are my little failures; nobody is perfect. God made me this way and anyway Jesus will forgive me."

Sin is so grievous to God that it could not go unpunished.

The Cross

The consequence of sin is separation from God – and that is spiritual death, God's just, holy and righteous judgment upon sin and the sinner. Jesus has suffered the punishment we deserved and has saved us from spiritual death. He needed to be sacrificed only once to make possible the forgiveness of all mankind, all men of all ages.

That is what He has made possible, but not all men receive God's forgiveness and become part of His Kingdom. Not all are restored to fellowship with Him and to the inheritance of His glory. It is faith in Jesus that makes actual in the believer what Jesus has made possible on the cross: "God offered him, so that by his death he should become the means by which people's sins are forgiven *through their faith in him*."

Jesus has paid the price for us. We have been redeemed "with the precious blood of Christ, a lamb without blemish or defect" (1 Pet. 1:19).

SINS FORGIVEN

Through the shedding of that blood, forgiveness is made possible and God will grant that forgiveness to those who confess their sins to Him.

> If we confess our sins, he is faithful and just and will forgive us our sins and purify us from all unrighteousness (1 John 1:9).

When God forgives us He declares us 'not guilty', even though we were guilty of the sins confessed. The blood of Jesus cleanses us from the guilt, through that perfect, sinless offering He made on our behalf.

Imagine a criminal coming into a court of law and confessing his crimes, only to have the judge declare him innocent and record a verdict of 'Not Guilty'. The criminal will be surprised, to say the least. He may think that he deserves to be punished. If he points this out to the judge, he will be told that he cannot be punished because someone else has already paid the penalty for his crime. It is not justice to punish the same offence twice.

It is only possible to have a clear conscience before God

because we believe in the power of the blood of Jesus to make us right in His sight. We can come before Him boldly, confident of the forgiveness we receive through Jesus. There is no need for us to be tentative, as if His blood could not possibly cover *our* sins, or that we are beyond His forgiveness, that He could not accept us or make us new. "The blood of Jesus, his Son, purifies us from *every* sin" (1 John 1:7).

It is sad that so many remain burdened for years because of some particularly grievous sin they have committed.

At the end of a meeting, a woman came to me in great distress. In her youth she had sinned sexually and for twenty years she had been pleading with the Lord for His forgiveness. She felt that her sin had made her so unclean in His sight that God would want nothing to do with her, and that His forgiveness was beyond her reach. It seemed to her that this particular sin was a barrier that separated her from God.

I showed her that the sin did not separate her from Him, but her unbelief did. When she first asked the Lord to forgive, He had forgiven her, because that is what He says in His word that He will do. But she did not believe His love and graciousness. She had been punishing herself ever since. Every day she asked God for His mercy; every day He gave it to her, and every day she rejected it because she knew she did not deserve it.

We never deserve His forgiveness, but God extends His love to us because the blood of Jesus is the worthy and acceptable offering for our sins. That blood always 'works' for the sinner who repents before God, unworthy though he or she is.

I told the woman that God had forgiven her twenty years ago, and together we could thank Him for that fact and for the love of Jesus on the cross that had made it possible. She went on her way rejoicing. Light flooded her being as she believed in the goodness of God and that He is "faithful and just to forgive us our sins".

Praise God for the power of the blood of Jesus! How awful are the consequences of unbelief!

God does not forgive you because He suddenly decided

to do so, but because Jesus died for you, He poured out His precious blood for you. God forgives you because of what has already taken place. He does not need to do a new thing when a sinner turns to Him in repentance. Jesus does not have to die on the cross all over again.

When you ask to be forgiven by God, you are appropriating the fruit of what He has already accomplished for you on the cross. He will not deny the blood of His Son. And in His word He says clearly that He will forgive all those who confess their sins to Him.

ACCEPTED BY GOD

When God has forgiven us, we are made righteous or acceptable in His sight. We are restored to fellowship with Him. Not everyone finds this easy to believe.

I once met a Christian girl who told me that she had great problems in believing that God had accepted her. She knew in her head that she was forgiven because Jesus died for her but she did not 'feel' forgiven. (That problem of feelings again!) And so she doubted her salvation. The enemy had a field day! He constantly taunted her and caused her to feel spiritually low. She was always questioning and fearful.

One night she had a dream in which she was shown the Book of Life in heaven. In this book are all the names of the redeemed, those who have been washed in the blood of Jesus and made acceptable in God's sight.

The page at which she was looking was divided into two columns. On the left was a list of names, and there among them she saw her own. At the top of the right-hand column she read the heading, 'Percentage of Doubt'. Against each name was a figure, 5%, 15%, 10%. When she came to her name she saw the figure 200%.

"How can I have 200%?" she asked in her dream.

She received the reply: "No matter how much you doubt you cannot alter the facts. Your name is written in the Book of Life."

When she awoke the following morning, she realised that she was a new person, accepted by God. That was true, not because of her dream, but because she had come to the cross some time before. Although her negative feelings had often resulted in a doubting attitude, nothing could alter the facts of what God had done for her. She was forgiven. She had been made acceptable in the sight of God. Her name was written in the Book of Life. But for the cross, the sinner would remain eternally separated from God. On the cross Jesus paid the price with His own blood so that the sinner could be forgiven, accepted and restored to fellowship with God.

THE ANSWER TO SATAN

Sin leads to a further problem. It is not only grievous in God's sight: it also produces guilt in the one who does it. Satan, whom Jesus describes as 'the accuser of the brethren', does not miss this opportunity. He can rightly accuse the sinner that he has offended God and deserves to have no part with Him. He is keen to do this because it was for his own sin and rebellion against the Lord that he was thrown out of heaven, together with all those who followed his example of disobedience. The blood of Jesus is the answer to Satan. Once we are forgiven, he has no right to accuse us before God, or to try to make us feel condemned. He often does so to make us doubt God's forgiveness. He will taunt and suggest that we do not 'feel' forgiven, that forgiveness could not be that simple, that we deserve to be punished, and, anyway, we shall only go and do the same thing over and over again.

Forgiveness is not a feeling; it is a fact. God is faithful and just, and will grant that forgiveness to those who ask Him. Satan has no right to disturb the peace that forgiveness brings to the believer. God the Father does not see you as guilty but as one who is forgiven. So the enemy can be told where to go! Do not argue with him. Refer him to Jesus, whose blood covers your sin.

There is nothing he can do to alter what God has said and done in Jesus. He can only try to make you disbelieve it. So he will continue to accuse you; he will point out the fact of your sin and how unworthy this makes you before God. He will tempt you to look within at your misery and wretchedness, and so cause you to feel that your situation is hopeless. If you listen to him, he will convince you that not only are you unworthy but, because of your weakness and failure, you will also inevitably go on sinning, and so can never become acceptable to God. A sense of hopelessness and despair enfolds some people because the enemy succeeds in confirming the low opinion of themselves that they have always held.

Satan achieves that in many, not because God does not love them or because he has rejected them, but because they do not believe the facts about the cross and the effectiveness of the blood of Jesus in not only securing their forgiveness, but also in making them totally worthy and righteous in His sight.

Some try to argue with the enemy. There is nothing that he likes more than an argument. They may try to argue that there are others worse than themselves and that, if God rejected them, He would have to reject a host of others as well. It is that idea of rejection that the enemy loves to foster. He wants us to doubt the power of the blood of Jesus; he does not want us to believe that His blood is the end of rejection for those who put their faith in Him.

Do not listen to 'the accuser of the brethren'. Even when he is right, and points to your sin and failure, you can point to the blood of Jesus. You do not stand before God guilty, but cleansed and forgiven. The blood of Jesus is the answer to all your sin and to every accusation that the enemy would bring against you. It is the answer to every feeling of self-condemnation.

Do not allow the enemy or your own self-pity to distract your attention from the cross. The more you look at yourself, the more you will certainly discover sin, weakness, failure, disobedience and negative unbelief. You will come to the same sorry conclusions over and over again, and wonder why God should persist in His love for you.

But as you continue to look at the cross you will grow in wonder at the immensity of God's love and the profound wisdom of His planning: that He has provided, not only the way of forgiveness for you, but also the means whereby the power of sin can be broken in your life.

You are helpless; you cannot please God of yourself. That is true. It is pointless to go searching within yourself to find something good with which to impress God. If you persist in contemplating your weakness and failure, and the fact of your sinfulness, you will only grow in weakness, continue to fail, and become more acutely aware of your guilt. You will go on believing your feelings and the enemy's lies.

If, instead, you look to the cross, to the love and the grace of God that is expressed there, if you seek to understand from the scriptures more of all that He accomplished for you, then you will grow in freedom. "The truth will set you free," and your heart will rejoice that once you were helpless, but now you are God's child. Once you were rejected; now you are accepted. Once you were in darkness; now you are light in the Lord.

Your words of faith: "GOD DEMONSTRATES HIS OWN LOVE FOR US IN THIS: WHILE WE WERE STILL SINNERS, CHRIST DIED FOR US." "GOD SHOWS THAT HE HIMSELF IS RIGHTEOUS AND THAT HE PUTS RIGHT EVERYONE WHO BELIEVES IN JESUS." "IF WE CONFESS OUR SINS, HE IS FAITHFUL AND JUST AND WILL FORGIVE US OUR SINS AND PURIFY US FROM ALL UNRIGHTEOUSNESS."

5

ETERNAL LIFE

A great gap existed between God and men; they were cut off from fellowship with Him. They could try to span that gap and relate to Him 'from a distance', but it was impossible for them to draw near to Him or know Him.

In this diagram X indicates you, at some point between your physical birth and your physical death. Most people think of God as being on the other side of death, living in heaven. If you manage to get there, you will receive eternal life. It is imagined that you must try to be good and to keep

Eternal Life

physical birth — X — physical death

God
heaven
eternal life

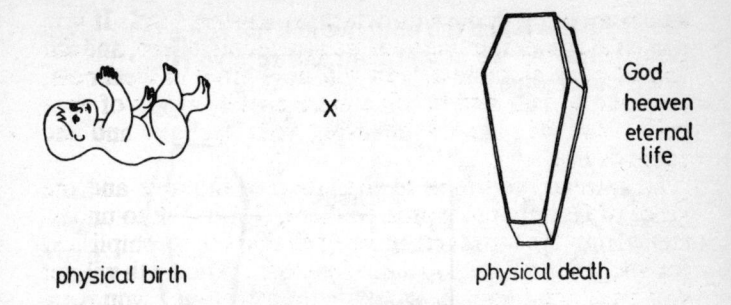

your record clean as you progress towards the grave, so that you will then receive a favourable judgment from God and be received into His eternal Kingdom.

That is a complete travesty of the Gospel. It is not what Jesus said; it is not what the New Testament teaches, and it takes no account of the cross.

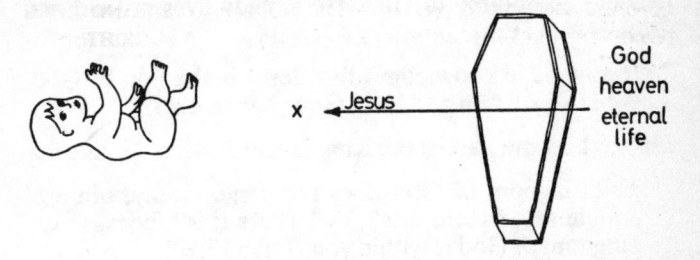

X ← Jesus ← God heaven eternal life

If it is possible to know God *now*, then the whole picture changes. For that to happen, God has to come to us, into the circumstances of our lives here and now.

This He has done in Jesus. And when He came, His message was, "Repent, for the kingdom of heaven is near" (Matt. 4:17). Jesus came bringing the life of God's Kingdom with Him, making the gift of eternal life available to men *now*. "I have come that they may have life, and have it to the full" (John 10:10). Not human life, for men already possess that. But eternal life, God's life, the life of His heavenly Kingdom.

Note which way the arrow is pointing in the diagram. It is

God who has taken the initiative and has come to us in His Son, Jesus. As we accept Him and receive Him, the diagram can change.

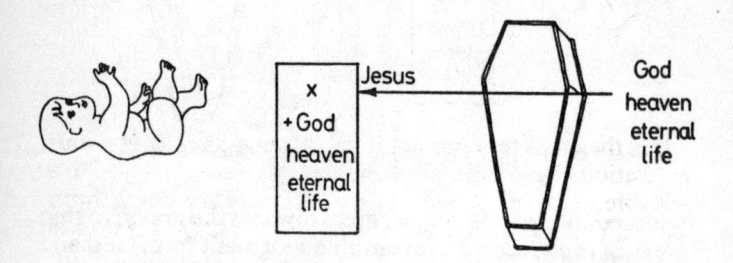

In receiving Jesus into our lives we receive God Himself; X no longer has to progress towards the time of his physical death on his own, trying to win favour with God and become acceptable to Him. He already lives in God and God lives in Him!

> If anyone acknowledges that Jesus is the Son of God, God lives in him and he in God (1 John 4:15).

He has become part of the Kingdom of heaven. Jesus said:

> The kingdom of God does not come visibly, nor will people say, "Here it is", or "There it is", because the kingdom of God is within you (Luke 17:20).

He has already received the gift of eternal life.

> I tell you the truth, whoever hears my word and believes him who sent me has eternal life and will not be condemned; he has crossed over from death to life (John 5:24).

If you are a Christian, you have already received the gift of eternal life because you believe what God has done for you through His Son. The Kingdom of heaven and eternal life will not begin on the other side of physical death; they begin during your earthly life-span. So we need to complete the picture by adding what has made that possible for you.

Eternal Life

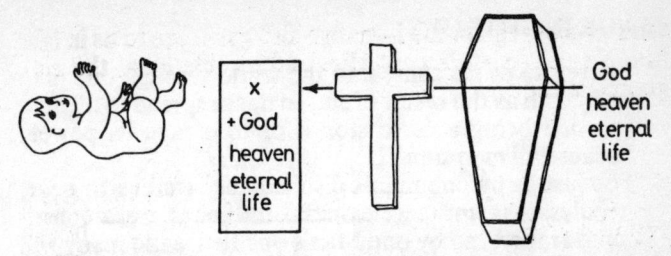

It is the cross that has made all this possible. There your separation from God ended. Now you have been raised to a new life, you are a new creature and have been 'born again'. You are a child of the Kingdom of heaven who has received the gift of eternal life. And it is Jesus who accomplished all this for you.

'God', 'heaven' and 'eternal life' still need to be represented on the other side of physical death. "Now I know in part," Paul says; "then I shall know fully, even as I am fully known" (1 Cor. 13:12).

What we know and experience of the Lord, of His Kingdom and life during our time on earth is only partial, compared to the total revelation that we shall receive when we see Him 'face to face'.

ACCESS TO GOD

At the moment when Jesus died on the cross "the curtain of the temple was torn in two from top to bottom" (Matt. 27:51). That curtain separated the Holy of Holies from the remainder of the temple. That 'Most Holy Place' was where the Presence of God dwelt, and could only be entered once a year by the High Priest, bearing the blood of animals because of the sinfulness of the people.

When Jesus shed His blood He made available, to all who believe in Him, access into the holy presence of God. We who believe belong to God and "in him we live and move and have our being" (Acts 17:28). We can live continually in His presence, in Him even, because the blood of Jesus cleanses us from all sin and restores us to fellowship with God. Jesus is our 'righteousness'; He has put us in right standing with God.

MADE RIGHTEOUS

> Therefore as sin came into the world through one man and death as the result of sin, so death spread to all men (no one being able to stop it or to escape its power) because all men sinned.
> For just as by one man's disobedience (failing to hear, heedlessness and carelessness) the many were constituted sinners, so by one Man's obedience the many will be constituted righteous – made acceptable to God, brought into right standing with Him (Rom. 5:12, 19 Amplified Bible).

In our human nature we have inherited the sin of Adam. He ignored the word of God and chose to act independently of Him. He was tempted to please himself and he yielded to that temptation. As a result he was excluded from paradise and lost fellowship with God. Instead of eternal life, he now had to face death.

The disobedience of Adam could only be redressed by the obedience of Jesus Christ. He is the second Adam. Through Him, and only through Him, can men be restored to a state of righteousness before God, being in right relationship with Him.

> If we claim to be without sin, we deceive ourselves and the truth is not in us. If we confess our sins, he is faithful and just and will forgive us our sins and purify us from all unrighteousness (1 John 1:8–9).

To be purified 'from all unrighteousness' means that we are made right before God, accepted and approved by Him. He looks upon us and sees nothing wrong with us, because we are cleansed by the blood of Jesus.

We do not have any right to be accepted by God because of what we are, or because of anything we have done. Self-righteousness is as filthy rags to God. We are acceptable to the Father because of the righteousness of Jesus. "Through the obedience of the one man the many will be made righteous."

Eternal Life

Well then, as one man's trespass – one man's false step and falling away – (led) to condemnation for all men, so one Man's act of righteousness (leads) to acquittal and right standing with God, and life for all men (Rom. 5:18 Amp.).

UNBELIEF

The blood of Christ has removed all the barriers that separate men from God. All except one: unbelief. God calls us to have faith in Jesus and in what He has done on the cross.

On many occasions people have said to me that they want to know God, or they need to receive healing or some other answer to prayer. They say that they *feel* they cannot get through to Him; something is blocking the way. Usually they have turned themselves inside out trying to find the cause of that blockage. They may have sought ministry and counsel of others to see if they could determine the nature of the barrier that prevents them from receiving what they need from the Lord.

In the vast majority of cases the problem is simply one of unbelief.

New life with Jesus begins with an act of faith. We cannot see Him and yet we believe in Him. We were not alive at the time of the crucifixion, and yet we believe that what happened then involved us and has eternal consequences for us:

> Surely he took up our infirmities
> and carried our sorrows . . .
> But he was pierced for our transgressions,
> he was crushed for our iniquities;
> the punishment that brought us peace was upon him,
> and by his wounds we are healed (Isa. 53:4, 5).

Many refer to themselves as 'doubting Thomases'. The disciple, Thomas, refused to believe that Jesus had risen and had appeared to the others, until he could see the Lord for himself and touch His wounds:

> Unless I see the nail marks in his hands and put my finger

where the nails were, and put my hand into his side, I will not believe it (John 20:25).

A week later Jesus again appeared to the disciples and this time Thomas was with them. "Put your finger here," Jesus said to him; "see my hands. Reach out your hand and put it into my side. Stop doubting and believe" (v. 27).

Thomas answered, "My Lord and my God!" Then Jesus told him, "Because you have seen me, you have believed; blessed are those who have not seen and yet have believed" (vv. 28–29).

A common saying in modern use is "Seeing is believing." Jesus says something totally different: "Blessed are those who have not seen and yet have believed." That is what God is asking of us. It is only by trusting what He says in His word that we discover the truth and are able to appropriate the benefits of that truth.

When teaching the disciples how to pray with faith, Jesus says:

Therefore I tell you, whatever you ask for in prayer, believe that you have received it, and it will be yours (Mark 11:24).

We may not be able to *see* an immediate answer to our prayers, yet we are to believe the answer although we see or feel nothing. And his promise is, "it will be yours."

BELIEVE NOW

You can ask God for His forgiveness now. You cannot see forgiveness, neither is it a feeling. As you believe that He has forgiven you, so *then* you will know His peace. That is His promise.

If you need to know that God has accepted you, believe that He has already done so on the cross. That you were made acceptable when Jesus died for you. Appropriate that great truth by faith now. Thank Him for all that He has already accomplished for you. You will have the joy of knowing "God has accepted me through Jesus."

What can you do if you do not believe? Confess your

unbelief to God, ask Him to forgive you and to give you faith. Once you have asked Him, you can be sure that He has forgiven you because we read in His word:

> If we confess our sins, he is faithful and just and will forgive us our sins and purify us from all unrighteousness (1 John 1:9).

Christ died for all – and that includes *you*. He did not leave you out when He went to the cross. He died that you might be put right with God and be given the gift of eternal life.

> I have complete confidence in the gospel; it is God's power to save all who believe. . . . For the gospel reveals how God puts people right with himself: it is through faith from beginning to end. As the scripture says, "The person who is put right with God through faith shall live" (Rom. 1:16–17 G.N.B.).

Your words of faith: "I HAVE COME THAT THEY MAY HAVE LIFE, AND HAVE IT TO THE FULL." "I TELL YOU THE TRUTH, WHOEVER HEARS MY WORD AND BELIEVES HIM WHO SENT ME HAS ETERNAL LIFE AND WILL NOT BE CONDEMNED; HE HAS CROSSED OVER FROM DEATH TO LIFE." "ONE MAN'S ACT OF RIGHTEOUSNESS LEADS TO ACQUITTAL AND RIGHT STANDING WITH GOD, AND LIFE FOR ALL MEN."

6

CONFLICT AND PEACE

THE BEGINNING OF CONFLICT
Before a man can come to repentance, God has to initiate a work within him that shows him he has sinned. He comes under 'conviction of sin'. That does not mean that he will

automatically repent, but he does realise that he has offended God and that he needs to be forgiven. Whether he asks for that forgiveness or not is the beginning of conflict. Part of him will want God's forgiveness, for he longs to be at peace, and senses that he will only have peace when he has been cleansed of the sin of which he is now conscious.

But another part of him wants to cling on to his independence, to the desire to please himself and do whatever he wants. Turning to God and asking for forgiveness is going to involve yielding his life to God and accepting His authority and direction.

The sinful nature will fight to the last to maintain control. There is a real sense in which we do not want God or anything to do with Him. Our flesh would much rather be left in control of us and what we do.

A good example of this conflict happened one evening when I was leading a mission in Bath. After the service many people were sharing testimonies of healings that had occurred during the meeting. Two girls in their late teens stood to one side, waiting to speak to me. When all the others had gone, one of the girls came forward and said that she believed God had told her to bring her friend to speak with me. The other girl was obviously very reluctant. I attempted to put her at her ease. As I spoke with her it became obvious that she did not know Jesus. "Do you want to know the Lord?" I asked her.

"No," she replied. I sensed this was not the whole truth, that here was someone in the conflict of decision. In one way, she wanted Jesus, and yet she wanted to maintain her independent control of her life.

"I think you do want to know Him," I said, "but you don't want to give yourself to Him." She nodded.

It transpired that her friend had become a Christian a few weeks earlier. The changes that were apparent in her life had stirred both jealousy and resentment within this girl. Against her wishes, she had allowed herself to be 'dragged' to the service that evening. She knew God had spoken to her, but still she did not want to say 'Yes' to Him.

After we had spoken together for a few minutes I said to her: "Although you do not *want* to give yourself to Him,

Conflict and Peace

will you do so because He wants *you*. This is an act of the will, not of the desire." Again she nodded her consent. I could see that she recognised her need and had to be helped through the conflict.

I led her through a simple act of repentance, thanked God that He had made her His child, and prayed for her to be filled with the Holy Spirit. I could see that she still lacked assurance that all we had prayed was really true for her. Quietly I asked the Lord what I should do.

"Now that you are a Christian," I said to her, "you will need to see yourself as God sees you. You will have to learn to speak about yourself in a new way because you are a new person."

She looked at me, her eyes full of doubt.

"You are only doubting because you have not experienced anything yet," I continued. "I want you to repeat these truths after me. Believe them as you say them, and you will receive all that you need to experience."

I began to speak affirmations of faith and she repeated each of them in a dead monotone.

"God has forgiven me."   "God has forgiven me."
"God loves me."   "God loves me."
"He has accepted me."   "He has accepted me."
"Jesus is my Saviour."   "Jesus is my Saviour."
"Jesus is my Lord."   "Jesus is my Lord."
"And I love Him."

The girl stopped. Her eyes had been closed, her head bowed. She looked up and stared me in the face. Slowly she began to smile, then to beam, and all at once she looked radiant. "And I love Him," she said, "I love Him. Oh, thank you, I love Him."

She embraced her friend in the love of Jesus and returned to her university lodgings rejoicing. Many people had come into the Kingdom of God earlier that evening, yet leading that girl to the Lord gave me a particular joy. She began by not wanting Him and ended by knowing that she loved Him. She had truly been born again and had experienced a complete transformation of heart.

A reluctant convert? Yes, but she was by no means the first.

THE RELUCTANT APOSTLE

Paul begins his First Letter to the Corinthians with these words: "Paul, called to be an apostle of Christ Jesus by the will of God". Almost identical words begin several of his other letters. For example, when he writes to Timothy he says: "Paul, an apostle of Christ Jesus, by the command of God our Saviour and of Christ Jesus our hope" (1 Tim. 1:1).

I used to pass quickly over these greetings so that I could get to the meat of the teaching that these epistles contain. And then one day I realised the amazing truth that God had to teach through this phrase, 'by the will of God'.

It was not Paul's idea to be an apostle. He never chose or elected to be an apostle; it was not his life-long ambition. He hated Jesus Christ and was devoted to the destruction of His Church. He had no intention of becoming a Christian, let alone an apostle to the Gentiles.

It was God's idea; it was by His command that Paul became first a Christian and then an apostle of Jesus Christ. The Lord took the initiative in his conversion. "Who are you, Lord?" Saul asked, when blinded by the light from heaven on his way to Damascus to carry out his threat against everything Christian.

Saul was by the standards of the Law a good man, utterly convinced that in persecuting the Church he was serving God by upholding and defending His Law. But for all his goodness and religious zeal, he was an enemy of Jesus Christ.

Saul did not choose Jesus. Jesus chose Saul. It was God's plan for him to become an apostle. Would Saul ever have known Jesus if He had not taken the initiative and called him?

CHOSEN BY GOD

Perhaps you think that you became a Christian because at some point in your life you chose Jesus. Your response of faith and repentance was the moment when you became a Christian, but it was not your faith that began the process. That repentance was the response to the initiative that God had taken in your life – as with St Paul – as with the university student in Bath.

Conflict and Peace

Jesus impressed upon His disciples:

> You did not choose me, but I chose you to go and bear fruit – fruit that will last. Then the Father will give you whatever you ask in my name (John 15:16).

The initiative in your life was taken by God and is still held by Him. He chose you, He called you. You could not have chosen Him if He had not chosen you. You could not have come to repentance unless His Spirit had first convicted you of sin and shown you the futility of your life without Jesus Christ: that, like Paul, you were persecuting Jesus.

> He who is not with me is against me, and he who does not gather with me scatters (Matt. 12:30).

You could not have put your faith in Jesus Christ as the Lord and Saviour of your life unless God Himself had somehow begun to open the eyes of your spiritual understanding.

It was God's purpose, not yours, to bring you into His Kingdom.

PEACE WITH GOD

When you place your faith in Jesus Christ, you respond to God's call and appropriate the salvation that He made possible for you. At that moment, the initial conflict ends and you find peace with God.

> Therefore, since we have been justified through faith, we have peace with God through our Lord Jesus Christ (Rom. 5:1).

To be justified is to be made innocent in God's sight. That means we can be without guilt in His presence. It is Jesus who has made that possible through taking all of our guilt to the cross. As we put our faith in what He has done, so we are actually justified before God. We can be at peace with Him because we have been cleansed of all our sin and guilt. We are no longer at enmity with God, cut off from Him and opposed to Him. Now we can know the fellowship of His peace, no matter how trying the circumstances around us.

You are at peace when you believe that He has accepted and forgiven you through Jesus. You know yourself to be at one with Him, that He loves you. In scripture, peace is not simply the absence of turmoil, noise or difficulty, but the positive gift from God that enables the believer to look to the Lord with confidence and trust, despite the negative situations in which he sometimes finds himself.

If you are at peace with God you need no longer believe the lying accusations of the enemy who wants to destroy that peace, and you do not have to heed the self-condemning thoughts of failure and uselessness which lead you to imagine that you are totally unacceptable to God.

What is more, when you are at peace with God you can believe more readily for His victory over the adverse circumstances and problems that confront you. Whenever people come to ask for healing, or want the Lord to meet some specific need in their life, I first lead them to repentance. They turn to Him afresh, seeking His loving forgiveness, and they renew the giving of their lives to Him.

The reason for doing this is simple: if there is no sin because Jesus forgives them, then guilt cannot be a hindrance to receiving healing or the answer to their prayer. More than that, they will be at peace with God, they will have awareness of well-being with Him, of His loving acceptance. They will know that God has already met with them in one fruit of the cross, forgiveness; so they will be able more readily to believe in another fruit of the cross, healing.

Also, when he is at peace with God, the Christian discovers that he can be at peace with others, and that is often a very important factor in the healing that God wants to perform in his life. Instead of negative feelings and reactions towards them, the peace of God overflows into a concern to forgive others for the wrongs that have been inflicted upon him. He wants to share with them the peace and well-being he has discovered with God. Attempts at reconciliation may sometimes prove futile because that desire for forgiveness is not mutual. But the Christian knows that he has done all he could to effect that reconciliation, that he has freely forgiven those who have wronged him, just as God has freely forgiven his sins.

Many will know Christians who have given a great witness of peace throughout long and painful illnesses. No one could doubt their awareness of God's love and their knowledge of His goodness. What a contrast to those who meet adversity with bitterness and resentment, murmuring against God and continually complaining to men! Where is their peace?

Those who seek freedom will only discover it when they know peace with God and with others. Paul speaks of "the peace of God, which transcends all understanding". That peace "will guard your hearts and minds" in the face of all difficulties. No matter what the situation, God loves you; He has accepted you and He is with you.

Your words of faith: "YOU DID NOT CHOOSE ME BUT I CHOSE YOU." "WE HAVE PEACE WITH GOD THROUGH OUR LORD JESUS CHRIST." "THE PEACE OF GOD, WHICH TRANSCENDS ALL UNDERSTANDING, WILL GUARD YOUR HEARTS AND YOUR MINDS IN CHRIST JESUS."

7

DEAD

Even though we have peace with God through Jesus, we are not necessarily at peace with ourselves. For our reconciliation with God does not mark the end of temptation or of the desire to sin and please ourselves.

OUR DESIRE TO SIN
Every believer experiences a conflict within himself. He is in conflict because he is being pulled in two directions at the same time. He can rejoice that he has peace with God, but he needs also to be at peace with himself.

We have seen that, when we were born into this world, we had a naturally sinful nature that was centred upon ourselves – the flesh. This term does not refer to the physical flesh of our bodies, but to this nature that is opposed to the purposes of God. Jesus said:

> Flesh gives birth to flesh but the Spirit gives birth to spirit (John 3:6).

The old nature is naturally sinful, hostile to God and cannot please Him. The new nature, which God gives when a man is 'born again', desires to please God by being obedient to Him. Clearly they are two opposites:

sinful nature ⟶ ⟵ new nature

These two natures cannot be reconciled; we must be clear about that. Anyone who tries to reconcile them only increases and prolongs the conflict that goes on within him.

> Those who live according to the sinful nature have their minds set on what that nature desires; but those who live in accordance with the Spirit have their minds set on what the Spirit desires (Rom. 8:5).

Sins are the bad fruit that result from a man's fallen, sinful, selfish human nature. The Christian will not be free to live in the power of the new life God gives him in Jesus, if that sinful nature is still able to control his life. Unless it is delivered a permanent death-blow, it will go on producing its bad fruit. It is not only forgiveness that is needed. The Christian has also to be set free from the power of sin in his life.

There is an inner impulse, a power even, that inevitably draws a man into sin, and God took this into account when He led Jesus to the cross. If He only dealt with sins without dealing with the root cause of sin, then that man would persist in disobedience and continue to bear bad fruit. He could receive forgiveness for his sins, but he would not be able to prevent himself from committing those same sins again. A man may try to control that impulse, but every time it breaks through his attempts at self-control, he sins. He needs something more effective to happen, in order to deal with the sinful nature itself that produces the bad fruit of sins.

The fact that this conflict exists at all is greatly disturbing to many Christians. They do their best to conceal it, imagining that others do not experience anything similar. They may attribute the cause of the conflict to a lack of faith on their own part. Or they may charge themselves with hypocrisy because what is going on within them is so different from the good Christian image that they try to portray to others.

The Christian can seek and receive God's forgiveness for his sins without that sinful impulse being touched. He must be set free from obeying that impulse that repeatedly drags him down into sin. He needs forgiveness not only for what he does that displeases God, but also for what he is in his natural state.

TEMPTATION

It is possible for a Christian to present the Lord with lists of things that need to be forgiven without realising that *he* is the problem, not his sins. That presents him with a dilemma. If he is a new creature, why should he go on sinning? Why are there still so many of these lists of sins to present to the Lord? They can hardly be explained as temporary lapses. He may excuse himself by saying that nobody is perfect or could hope to measure up to the perfection of Jesus.

He may summon up all his self-control to resist temptation which is still real, even though he is now a Christian. He may fall into the trap of thinking it is wrong to be tempted, that the temptation itself is sinful. If he does, he is likely to be plagued by negative reactions: "If I wasn't such a failure as a Christian, I wouldn't be tempted in that way."

Temptation is *not* sin. The sin is giving in to the temptation. Jesus was tempted by the enemy when in the wilderness, prior to the beginning of His teaching and healing ministry. During His human life He was "tempted in every way, just as we are – yet was without sin" (Heb. 4:15). That was the difference between Jesus and us. When tempted, He never yielded to the temptation. He never gave in; He did not say 'Yes' to it.

Unfortunately temptation will be with us throughout our lives on earth. The tempter will try to disrupt our Christian lives by leading us away from the purposes of God, and he knows the points where each of us is most vulnerable.

Sometimes a Christian does not want to yield to temptation. It is not long before he discovers, to his dismay, that there are occasions when he *does* want to do what he knows will be sinful. He is willing to act in direct disobedience to the Lord. That increases the sense of conflict within him. He still has many earthly desires and is prepared to be manipulative to get his own way, irrespective of God's purpose.

This may increase his resolve to turn away from temptation and resist it. He may pray with great fervour and intensity 'Lead us not into temptation'. But he is still left with the knowledge that he *wants* to sin, he *wants* his own way, and he does not want God to interfere with his plans for his life.

Some try to reach a place of compromise with God, by giving part of their lives to Him, while the rest is kept for themselves. This is the attitude of the small child. The toddler wants his own way and does what he wishes, unless he is made to do what he is told. He will escape from authority and discipline whenever possible. He does not see anything wrong with what he is doing. He simply wants to do what he wants to do.

His parents train him to discriminate between what he should do and what is forbidden. As he grows older, things that used to be allowed are no longer permissible. The temptation is still there, but so is the knowledge of what may happen if, now that he is older, he still behaves like a small, self-willed child.

When we are new-born Christians, God is not continually disciplining us for every incorrect thought or word, for every wrong attitude or action. He patiently sets about the business of training us, teaching us to be responsible, and showing us that sin may gratify our desires, but it does not please Him, nor is it good for us.

At some point in the process of growth there comes the revelation that the believer does wrong because *he is wrong*. He sins because he wants to – just like the self-willed toddler. He has to face the fact that there is something about him that still does not want to please the Lord, and that he chooses to remain deliberately disobedient in some areas of his life.

There is something within him that deliberately opposes the purposes of God. He is perplexed. He knows that, on the one hand, he wants to please God and obey Him. Yet, on the other hand, there is this desire, this urging, this prompting to do what he wants. For example, he knows that he should not criticise others, but he wants to, and even feels justified in doing so. And so he does. He knows he should be humble, but cannot resist the temptation to make proud statements, even though he may regret having done so afterwards. If he tries to resist the impulse, it seems to build up in him until he can resist no longer, and out pours the criticism or the proud statement.

Then one day comes the revelation: "*I am wrong*. I do wrong because *I am wrong*. Lord, please do something about *me*!"

At this point he will not understand that God has already answered that cry from his heart.

THE ANSWER TO THE CONFLICT
Jesus has made you right with God. It is not His purpose that you should still be under the power of an unholy and unrighteous nature that is constantly pushing you into sin and disobedience. But unless that sinful nature is put to death, it will still influence you, even though you are given a new nature.

The only way that you can be cut off from the sinful nature with which you were born is by death! That old nature needs to be dead and buried. God does not want you to put the new nature of Jesus on top of the old nature of sin. That would be like putting on your best coat over your oldest, scruffiest jeans – and hoping that 'they' wouldn't notice.

It is only through death that you can be free to live in the power of the new nature. Not physical death, but the death of the old sinful nature. *The good news is that your death has already taken place*! When Jesus went to the cross, He not only took your sins, He also took you!

> For we know that our old self was crucified with him so that the body of sin might be rendered powerless, that we should no longer be slaves to sin – because anyone who has died has been freed from sin (Rom. 6:6–7).

Paul is referring the Romans to something they already know: 'We *know* that our old self was crucified with Him.' He is not referring to some personal, subjective experience of crucifixion. He is pointing to an objective fact: what happened to them when Jesus died on the cross.

God calls us to believe not only the death of His Son, Jesus, but also our own death with Him.

We believe in the death and the resurrection of Jesus Christ because that is the revelation of God's word. It is equally the revelation of His word that we have died with Him. That is not a matter for argument; it is presented to us as a fact, something that has happened and that we need to believe. It is a truth to enter into, not deny.

It is not a question of whether you *feel* dead. Whether you *feel* that Jesus died or not makes no difference to the fact of His death. Whether you *feel* that *you* have died or not makes no difference to the fact of *your* death on the cross with Jesus. Your death is as much a fact as the death of Jesus Himself.

It is a great temptation to adopt this kind of attitude: "I don't feel dead. In fact, I am so conscious of my fears and doubts and sinfulness that my feelings tell me the opposite. My old nature is not dead; it is very much alive."

That is conclusive evidence that you should not trust your feelings! Being crucified with Christ is not a feeling. You can be truly thankful that you have been spared the feelings of such an experience as crucifixion.

No matter how you feel about it, you cannot undo what God has already done. He wants you to live, not by your feelings, but by faith in all that He has accomplished. Your feelings will often contradict the truth. But Jesus has said, "The truth will make you free."

YOU WERE INCLUDED
Some may want to ask "How can I be sure that I was included in what Jesus did on the cross?" Paul explains to the Corinthians:

> One died for all, and therefore all died (2 Cor. 5:14).

"All died", and that includes *you*. If you do not know that you have been crucified with Christ, you cannot believe it. And if you do not believe it, then you will continue to think that sin still has a powerful and controlling interest in your life. For that old nature, the person you used to be before you were born again, was under the control of the power of sin.

When Jesus took you to the cross, your old nature was put to death and the control of the power of sin over you was broken. Paul's personal testimony was:

> I have been crucified with Christ and I no longer live, but Christ lives in me. The life I live in the body, I live by faith in the Son of God, who loved me and gave himself for me (Gal. 2:20).

At the time of the crucifixion, Saul of Tarsus was an enemy of Jesus; later he became the arch-persecutor of the Church. After his conversion he came to appreciate that when Jesus went to the cross He had taken Saul with Him. He had crucified the old Saul, with his naturally sinful, selfish nature. That had made possible the new birth that he was to experience when he was made a 'new creature', a new man with a new nature. Saul could become Paul.

> Therefore, if anyone is in Christ, he is a new creation; the old has gone, the new has come! All this is from God,

who reconciled us to himself through Christ . . . (2 Cor. 5:17–18).

In this Paul saw the magnitude of God's grace. He described himself as 'the chief of sinners', and yet he had been reconciled with Him. God did not try to reform him or change him. He made him new. A new creation!

That is true for all Christians. God does not try to reform or change that old, naturally sinful, selfish nature. He knows that it will never change. What is selfish by nature will always be selfish. What is sinful by nature will always be sinful.

There was only one way to deal with this old nature – death! Crucifixion!

> I will give you a new heart and put a new spirit in you; I will remove from you your heart of stone and give you a heart of flesh (Ezek. 36:26).

God, through His prophet, does not say that He will change our hearts by trying to influence or reform them. He knows that would never work. What we need is new hearts, to become new creatures who possess new life.

When preaching in a prison in the north of England, I told the large congregation of prisoners that God did not want to reform them. That was the best news they had heard for a long time! Instead, I continued, God wanted them dead! That did not sound like such good news, until I explained that Jesus took men to the cross and put them to death. That naturally sinful nature was put to death so that they could receive a new nature and be made new men with new life. Several came to the Lord that day, and experienced the radical change in their lives that is evidence of new birth.

It is because the work of the cross is complete and deals with both sins and the sinful nature that Christians can know personal victory over the temptations of the world, the flesh and the devil, and so enjoy the fellowship of love that God has made possible for them to have with Him.

It is through the event of being born again that, Jesus says, we become part of the Kingdom of heaven. He did not come to tell us about the Kingdom of God, and that His Father wanted us to be part of that Kingdom, without making it possible for us to enter it and live as children of the King.

It is folly to imagine that we can pay our own debts to God, or can try to make ourselves acceptable to Him. It is folly to think that we have any righteousness of our own, any right to stand before God and make demands upon Him. It is folly to imagine that we can break, or even control successfully, the power of sin in our lives.

Only God could accomplish all these things. And the good news of the Gospel is that He has done so. He has accomplished all this through the cross of Jesus.

Through the cross, Jesus has paid your debts and suffered the punishment you deserved because of your sins.

Through the cross, Jesus has made you acceptable to God; you have been made righteous in His sight.

Through the cross, Jesus has broken any hold that Satan could have over you.

Through the cross, Jesus has broken the power of sin in your life and made it possible for you to be a 'new creation'.

Your words of faith: "WE KNOW THAT OUR OLD SELF WAS CRUCIFIED WITH HIM SO THAT THE BODY OF SIN MIGHT BE RENDERED POWERLESS." "ONE DIED FOR ALL, AND THEREFORE ALL DIED." "I HAVE BEEN CRUCIFIED WITH CHRIST AND I NO LONGER LIVE, BUT CHRIST LIVES IN ME."

8

AND BURIED

You were in Christ when He died on the cross; you died with Him. Your old sinful nature was crucified to set you free to live in the power of your new nature. For a Christian this death is not something that lies ahead of you. It is pointless to say: "I must die; I must die." You have already died.

> For you died, and your life is now hidden with Christ in God (Col. 3:3).

Paul is talking to people who are physically very much alive. He reminds them, for they needed to be reminded, of the great spiritual truth "You died." The consequence of their deaths is that their lives can now be lived in God.

What was true for those Christians at Colossae is true for us. We have died and our lives are now hidden with Christ in God.

BURIED WITH CHRIST

Travelling to many parts of the world means that I meet many Christians. I have discovered that very few have any real revelation of the fact of their death on the cross. And yet that is what is signified in their baptism. God is not concerned with how much water is used in baptism, whether people are immersed or sprinkled. He is much more concerned that they live in the power of what He has done on the cross and what is signified by baptism. Those who are baptised are dead men raised to new life in Jesus Christ.

> Or don't you know that all of us who were baptised into Christ Jesus were baptised into His death? We were therefore buried with him through baptism into death in order that, just as Christ was raised from the dead through the glory of the Father, we too may live a new life (Rom. 6:3–4).

Paul reminds the Romans of the meaning of their baptism in water. Baptism signifies that the new believer is not only a participant in the death of Jesus, but is also buried with Him. The old sinful nature is dead and buried.

Being submerged in water signifies the drowning of the old life by faith in Jesus. The candidate comes out of the water as a new man, cleansed not only from sin but also from the power of sin, the power of that old nature.

In the ancient Church it was customary for baptism to

And Buried

take place in the open at a river or stream. The candidate had been suitably prepared, often over a prolonged period of time. At the actual baptism he first removed his outer garments to signify that he was taking off the old life of sin and corruption. He would then descend into the water, where he was immersed in the name of God, Father, Son and Holy Spirit. That old nature was dead and finished with.

When he emerged from the water he was given a white garment to wear, signifying that he had now put on the new life of Jesus. He would then receive the laying on of hands, with the prayer that he would be filled, or baptised, with the Holy Spirit.

> I tell you the truth, unless a man is born of water and the Spirit, he cannot enter the kingdom of God. Flesh gives birth to flesh, but the Spirit gives birth to spirit (John 3:5–6).

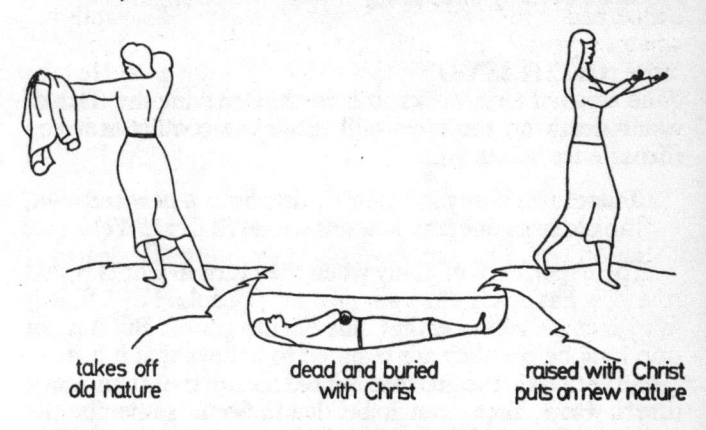

takes off old nature | dead and buried with Christ | raised with Christ puts on new nature

Your baptism in water signifies that you have not only died with Christ; you have also been buried with Him. That naturally sinful self you have been fighting, with its impulse to drag you into sin and disobedience, is already crucified with Christ and buried with Him.

JESUS TOOK YOUR SINS TO THE CROSS.
JESUS TOOK YOU TO THE CROSS.

Many things will tempt you to disbelieve the fact of your death on the cross:
   your feelings,
   your reason,
   your experiences,
   the enemy.
Until you do believe it, those same feelings, your human reason and the arguments of Satan will continue to have a controlling effect upon your life. Without the revelation that your old nature was crucified with Christ, you will continue to fight a battle that has already been fought and won by Jesus. You will fight yourself, you will fight the enemy – and often you will think that you are the loser and the task hopeless.

Don't fight a battle that Jesus has already fought and won. Live in the power of the victory He gained on the cross. Every time you lose sight of that victory you will find yourself battling once again in your own strength.

THE OLD HAS GONE
The word of God works. It is truth. Believing the truth of your death on the cross will settle the conflict that you experience within you.

> Therefore, if anyone is in Christ, he is a new creation; the old has gone, the new has come! (2 Cor. 5:17).

The experience of many when they turn to Christ is that the new has come; they are now new people. For a time it also seems true to say that "the old has gone". But it is not too long before they are tempted to believe that it has not gone very far! It seems that this old nature tries to re-assert itself. How, then, can it be dead? Some settle for the attitude "My old life has died, but it won't lie down!" That will not do. What is dead and buried cannot sit up!

Paul is emphatic: "the old *has* gone." He is not speaking of what will happen, but of what has already taken place in the life of the believer. God, by His sovereign grace, has caused the old nature to pass away and has given His child a new nature.

And Buried

Because Christians become aware of the conflict within them, one part of them wanting to do God's will, another part not wanting to, they are often tempted to pray to God and ask Him to crucify them. Or else they subject themselves to rigorous, ascetical practices to try to contain 'the flesh', or even put it to death themselves.

We can see that both are based on a lack of appreciation of what God has already done. We need not to be crucified, but *to live in the power of our crucifixion that has already taken place*. No amount of rigorous asceticism will ever put the flesh to death. God has already done that. He wants us to live in the joy of that fact.

We do not walk away from the cross as the same person who went to the cross. We have died and are made new.

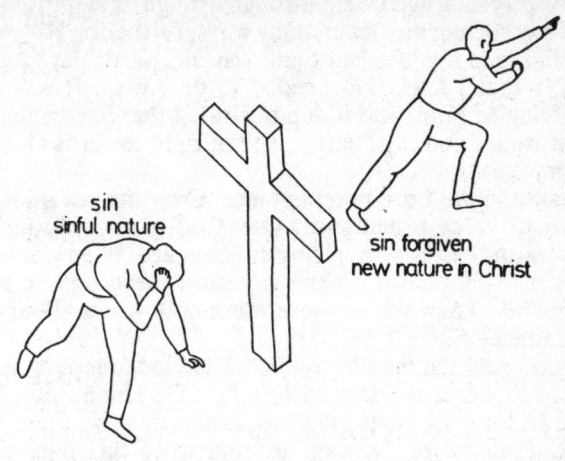

sin
sinful nature

sin forgiven
new nature in Christ

It is impossible to understand with human reason how God could have accomplished this. That does not matter. What is important is to believe that it has been accomplished and to apply this great fact to our lives. It is only then that we shall be able to see the answer to our dilemma of needing to know that we are free from bondage to the sinful, rebellious nature. It is only then that we shall know victory in this conflict of wanting to please God and yet not wanting to.

Christ did not send me to baptise, but to preach the gospel – not with words of human wisdom, lest the cross of Christ be emptied of its power. For the message of the cross is foolishness to those who are perishing, but to us who are being saved it is the power of God. For it is written: "I will destroy the wisdom of the wise; the intelligence of the intelligent I will frustrate" (1 Cor. 1:17–19).

EASY TO FORGET

This is a truth that I have known for several years, and it has been a powerful influence in both my personal life and my ministry. And yet I have to confess that there are times when I lose sight of this truth myself.

Not very long ago I went through a tough time spiritually. God was sorting me out in many ways, furthering His work of refining in my life. But there was one particular area of my life that I knew He needed to deal with. It was not glorifying to Him, and it demonstrated that in some ways my attitudes and my heart were not right towards God or others.

I came to the Lord in repentance. Over the years I have grown to value repentance. Our God is so faithful; He forgives and restores us, giving us His peace, when we come humbly to Him. But on this occasion there was no real peace and I knew why – there was a hollowness about the repentance.

I was caught in the old conflict. I needed to repent and I wanted to, because I desired the will of God for my life. Yet I had to face the shattering realisation that, on the other hand, I didn't really want to repent of this particular matter. There was an area of self-love to which I wanted to hold on.

I asked the Lord to deal with my heart and the wrong attitude. Nothing seemed to happen, although I persisted in this prayer for days. By discipline I tried to control the problem, was not always successful, and was continually aware that I still desired disobedience to the Lord.

Satan revelled in the situation. I seemed to be living under a cloud of condemnation; he was for ever accusing me and trying to convince me that I did not have a scrap of true love for God in me.

Instead of the conflict easing it grew more and more intense. I reached the point of yielding my self-love to God, and I longed for Him to deal with me. I wanted to be set free from the mess and confusion I felt inside me. I could not understand why He did not answer my prayer and the earnest desire of my heart.

Then one day He did. He didn't still the turmoil. He didn't need to. He simply said to me: "Colin, you have died!"

Flashes of light! Revelation! Of course! "You fool, Colin," I said to myself.

Jesus had taken me, my old heart and desires, all my wrong attitudes, everything about my sinful nature, to the cross. I prayed aloud in my study: "Father, thank you that I have been crucified with Christ. Thank you that this problem has already been dealt with; you have already given me a new heart and I do not need to desire this sin nor yield to any temptation. I proclaim the victory of Jesus in my life and I tell Satan, in the name of Jesus, that he has no right to accuse me concerning this matter again."

And I was free. After weeks of torment I was free. Why? The truth had set me free. The Holy Spirit had spoken the truth of God's word to my heart: "You have died." All those weeks of useless, senseless battling, when all I had to do was to believe what God had done for me on the cross!

Of course, while it was going on I was justifying the battle. I was telling myself that, when I came through, my faith would be stronger, my heart purer; that I would have learned more about how to persevere in prayer. And all the time I was doing completely the wrong thing.

There was no excuse for me. Over the years I have ministered this truth to countless others. "Reckon yourself dead to that old life; you are already a new creature. You don't have to fight what you were; simply turn away from the past and live in the power of your new nature." And on this occasion I failed to apply the truth to myself.

The word of God works. It is truth. I pray that I will never fall into the same trap again, but will always live as one who has died, knowing that the old nature is buried with Christ. It is amazing how believing that truth settles the conflict within you.

> Therefore, if anyone is in Christ, he is a new creation; the old has gone, the new has come! (2 Cor. 5:17).

APPLY THE TRUTH

Are you making a similar mistake to mine? Are you fighting against something that has already been defeated on the cross? If so, apply this truth to yourself, relating it especially to that situation: you have been crucified with Christ. The old has passed away; the new has come!

Do not listen to your desires, or to the enemy's ridicule. Listen to the truth that God reveals about you in His word. And remember, you are as deeply involved in the resurrection of Jesus as you are in his crucifixion. You were buried with Christ in baptism so that "just as Christ was raised from the dead through the glory of the Father", so you too may live a new life.

Your words of faith: "FOR YOU DIED, AND YOUR LIFE IS NOW HIDDEN WITH CHRIST IN GOD." "WE WERE THEREFORE BURIED WITH HIM THROUGH BAPTISM INTO DEATH IN ORDER THAT, JUST AS CHRIST WAS RAISED FROM THE DEAD THROUGH THE GLORY OF THE FATHER, WE TOO MAY LIVE A NEW LIFE." "IF ANYONE IS IN CHRIST, HE IS A NEW CREATION: THE OLD HAS GONE, THE NEW HAS COME!"

9

COUNT YOURSELF DEAD

Death is something that cannot be undone; it is final. The death of your old nature is an accomplished fact; it has happened. It is not the old nature that is raised to new life.

When you were born again you were given a new nature and became a new creation.

> Count yourselves dead to sin but alive to God in Christ Jesus (Rom. 6:11).

To 'count yourselves dead' means that you believe the fact of your death on the cross and live accordingly.

You cannot 'count yourself dead' without *knowing* that you are dead. If you are trying to convince yourself that you have died with Christ, that is evidence that you do not believe your death has already taken place with Him.

There is nothing Satan can do about facts except encourage you to disbelieve them. When you are conscious of selfish desires that you associate with the old nature, he will be quick to suggest that this is ample evidence that you have not truly died. Actually to commit sin, he will suggest, is the absolute proof that you cannot have died to sin.

When you put your faith in the fact of the cross and believe that "the old has passed away", that does not mean that sin has been eradicated. Even though the sinful nature is dead, sin itself is very much present and, given the opportunity, will overpower you and cause you to commit sins again, whether consciously or unconsciously.

It is your sinful nature that is dead, buried and finished with – not sin itself.

Because God does not interfere with the free will of the soul, sin is always a possibility for every one of us. It would be wonderful if our new birth led to an immediate and instant state of perfection that made it impossible for us to sin. Unfortunately that is not the case.

Because God has dealt with your old nature on the cross, that sinful nature is no longer the guiding principle within you. You are now born of the Spirit, and God Himself has come to live in you that He may be the guiding principle of your life.

When the old nature dies, God does not destroy *you*; He does not kill the soul. Your soul still exists in all its human frailty and weakness, but can now come under the influence of God living in you by the power of His Spirit.

'The body of sin' is rendered powerless now that the old

life has been crucified with Christ. You are no longer a slave to sin. It no longer has control over you. It is no longer your master.

But because you have free will you can still choose to sin, to disobey God, to disbelieve His word, to elect for your own will instead of His.

Before conversion a man sins without thinking about it, without considering that what he is doing is sinful. Often he feels powerless to resist the temptation to sin because he only has his own human self-will to fight against his naturally sinful nature.

That is not the case with the Christian. Sin is no longer in control of his life; it is not natural for him to sin, neither can he fall back upon the excuse, "I couldn't help it." That is not true for the born-again man, for if he was trusting to the resources of Jesus working through his new nature, he would be able to resist every temptation to sin.

He is still prone to the temptation of the world around him; Satan will want him to sin and he will often feel inclined to please himself rather than obey God.

> No temptation has seized you except what is common to man. And God is faithful; he will not let you be tempted beyond what you can bear. But when you are tempted, he will also provide a way out so that you can stand up under it (1 Cor. 10:13).

Temptation need not be regarded as negative and destructive. God uses it positively to test and prune us. When we sin by yielding to temptation, we demonstrate that we still want our own way rather than His; we still trust in ourselves rather than Him; we still do not count ourselves dead to sin. For that we need His forgiveness.

When Paul says "count yourselves dead to sin", he clearly implies that sin itself is a present reality. But it no longer controls the man who has died with Christ. He does not need to live any longer under the power of sin.

> For he has rescued us from the dominion of darkness and brought us into the kingdom of the Son he loves (Col. 1:13).

FROM DARKNESS TO LIGHT

God has already rescued you from the dominion of darkness and brought you into the Kingdom of His Son. He wants you to live as a child of light. Jesus said:

> I have come into the world as a light, so that no one who believes in me should stay in darkness (John 12:46).

Therefore, "let us put aside the deeds of darkness and put on the armour of light" (Rom. 13:12).

> For you were once darkness, but now you are light in the Lord. Live as children of light (for the fruit of the light consists in all goodness, righteousness and truth) and find out what pleases the Lord. Have nothing to do with the fruitless deeds of darkness, but rather expose them (Eph. 5:8–11).

Although you are "light in the Lord" it is still possible for you to be guilty of doing works that belong to the dark. There needs to be, therefore, a constant turning away from everything that belongs to darkness. You can regard yourself dead to all that. You do not need to behave like that any longer, nor do you need to gratify those desires to have what the world counts dear.

> You are all sons of the light and sons of the day. We do not belong to the night or to the darkness (1 Thess. 5:5).

If we do not belong to the night, there is no need for us to live as if we do. If we have been freed from sin there is no need for us to live as if we are still bound by sin. But darkness and sin are always a possibility. John warns us:

> God is light; in him there is no darkness at all. If we claim to have fellowship with him yet walk in the darkness, we lie and do not live by the truth. But if we walk in the light, as he is in the light, we have fellowship with one another, and the blood of Jesus, his Son, purifies us from every sin (1 John 1:5–7).

Either is possible. We belong to the light. We can walk in either light or darkness. Before our new birth, we could only walk in darkness. Now we can leave all that darkness behind and live as the children of light.

BELIEVE THE VICTORY
Many bemoan their weakness, thinking that if only they were spiritually stronger, they would be able to fight more adequately against the temptation to sin and "walk in the darkness". They may seek more power from God to fight against their weakness, and wonder why He does not give it.

He does not give it because that is not His answer to the need. "Anyone who has died has been freed from sin" (Rom. 6:7).

Many Christians are fighting battles with themselves that are unnecessary. They need to believe the victory that has already taken place on the cross. It is not that they need to ask God to do something to strengthen their resolve to fight against sin; they need to live in the power of what He has already done for them in Jesus. They need to count themselves dead to sin and know that they no longer need to walk in darkness.

It is not power that gives you victory over sin, but the cross of Jesus Christ.

God did not try to strengthen your old nature so that it could resist its own desires and impulses. He put it to death. It was no good to you or to Him. It was in rebellion against Him and would only keep you in rebellion and disobedience to Him.

Human resources are of little use in fighting sin. God desires to see you trusting in the victory that He has already won on the cross.

KNOWING THE TRUTH
For the truth to be effective in our lives, we need to know it, not in our heads, but in our hearts. Each Christian needs to receive personally from God the revelation that he has been crucified with Christ. It is only the Holy Spirit that can witness this truth to the heart of a believer.

A man can know that his sins are forgiven. That is not a feeling but a knowing that results in being at peace with

God. In the same way, he needs to know that he is crucified with Christ. It becomes a fact for him, not some spiritual theory locked up in a holy book.

At first he will not understand all the implications of this truth. Nevertheless he *knows* it. "For we *know* that our old self was crucified with him . . ."

You often hear people say: "I am trying to be dead." No amount of trying will ever make you dead. Your death is a fact to reckon with: "you died, and your life is now hidden with Christ in God" (Col 3:3).

Your words of faith: "COUNT YOURSELVES DEAD TO SIN BUT ALIVE TO GOD IN CHRIST JESUS." "FOR HE HAS RESCUED US FROM THE DOMINION OF DARKNESS AND BROUGHT US INTO THE KINGDOM OF THE SON HE LOVES." "FOR YOU WERE ONCE DARKNESS, BUT NOW YOU ARE LIGHT IN THE LORD."

10

SPIRIT, SOUL AND BODY

Every human being possesses a spirit, soul and body. It is important for us to understand the function of each of these parts of the whole person, and the relationships between them.

THE HUMAN SPIRIT

"Flesh gives birth to flesh," Jesus says, "but the Spirit gives birth to spirit."

In the natural man, born of the flesh, the human spirit is, to all intents and purposes, useless. It is inactive because he is spiritually dead; he does not have communion or fellowship with God. His human spirit is not alive, because he is not yet 'born of the Spirit'. Jesus says:

> God is spirit, and his worshippers must worship in spirit and in truth (John 4:24).

But the natural man cannot worship in spirit; he is not yet spiritually alive and cannot understand the things of God. He must be born of God's Spirit if he is to do so.

> The man without the Spirit does not accept the things that come from the Spirit of God, for they are foolishness to him and he cannot understand them, because they are spiritually discerned (1 Cor. 2:14).

Although he has a human spirit, it does not exercise any real influence upon him until that spiritual rebirth takes place. Then he can know God; he is able to hear Him and speak to Him personally. His body becomes a temple of the Holy Spirit because God has come to live in him.

THE SOUL
Your soul consists of three main areas of your life:
a) the mind – your thinking and intellectual processes;
b) the emotions – your affections and feelings;
c) the will – your ability to choose and determine what you will do.

The word Jesus used in His teaching can be translated either 'soul' or 'life'. The soul is the non-physical part of the natural man, the person that he is, his personality and character.

We shall have to pay particular attention to these three functions of the soul: the mind, the emotions and the will. Until a man is born of the Spirit, his soul will run his life. He is used to assessing situations with his mind, and reaching his own conclusions. He pays considerable attention to his emotions, and often allows them to rule him. He makes his own decisions, based upon the reasoning of his mind, or as a result of the emotional desires he has, or by a combination of the two.

THE BODY
The physical body houses the soul and the human spirit. Whatever goes on in your soul determines what you do with your body. The body reacts to the thoughts of the mind, it expresses the emotions and responds to the decisions of the will.

Spirit, Soul and Body

When a man is born again, his body becomes a temple of the Holy Spirit.

> Do you not know that your body is a temple of the Holy Spirit, who is in you, whom you have received from God? (1 Cor. 6:19).

THEIR RELATIONSHIP

Because of the presence of God within him, the Christian can live under the direction of the Spirit. God desires the entire life of the soul (the mind, the emotions and the will) to be under the influence of His Spirit working through the human spirit, which has come alive as a result of his new birth. It will help us to see this diagramatically.

```
                          flesh
                          self
(spirit)        |      soul ——— body
                |       |
                |      mind
                |      emotions
                |      will
```

When Paul uses the term 'flesh' he means that the soul and body are operating independently from the Spirit. Because of the sinful, fallen nature they inherit, that is how all men operate before their conversion to Jesus Christ. They could not understand the things of the Spirit; they were dependent upon their own thinking and wills to determine what they would do, and were largely at the mercy of their emotions. They were naturally independent and self-willed.

When a man is born again the picture changes dramatically:

```
HOLY
SPIRIT
   |
   ↓
spirit ——→ soul ——→ body
             |
            mind
            emotions
            will
```

The human spirit no longer lies dormant. It has now been brought to life by the Spirit of God. It can, therefore, begin to exercise its proper influence upon the soul, informing the mind, emotions and will of God's purposes. The body can then be directed by the Spirit working through the soul, to accomplish the will and purpose of God.

That would be straightforward if the new birth meant that the Christian always listened and obeyed the voice of the Spirit of God within him, that "still small voice of God". In practice it is often drowned by the clamour of the soul. For although he can now know the will of God and decide to do it, he will not necessarily do so. God does not interfere with his mind, emotions or will. He desires to influence them, but with his co-operation. The soul has always run his life in the past and still demands to do so. The Christian still has a mind of his own; he can make his own rational appraisal of a situation, and need not seek to know the mind of Christ. He still has a will of his own and may choose to ignore God's will. He can allow his feelings to rule him instead of trusting to the leading of the Holy Spirit.

The soul will not easily give place to the Spirit.

So, although he is now spiritually aware, there is no guarantee that he will allow "the Spirit to direct his course". That is why he suffers what appears to be a conflict between the old and the new natures. He can think in a new way, make decisions in a new way, control the selfish emotions and feelings in a new way, his body can radiate the new life that he has received, and can do the things that are the outworking of a new motivation that comes from the 'new spirit' that he has.

Or he can go on as he did before his conversion, his new birth and his baptism. He can be as selfish as ever he was; he may be spiritually blind because he does not listen to God. So, unfortunately, we have to bring the two diagrams together.

That seems confusing – and it is! This describes the conflict that the Christian experiences, with the soul being pulled in two opposite directions, by the flesh and the Spirit of God working through his human spirit. Sometimes he obeys one, sometimes the other.

```
        HOLY
        SPIRIT
          │
          ▼              flesh
                         self
    spirit ──────► soul ──────► body
                    │
                   mind
                   emotions
                   will
```

Because he has been crucified with Christ, he no longer has to be ruled by the flesh. He is to reckon that his old nature is dead. However, it is still possible for him to ignore the Spirit and allow his soul and body to act independently of God. When he does that, he denies his new life in Jesus.

With God's Spirit within him, the Christian has all the resources to be able to deal with the pressures of the world, the flesh and the devil around him. What he needs is for the power of the Holy Spirit to fill his soul and body, to influence every part of His being.

THE HOLY SPIRIT

The Holy Spirit is God. To say that the Holy Spirit lives in us is to say that God lives in us, that our bodies are temples that house the presence of God Himself. When a man is born again, He is born of the Spirit; He is born of God. His human birth was the result of a physical act between his mother and father. His second birth is by the direct activity of the Holy Spirit. God comes to live in him.

The Holy Spirit could not be given to those who believed in Jesus until He had been glorified, until He had returned to be with His Father in majesty and honour. God the Father gives this precious gift of the Holy Spirit, not because of what we are or have done, but because of who Jesus is and what He has done. He is the obedient Son who gave His life as a ransom for us, who was raised from the dead and now reigns in glory with His Father.

> I will ask the Father, and he will give you another Counsellor to be with you for ever – the Spirit of truth. The world cannot accept him, because it neither sees

him nor knows him. But you know him, for he lives with
you and will be in you (John 14:16–17).

The Spirit is given in response to the Son's request of His
Father. He gives the Holy Spirit to those who believe in
Jesus, not as a reward for their faith, but out of love for His
Son. He is the Spirit of truth and will guide God's children
into all truth. He will teach them everything and will
remind them of all that Jesus has said. He is the voice of
God within the believer.

The Counsellor, the Holy Spirit, whom the Father will
send in my name, will teach you all things and will
remind you of everything I have said to you (John
14:26).

He is also the 'Counsellor', our 'Advocate', the one who
helps us, speaks on our behalf, teaches us what to say, and
pleads our cause.

EMPOWERED BY GOD

Jesus Himself was conceived of the Holy Spirit; His birth
was the direct result of the Spirit's activity. Before His
public ministry began, the Holy Spirit came upon Him after
He had been baptised by John.

As soon as Jesus was baptised, he went up out of the
water. At that moment heaven was opened, and he saw
the Spirit of God descending like a dove and lighting on
him. And a voice from heaven said, 'This is my Son,
whom I love; with him I am well pleased' (Matt. 3:16–17).

John had prophesied that Jesus would practise a baptism
different from his. John had been baptising people with
water, signifying that in response to their repentance, God
had washed away their sins. Speaking of Jesus he said: "He
will baptise you with the Holy Spirit and with fire" (Matt.
3:11).

Jesus does not allude directly to this prophetic word until
He appears to the disciples in His risen body. The promise
of the Spirit could not be fulfilled until He returned to be

Spirit, Soul and Body

with His Father. That time was now imminent and so Jesus renews this promise Himself:

> Do not leave Jerusalem, but wait for the gift my Father promised, which you have heard me speak about. For John baptised with water, but in a few days you will be baptised with the Holy Spirit (Acts 1:4–5).

And Jesus explained what the implications of this baptism in the Holy Spirit would be:

> But you will receive power when the Holy Spirit comes on you; and you will be my witnesses in Jerusalem, and in all Judea and Samaria, and to the ends of the earth (Acts 1:8).

The promise was fulfilled on the day of Pentecost: 'All of them were filled with the Holy Spirit and began to speak in other tongues as the Spirit enabled them' (Acts 2:4).

It was that event that revolutionised the ministries of those men, as the early chapters of Acts demonstrate. Jesus had warned them to wait until they had received this empowering of His Spirit before they went out to fulfil their apostolic ministries. They were changed from frightened believers into those who were bold in their faith and witness. It is this experience of being baptised with the Holy Spirit that is presently renewing the lives of countless numbers of Christians around the world.

To be filled with the Holy Spirit is not the same as being born of the Spirit. Many Christians have missed the empowering that God has wanted to give them, because of their confusion about this. It is essential to God's purpose that they are born of the Spirit. If they are to live lives of faithful witness, it is equally essential that the power of the Holy Spirit is released through their souls and bodies. Jesus speaks of the Spirit as flowing out of Christians like rivers of living water:

> "If a man is thirsty, let him come to me and drink. Whoever believes in me, as the Scripture has said, streams of living water will flow from within him." By this he meant the Spirit, whom those who believed in

him were later to receive. Up to that time the Spirit had not been given, since Jesus had not yet been glorified (John 7:37–39).

It will help us to look again at the illustration of the spirit, soul and body. At the moment of spiritual rebirth, the Holy Spirit brings the human spirit to life. God does not want His Spirit locked up within the believer; He desires to see the life, the love and power of the Spirit released through his soul and body, so that the presence of Christ is manifested powerfully in his life.

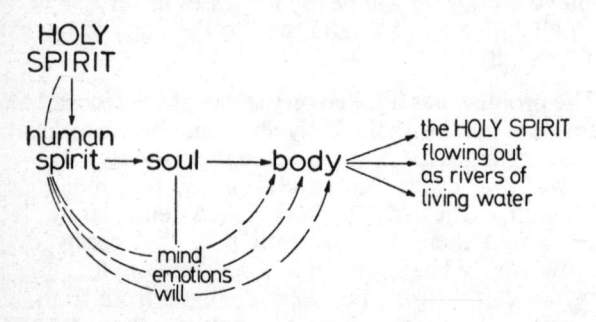

```
HOLY
SPIRIT
   ↓
human                          the HOLY SPIRIT
spirit → soul → body           flowing out
                               as rivers of
                               living water
         mind
         emotions
         will
```

As Christians, we shall not be able to glorify the Father by manifesting lives that are 'clothed in Christ' unless we are 'submerged' in the Holy Spirit. That is what it means to be baptised in the Spirit of God, to be saturated and drenched in Him.

To recognise that you need to be baptised in the Holy Spirit does not call into question the reality of your new birth by the Spirit when you became a Christian. To be baptised by Jesus with His Spirit is not the same as to be baptised with water *into* Jesus. Water baptism signifies that the new believer is totally identified with the death of Jesus on the cross; his old nature is buried with Him, and he has been given a new nature. He is baptised into Jesus and is born of the Spirit.

It is Jesus Himself who baptises, or submerges, the believer in the Holy Spirit. This event releases the power of the Spirit in his life and enables him to live more fully in the power of his new nature. That release of God's love and power is a definite event in the life of a Christian. But there is still the need to go on being filled with the Holy Spirit, as Paul makes clear to the Ephesians, and as the disciples themselves realised.

Despite the great event of Pentecost, when they were baptised in the Holy Spirit, the disciples continued to seek God's empowering, and He answered their prayers by filling them with the Holy Spirit *again*.

> "Enable your servants to speak your word with great boldness. Stretch out your hand to heal and perform miraculous signs and wonders through the name of your holy servant Jesus." After they prayed, the place where they were meeting was shaken. And they were all filled with the Holy Spirit and spoke the word of God boldly (Acts 4:29-31).

If we are to see God working in powerful ways, we shall need to see the continual release of His Spirit in our lives. He is not concerned with experiences that we claim, or particular doctrines of the Holy Spirit that we believe. God wants to see the evidence of His life and power in our lives. He desires to see those rivers of living water flowing freely out of our innermost beings.

RECEIVING THE SPIRIT
God does not withhold the gift of the Spirit from any who truly seek Him. Jesus promised:

> Ask and it will be given to you; seek and you will find; knock and the door will be opened to you. For everyone who asks receives; he who seeks finds; and to him who knocks, the door will be opened . . . how much more will your Father in heaven give the Holy Spirit to those who ask him! (Luke 11:9-10, 13).

It is God's purpose to give us the power we need to live as His children, being obedient to Him and ministering His love and power to this needy world. He will not refuse those who seek Him, because the Holy Spirit has already been given. Just as Jesus does not have to die on the cross again when a sinner repents, so God does not have to pour out His Spirit again because a believer somewhere decides he needs more power in His life. The gift is given and awaits those who ask. It is at that time that the gift is appropriated and the power released in men's lives.

God does not desire to withhold what He has already given. The Spirit has been given because Jesus has been glorified. At any time you can reach out to Him for His precious gift, or you can know a release of the gift that is within you.

In my ministry I see many thousands baptised in the Spirit every year. Some are new Christians who have only just come into the Kingdom of God; others have been believers for years, but know that their witness is lacking the power of God.

And I see countless others asking God to renew the gift within them, to release those rivers of living water afresh. That is my constant prayer. Without a continual dependence upon the Holy Spirit and the freshness of His anointing, we grow spiritually dull and weak.

The experience of receiving the Spirit will differ widely from one person to another. It is folly to covet someone else's experience, or to think that you have received only if your experience tallies with that of another. The Lord asks you to believe His promise, not an experience. The Spirit has been given because Jesus has been glorified. It is unbelief that keeps some from knowing that God has graciously fulfilled His promise in their lives. They experience the anguish of constantly asking Him to give to them without ever believing that He has.

> Therefore I tell you, whatever you ask for in prayer, believe that you have received it, and it will be yours (Mark 11:24).

God does not want His Holy Spirit locked up in you. He wants to see His love, His life and power flowing through your soul and body, flowing out of you as 'rivers of living water'. Is God working freely through you, so that His life can pour out of you to affect people around you and the situations in which you are placed?

Spirit, Soul and Body

Like those early disciples, don't be afraid to ask Jesus to baptise you in the Holy Spirit, or to seek Him for a further release of His love and power in your life. It is His purpose to give to *you* because His Spirit has been given as Jesus is now glorified. If you want to live in the power of your new nature, you will need to use all the resources of His Holy Spirit that God makes available to you.

Your words of faith: "HOW MUCH MORE WILL YOUR FATHER IN HEAVEN GIVE THE HOLY SPIRIT TO THOSE WHO ASK HIM." "DO YOU NOT KNOW THAT YOUR BODY IS A TEMPLE OF THE HOLY SPIRIT, WHO IS IN YOU, WHOM YOU RECEIVED FROM GOD?" "THE COUNSELLOR, THE HOLY SPIRIT, WHOM THE FATHER WILL SEND IN MY NAME, WILL TEACH YOU ALL THINGS AND WILL REMIND YOU OF EVERYTHING I HAVE SAID TO YOU." "YOU WILL RECEIVE POWER WHEN THE HOLY SPIRIT COMES ON YOU; AND YOU WILL BE MY WITNESSES."

Here is a simple way in which to ask the Lord to baptise you in the Holy Spirit, or to release afresh the power of His Spirit in your life:

1. *Give* yourself to the Lord.
   Ask Him to forgive the sins, the fear and doubt. Offer your life to Him, telling Him that you want Him to be Lord of your body, your mind, your will, your affections; give Him your relationships, work, time, future, your money and possessions – for you want His life to flow through every area of your life.
2. Believe His forgiveness and know that He accepts the offering of your life that you make from your heart.
3. Ask him to fill you to overflowing with His Holy Spirit, to fulfil the promises set out in the words of faith above.
4. Believe God has answered your prayer of faith whether you immediately experience anything or not. Remember that Jesus said:

   "Therefore I tell you, whatever you ask for in prayer, believe that you have received it, and it will be yours" (Mark 11:24).

> If you believe, then you will be thanking God for His precious gift to you.

All you need to know and experience of God's love, joy, peace and the gifts of the Holy Spirit will be given you as you believe God's faithfulness in honouring His promise.

11

IN CHRIST

The Christian has not only been rescued from the dominion of darkness and brought into the Kingdom of God's Son. He also lives in Christ Himself. He lives in Christ because that is where God has placed him:

> It is because of him (God) that you are in Christ Jesus. (1 Cor. 1:30).

Jesus took all sinful humanity to the cross, but Paul uses the phrase 'in Christ Jesus' countless times to refer to the position of the believer. For the Christian is not only crucified with Christ, he is raised to new life in Him. In some mystical sense he is living 'in Christ Jesus'.

Obviously there is no sin in Christ Himself. So there should be no sin in those who live in Him. If we do sin and fail God, can we really be said to be living in Christ, in whom there is no sin?

The short answer is 'Yes'. We have been made 'sons of light', but we are still capable of performing deeds of darkness.

The old sinful nature has been crucified. That is a fact, but we can still live in ignorance or unbelief of that fact and imagine that we are still bound by sin. God has placed us in His Son, Jesus, but it is still possible for us to live as if we were not in Him, to deny our wonderful inheritance and seek our own purposes instead of His. That is not what God wants, but it remains a possibility. He will never force us into submission and obedience, because He desires a loving response from us. He wants us to submit our free will to the leading and guiding of His Spirit; He does not force us to do so.

If we deny that we are in Christ, we not only argue with the teaching of scripture, we also render ourselves ineffective in combating sin. It is because we are in Him that we can be built up in His life and His truth, and so be set free from the desire to please ourselves and oppose Him.

It will be important for us to build up a picture from the scriptures of what it means to live 'in Christ Jesus'. For only then shall we see ourselves as God sees us. He does not see us separated from Him, but as living in Him. He is not divorced from the needs and circumstances of our lives. He cannot be, for God has placed us in Him and He is in us.

> We know that we live in him and he in us, because he has given us of his Spirit (1 John 4:13).

It is certain that God wants us to manifest lives that are a reflection of this great truth, both by what we are and by the things we do. Yet at any moment it is possible to sin and disobey.

Once we know and reckon ourselves to be dead in Christ, then the way is clear for us to be built up in our understanding of the new nature that God has given us, the truths that apply to us as those who live in Him, and the power that He makes available to us.

> To live in the revelation that you are a new creature living in Christ, and no longer bound by the old, sinful nature, will enable you to die daily to sin.

THE PLACE OF FAITH
If you do not believe the revelation of what God has done on the cross, that work is of no value to you. In the same way, if you do not believe that you have died with Christ, or do not apply that truth to your life, then that fact does you no good. If you do not believe that you have been set free from sin, then you will allow yourself to fall into sin again

and again, because you will fail in your desperate attempts to resist temptation in your own strength.

The enemy will try to undermine your assurance of the facts that God reveals in His word. Stand firm against him and he will flee from you. When Jesus resisted the devil in the wilderness, He said: "It is written . . ." in answer to every temptation.

The word of our God stands for ever. We need to stand on what He says, not on what 'the father of all lies' would have us believe. He encourages us to look at ourselves, our feelings, our doubts, our experiences – anything that will cause us to take our eyes off Jesus and what He has done for us.

God does not want us to reduce His word to the level of our experience; he wants our experience raised to the level of His word.

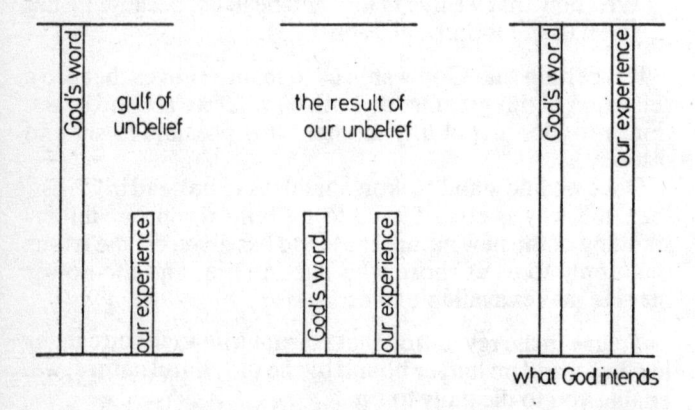

God's word	gulf of unbelief	the result of our unbelief	God's word	our experience
	our experience	God's word / our experience		

what God intends

Our experience will only be raised to the level of God's word if we learn to affirm positively the truth of that word in the face of every difficulty and temptation to doubt.

We are dead in Christ – not in ourselves. If we look within ourselves, in our own souls, we shall see weakness, failure, sin. God has done His work in Jesus, not in ourselves. In Him we are dead, made righteous, holy and acceptable to God, despite all that we are in ourselves.

In Christ

Count yourselves dead to sin but alive to God *in Christ Jesus* (Rom. 6:11).
For you were once darkness, but now you are *light in the Lord* (Eph. 5:8).
For you died, and your life is now hidden *with Christ in God* (Col. 3:3).
If anyone is *in Christ*, he is a new creation; the old has gone, the new has come! (2 Cor. 5:17).

Some of the modern techniques of ministry are not only dangerous, but also anti-scriptural, for they point the Christian more and more deeply into himself, instead of teaching him to see himself dead and raised to new life with a new nature in Christ. If we keep on looking at our weakness and failure, we shall believe even more strongly in our weakness and failure. The only positive result of that is that we learn the futility of trusting in ourselves. As we look to Jesus and what God has made us because we are in Him, so we are able to trust Him more fully. And He is the one who is Almighty and never fails.

LIVING IN JESUS

In Him I have died and can count myself dead to sin. Of myself I am still prone to sin. In Him my old nature has no power, sin is not my master and cannot control me. But if I set my mind on the things of the flesh, on pleasing myself, on my own weakness and failure, I shall fear, doubt, sin – and deny my inheritance in Christ every time I do so.

Does that mean that there is no need for self-examination before confessing our sins to God? No; but self-examination is not a matter of trying to impress God with what weak, miserable wretches we are. Rather, we need to ask the Lord to show us the ways in which we have denied our rich inheritance as those who live 'in Him'; to show us when we have not acted in the power of the new nature He has given us, and when we have listened to the deceiving lies of the enemy. We need to confess the ways in which we have not submitted to His Lordship and the leading of His Holy Spirit.

The more we are built up in the revelation of who and

what we are 'in Christ Jesus', the more we shall be able to please God and resist the pull of sin to please ourselves.

Spiritual growth does not come from seeking one spiritual experience after another; it comes from learning to trust the facts of what God has done for us in Jesus and to see ourselves as He sees us.

You cannot look to a particular moment in your experience and say that on that day you were crucified with Christ. At some time you realised the truth that when Christ died, you died with Him. It was then that you identified personally with what happened on the cross, with what happened to Him.

Genuine spiritual experience, for all Christians, is an entering into what He has done. That leaves no room for pride on our part. There can be no suggestion that we could achieve any of this for ourselves. The whole Christian life is a continual revelation of the grace of God.

That is offensive to the man who considers that he is of any value to God apart from Jesus. It is music to the ears of the man who knows his total dependence upon the Lord; apart from Him he can do nothing and would be unacceptable to God.

As we enter more fully into the revelation of all that God has done for us in Jesus, we discover that whatever is true of Him becomes true for us because we are 'in Him'. That leads us to some startling conclusions – as we shall see.

If, on the other hand, we look back at the old nature, we shall easily be led to believe that this is still the truth about us. In Him we find everything we need for every situation in

In Christ

our lives; in ourselves, we find only weakness, failure and sin.

The Christian is able to look in either direction. The reason why the lives of so many Christians appear to be a dismal catalogue of fear, failure, sin and powerlessness should, by now, be easy for us to see. They are looking in the wrong direction. They are looking at themselves, their weakness, their failure, their darkness, their problems. Anyone who does that will see himself as one big problem!

A woman came to receive ministry from members of our community. Her husband, himself a minister, had telephoned in desperation. His wife was such a problem! Her lack of spiritual vitality was hindering the developing work of the Spirit in that congregation. Many had tried to help her, but she had a problem deeper than anything they could fathom. Perhaps, with our experience, we could get to the root of her problem.

The 'problem' duly arrived. My colleague, David, sat with her and listened as she talked for an hour about her failure and the way in which she was hindering everybody else.

Then David said to her: "What would you say if I told you that you are not a problem at all?"

"I wouldn't believe you," she answered.

David then opened the scriptures for her, and showed her that she was dead 'in Christ' and made alive in Him; that all the scriptures relating to what it means to be 'in Christ Jesus' were truths about her.

Even as he talked the woman changed, not only inside; her physical appearance also changed. The lost, frightened, haggard look gave way to wonder and joy. The truth was setting her free. Not the truth of some deep, hidden problem, but the truth of who she was as a child of God, living in Christ Jesus.

David then left her to discover more of these great truths for herself by turning the pages of the New Testament, especially Paul's epistles.

That woman is not an isolated case; she is a typical example of people who come to us seeking help. They come thinking that they are big problems, and the ministry they have received in the past supports that low appraisal of themselves. If they were not Christians, that appraisal would be true. But it is not true of those who belong to Christ Jesus. God does not see His children as big problems, but as those who have had all their needs met on the cross.

When people are subjected to 'hunt-the-problem' type of ministry, they certainly end up with one if they didn't start with one!

> And we, who with unveiled faces all reflect the Lord's glory, are being transformed into his likeness with ever-increasing glory, which comes from the Lord, who is the Spirit (2 Cor 3:18).

That is a more positive and truthful way of seeing yourself. That is the purpose that God is wanting to work out in you. See yourself as one who reflects the Lord's glory; that you are being transformed in His likeness with ever increasing glory. It is the Lord who is doing this work in you by His Spirit.

This is not a question of mind over matter. It is seeing the spiritual truth about yourself, and allowing the Spirit of God to transform your soul (mind, emotions, will) and radiate His Presence through your body.

Yours words of faith: "IT IS BECAUSE OF HIM THAT YOU ARE IN CHRIST JESUS." "WE KNOW THAT WE LIVE IN HIM AND HE IN US, BECAUSE HE HAS GIVEN US OF HIS SPIRIT."

PART 2

YOUR NEW LIFE IN JESUS

12

RECEIVING THE TRUTHS

From the New Testament, we are going to build a picture of the new life that we have 'in Christ Jesus'. Because the old has passed away and the new has come, we need to see what our inheritance is as God's new creation. If we are to combat the negative feelings of failure and doubt, we shall need to know the truth about ourselves as God sees us.

We are going to keep close to the words of scripture. That will involve some repetition of truths we have already discussed. That does not matter. It is by continually receiving these words that "you will know the truth, and the truth will set you free."

BECAUSE YOU LIVE 'IN CHRIST JESUS', ALL THESE TRUTHS RELATE TO YOU. THEY ARE TRUTHS ABOUT YOU. GOD IS SPEAKING TO YOU AND TELLING YOU HOW HE SEES YOU.

This second part of the book is divided into short sections, each concentrating on one or more scriptures which will speak to you of what it means to live in Jesus. At the end of each section certain truths about you as a new creation are emphasised. Take these truths to heart.

These short sections are arranged so that they are suitable for daily meditation. Having read this book, come back to the second part and work through the sections one by one each day. Absorb the truth which God is saying to you about yourself and what He has done for you. Believe the promises He gives you, and put into operation the things He says you are to do.

Where there is repetition that is because the scriptures are repetitive, as the same truths are emphasised again and again. Obviously God wants His children to take these truths to heart.

A WAY OF MEDITATING

It is important to do more than think about these great truths that you will discover. You need to hear these scriptures in your heart. Allow God to speak them to you personally. Here is a simple way of doing this.

Sit down quietly and read one section two or three times, realising that God is speaking about you in His word because you are in Christ.

Then repeat the scripture at the beginning of the section several times. It is best to speak the sentence softly but audibly. This will aid concentration. Do not try to work out what the sentence means with your mind. Receive it in your heart. At first you may find that you can only repeat the scripture meaningfully a few times. As you become used to receiving the word in this way, you will be able to spend several minutes allowing the Lord to speak to you through that particular verse.

Finally, have a brief time of thanksgiving for the truths about you that are in bold print at the end of each section. Allow that thanksgiving to develop into praise for God, who loves you so much that He has called you to live 'in Christ Jesus'.

You can remember this method easily in three words: READ, RECEIVE, REJOICE.

It is only by receiving and constantly affirming the truths about your new life that are revealed in the scriptures that you will be able to live in the power of them. Chapter 25 will show you how to affirm these truths about yourself.

13

SET FREE

ALIVE WITH CHRIST

> Now if we died with Christ, we believe that we will also live with him (Rom. 6:8).

When Jesus went to the cross He took not only your sin and guilt; He also took you. That is not a feeling, it is a historical fact. *You died with Him and have been raised to new life with Him.* Now you can live in Him in this life, and reign with Him in His eternal Kingdom. You have put your faith in what He has done on the cross; now He wants you to believe all that He promises you as your inheritance because you are a child of God.

YOU HAVE DIED WITH CHRIST.
BY FAITH YOU WILL ALSO LIVE WITH HIM.

CRUCIFIED WITH CHRIST

> I have been crucified with Christ and I no longer live, but Christ lives in me. The life I live in the body, I live by faith in the Son of God, who loved me and gave himself for me (Gal. 2:20).

You can identify with Paul's personal testimony. Jesus took you to the cross that your old sinful nature might be put to death: "I no longer live." Replacing that old 'I' is the new nature: *Christ lives in you. Your body is a temple of His presence.* During the rest of your life, it is His purpose for you to live "by faith in the Son of God", trusting to the infinite resources of His power and love. Jesus loved you by giving His life for you to make that possible. He does not want you to squander that inheritance by continuing to trust in yourself, in your own weakness and failure.

YOU HAVE BEEN CRUCIFIED WITH CHRIST.
CHRIST LIVES IN YOU.
YOU CAN LIVE YOUR LIFE BY FAITH IN HIM.

OLD SELF CRUCIFIED

For we know that our old self was crucified with him so that the body of sin might be rendered powerless, that we should no longer be slaves to sin – because anyone who has died has been freed from sin (Rom. 6:6–7).

Your old self was crucified with Christ. The 'body of sin' has been rendered powerless and no longer needs to control your life. *You have been set free from slavery to sin; it is not your master*. You are no longer under any compulsion to be disobedient to the Lord. You have been freed from the power of sin. Remember that sin itself still exists and there will always be the temptation to sin. But you do not need to yield to that temptation. You can count yourself dead to sin and alive in Christ, able to live His new life for His glory.

YOUR OLD SELF WAS CRUCIFIED WITH CHRIST.
YOU HAVE BEEN FREED FROM SIN.
YOU ARE NO LONGER A SLAVE TO SIN.

BAPTISED INTO HIS DEATH

Don't you know that all of us who were baptised into Christ Jesus were baptised into His death? We were therefore buried with him through baptism into death in order that, just as Christ was raised from the dead through the glory of the Father, we too may live a new life (Rom. 6:3–4).

Your baptism signifies that when Christ died you died with Him, and because He has been raised, so you too have been raised to a new life with Him. *That old life is dead – and buried!* It is not to be resurrected. Now God wants you to live in the power of your new nature, seeing yourself as He sees you.

YOU WERE BURIED WITH JESUS THROUGH BAPTISM.
YOU ARE FREE TO LIVE A NEW LIFE.

HIDDEN WITH CHRIST

For you died and your life is now hidden with Christ in God (Col. 3:3).

Your life is now hidden with Christ in God. You can only live in Him because of your death that took place on the cross. God will continue to reveal to you more of the truths of this new life. He will continue to show you what it means for your life to be hidden with Christ in God. Realise now how you are identified with Christ because you live in Him and He lives in you. As He lives in union with the Father, so can you, by virtue of the fact that you are 'in Christ Jesus'.

YOU DIED.

YOUR LIFE IS NOW HIDDEN WITH CHRIST IN GOD.

DEAD TO THE WORLD

You died with Christ to the basic principles of this world . . . (Col. 2:20).

To say that "your life is now hidden with Christ in God" is not simply a great spiritual truth to rejoice in. It brings considerable responsibilities. God calls you to a life of dependence upon Him and the working of His Spirit within you, so that 'rivers of living water' will flow out of your life. To live in the power of your new spiritual nature will involve counting upon the fact that "you died with Christ to the basic principles of this world". Unless you do that, your life will continue to be worldly: "Do not conform any longer to the pattern of this world, but be transformed by the renewing of your mind. Then you will be able to test and approve what God's will is – his good, pleasing and perfect will" (Rom. 12:2). *Your citizenship is now in heaven. God wants you to live as a child of His Kingdom.* You will please Him if the values of your life are the values of that Kingdom.

These values are centred upon the Lord and His purposes. The basic principles of this world are centred upon the self: self-pleasing, selfishness, self-concern, self-pity, self-adulation, self-effort. You have died to that life of 'self'.

May I never boast except in the cross of our Lord Jesus Christ, through which the world has been crucified to me, and I to the world (Gal. 6:14).

YOU DIED WITH CHRIST TO THE BASIC PRINCIPLES OF THIS WORLD.
YOU HAVE BEEN CRUCIFIED TO THE WORLD AND THE WORLD TO YOU.

DEAD TO THE LAW

So, my brothers, you also died to the law through the body of Christ, that you might belong to another, to him who was raised from the dead, in order that we might bear fruit for God (Rom. 7:4).

Through the death of Jesus, you have died to the law. No longer do you have to try to make yourself acceptable to God through religious observance. You do not belong to a religion; *you belong to a Person*, "to another, to him who was raised from the dead". You do not live as part of a religious system; *you live 'in Christ Jesus'*. And the reason why God has placed you in Him is that you might bear fruit for God. The law could not bear fruit because the law cannot produce new life; neither can religious observance. Only the Spirit of God can produce that new life, and it is the fruit of His Spirit that God desires to see in you.

A man is not justified by observing the law, but by faith in Jesus Christ. So we, too, have put our faith in Christ Jesus that we may be justified by faith in Christ and not by observing the law, because by observing the law no one will be justified (Gal. 2:16).

YOU "DIED TO THE LAW THROUGH THE BODY OF CHRIST".
YOU "BELONG TO ANOTHER, TO HIM WHO WAS RAISED FROM THE DEAD" TO BE FRUITFUL.

NO CONDEMNATION

Therefore, there is now no condemnation for those who are in Christ Jesus, because through Christ Jesus the law of the Spirit of life set me free from the law of sin and death (Rom. 8:1–2).

Because you are made acceptable before God, you are not under condemnation and judgment. He does not look upon you with anger, but with love. You can resist all attempts of the enemy and other people to make you feel condemned. There is no need to fear judgment, because you have been set free from the law of sin and death. It is now the Spirit of life that is operating in you. As you allow the Spirit pre-eminence in your life, so He shall lead you in obedience to Jesus. You have been set free from the old life of sin and disobedience.

This verse of scripture is quoted often, and it needs to be. *There is no condemnation for you, because you are in Christ Jesus.* Outside of Jesus, the law of sin and death operates and men need to fear the anger and judgment of God. The blood of Jesus stands between you and that judgment. In Jesus there can be no condemnation, and you are in Him.

You will have a false sense of condemnation if you take your eyes off Jesus and look in upon your own weakness and failure. You will feel condemned if you listen to the lying taunts of the enemy. But in Christ there is no condemnation, and you are in Him.

THERE IS NO CONDEMNATION FOR YOU BECAUSE YOU ARE IN CHRIST JESUS.

THROUGH HIM THE LAW OF THE SPIRIT OF LIFE HAS SET YOU FREE FROM THE LAW OF SIN AND DEATH.

FREE BY GRACE

But by the free gift of God's grace all are put right with him through Christ Jesus, who sets them free (Rom. 3:24 G.N.B.).

Again and again the scriptures proclaim these central truths of the gospel to your heart. The only way to be put right with God is by the free gift of His grace expressed through Jesus Christ. God has extended that free gift of His grace to you. *You are put right with Him through Jesus Christ. Your salvation is God's gift to you,* and it has been accomplished through His Son, through whom you are set free. Believe that. God has set you free from sin and the power of sin; He has set you free from your old nature and from "the law of sin and death". He has freed you from the kingdom of darkness and from the power of Satan, and brought you into the glorious liberty of the sons of God.

BY THE FREE GIFT OF GOD'S GRACE YOU ARE PUT RIGHT WITH HIM.

THROUGH JESUS CHRIST YOU ARE SET FREE.

FREEDOM MAINTAINED

> (This matter arose) because some false brothers had infiltrated our ranks to spy on the freedom we have in Christ Jesus and to make us slaves (Gal. 2:4).

In Christ you have been set free from religious legalism, even from Christian religious legalism. You need no longer try to please God by your own efforts or through traditional practices. It is only through the blood of the cross that you can please Him, and through the power of the Holy Spirit that you can bear fruit for Him. The freedom that you have in Christ is the knowledge that you do not have to do anything to make yourself righteous before God. Jesus has already done that, and so you can now live in His righteousness and perform the works of God.

'This matter' to which Paul alludes involved the rite of circumcision. It was a matter of contention in the earliest days of the Church as to whether a Gentile believer in Jesus needed to undergo the Jewish rite of circumcision. Paul contended that to belong to Christ meant that a man was freed from the law by the grace of God, and he strongly opposed those who tried to impose their old legalistic attitudes on to the new converts. Jesus is the fulfilment of the law; you do not have to be 'under the law' before knowing Him and the work of His grace in your life.

Beware of any corresponding attitudes of legalism today. Enjoy with St Paul the freedom you have in Christ, and do not allow your faith to be confined by man-made rules and traditions – religious, restrictive practices. Heed Jesus's warning: "You nullify the word of God for the sake of your tradition" (Matt. 15:6).

> In him you were also circumcised, in the putting off of

the sinful nature, not with a circumcision done by the hands of men but with the circumcision done by Christ, having been buried with him in baptism and raised with him through your faith in the power of God, who raised him from the dead (Col. 2:11–12).

Physical circumcision means nothing in the new life: "Neither circumcision nor uncircumcision means anything; what counts is a new creation" (Gal. 6:15). "For in Christ Jesus neither circumcision nor uncircumcision has any value. The only thing that counts is faith expressing itself through love" (Gal. 5:6). You have received the circumcision 'done by Christ' that gives you a new heart that desires to please God rather than yourself, to know His will for your life and His grace to enable you to do it.

Your baptism signifies that the old nature lies buried with Him. You cannot resurrect the past, for now, by your faith in Him, you are raised with Christ to new life.

When you were dead in your sins and in the uncircumcision of your sinful nature, God made you alive with Christ. He forgave us all our sins, having cancelled the written code, with its regulations, that was against us and that stood opposed to us; he took it away, nailing it to the cross. And having disarmed the powers and authorities, he made a public spectacle of them, triumphing over them by the cross (Col. 2:13–15).

From death and separation from God, you have been brought to life; you are made 'alive with Christ'. He has forgiven you and freed you from legalistically trying to win God's approval through the keeping of a written code of laws. That was impossible to achieve and only left you condemned in God's sight. The written code with its regulations was against you, and stood opposed to you because you could not obey everything demanded of you by those laws. *Through the cross God has opened up for you the new way of God's grace*. Through that same victorious cross, He has rendered the spiritual forces of wickedness powerless. He disarmed them and triumphed over them. *Because you live in Him, you live in His victory and need to believe that those powers and authorities cannot prevail against you in any way.*

YOU HAVE FREEDOM 'IN CHRIST JESUS'.
YOU HAVE RECEIVED 'THE CIRCUMCISION DONE BY CHRIST'.
YOU HAVE BEEN RAISED WITH CHRIST "THROUGH YOUR FAITH IN THE POWER OF GOD".
GOD MADE YOU ALIVE WITH CHRIST.
HE HAS CANCELLED THE WRITTEN CODE WHICH STOOD OPPOSED TO YOU.
HE HAS DISARMED THE POWERS OF DARKNESS THAT OPPOSE YOU. YOU LIVE IN THE VICTORY OF JESUS.

14

WHAT JESUS HAS DONE

GOD LOVES YOU

This is love: not that we loved God, but that he loved us and sent his Son as an atoning sacrifice for our sins (1 John 4:10).

Because God loves you, He took the initiative in making your reconciliation with Him possible. *Your love for Him is the response to His love for you* that was shown in sending "his Son as an atoning sacrifice" for your sins. That perfect offering of Himself on your behalf satisfies the righteousness and holiness of God. Because of Jesus, He accepts you and declares you innocent in His sight.

YOU ARE LOVED BY GOD.
JESUS HAS PAID THE PRICE FOR YOUR SINS.

CHRIST DIED FOR YOU

For Christ died for sins once for all, the righteous for the unrighteous, to bring you to God. He was put to death in the body but made alive by the Spirit (1 Peter 3:18).

Jesus is righteous. He has always been 'right' in God's eyes and has always done 'right' in obedience to Him. He offered His life for you, "the righteous for the unrighteous". *He has brought you to God and made you 'right' in His sight*, not with any righteousness of your own, but through the righteousness of Jesus. You have been put to death with Him and have been made alive with Him 'by the Spirit'.

YOU ARE MADE RIGHTEOUS IN GOD'S SIGHT.

THE VEIL REMOVED

To this day the same veil remains when the old covenant is read. It has not been removed, because only in Christ is it taken away (2 Cor. 3:14).

Jesus, by His death on the cross, has torn the veil apart, the veil that has separated you from God. *Because you live in Him, you have clear access to the throne of God, your Father*. You can enter "the gates of thanksgiving" and come into "the courts of praise". This is only possible through Jesus. You can only come to the Father through Him and because of Him.

Whenever anyone turns to the Lord, the veil is taken away. Now the Lord is the Spirit, and where the Spirit of the Lord is, there is freedom (2 Cor. 3:16–17).

The veil has been taken away for you because you have turned to Christ; you have been washed and cleansed in God's sight through His blood. His Spirit has come to live in you and "where the Spirit of the Lord is, there is freedom"; freedom from the power of sin and death, freedom to live in Christ, freedom to come before the throne of God in true worship and adoration.

YOU HAVE DIRECT ACCESS TO GOD THE FATHER THROUGH JESUS.

THE SPIRIT OF GOD LIVES IN YOU THAT YOU MIGHT LIVE IN FREEDOM.

VICTORY OVER DEATH

Since the children have flesh and blood, he too shared in their humanity so that by his death he might destroy him who holds the power of death – that is, the devil – and free those who all their lives were held in slavery by their fear of death (Heb. 2:14–15).

Jesus shared your humanity totally. He even endured every temptation to which you have been subjected, and never sinned. He did not need to die Himself for, even in His humanity, He was perfect. He died for the sake of all men, for they deserved death, as they had sinned against God.

You are freed from God's judgment of death, of eternal separation from Him, because of the sinless death of Jesus. He has destroyed "him who holds the power of death – that is, the devil". You no longer need to fear physical death for, although your body will pass away, you will live with the Lord eternally. He has given you the gift of eternal life in His Son, Jesus.

YOU ARE SET FREE FROM THE FEAR OF DEATH.

HEALED

This was to fulfil what was spoken through the prophet Isaiah:

"He took up our infirmities
    and carried our diseases" (Matt. 8:17).

During His earthly ministry, Jesus healed multitudes of sick people from every kind of illness: "people brought to him all who were ill with various diseases . . . and he healed them" (Matt. 4:24). He demonstrated His Father's desire and power to heal: "My food," said Jesus, "is to do the will of him who sent me and to finish his work" (John 4:34). On the cross, Jesus paid the price for your sins; He destroyed the devil and set you free from the fear of death. *But He also took your infirmities and diseases to that cross.* "By his wounds we are healed."

Jesus has accomplished all that is necessary for your

What Jesus Has Done

healing and wholeness – spiritual, mental, emotional and physical healing: "and by his wounds we are healed" (Isa. 53:5). When you pray for healing, you appropriate part of the fruit of the cross.

YOUR TOTAL HEALING OR WHOLENESS WAS ACCOMPLISHED ON THE CROSS.

CHRIST ASCENDED FOR US

He entered heaven itself, now to appear for us in God's presence (Heb. 9:24).

When Jesus had finished all that the Father wanted Him to do on earth, He ascended to heaven and was restored to His rightful place of majestic glory. But His ministry to you has not ended. *He takes you into the heavenly places with Him, as one of those who is 'in Christ Jesus'. He appears in God's presence for you. God the Father does not see you separated from Jesus; He sees you living in Him.* He does not look upon the awfulness of your sin; He sees the sacrifice of His Son for you, that His blood has cleansed you from all sin.

JESUS HAS ENTERED HEAVEN AND APPEARS BEFORE GOD FOR YOU.

OUR GREAT HIGH PRIEST

Because Jesus lives for ever, he has a permanent priesthood. Therefore he is able to save completely those who come to God through him, because he always lives to intercede for them (Heb. 7:24–15).

Jesus, already enthroned in heaven, is always interceding for you. *God will not deal with you in anger or wrath, because His Son pleads your cause before Him constantly.* You can be bold in coming directly to the Father in prayer, because you come through Jesus. He will not deny any who come in the name of His Son.

Such a high priest meets our need – one who is holy, blameless, pure, set apart from sinners, exalted above the heavens (v. 26).

He suffered in order to make you like Himself:

> Jesus also suffered . . . to make the people holy through his own blood (Heb. 13:12).

Jesus's purpose is to present you holy and blameless before God that you may know His glory.

JESUS MEETS YOUR NEED.
HE LIVES TO INTERCEDE FOR YOU.
HE SUFFERED TO MAKE YOU HOLY.

JESUS THE SAME FOR EVER

> Jesus Christ is the same yesterday and today and for ever (Heb. 13:8).

Because He is God, Jesus does not change. His love for you remains constant; you can always depend on His faithfulness. He keeps His word because He is the Word. He promises that He will never leave you nor forsake you.

Whatever He did yesterday, He can do today. You do not need to look wistfully at the mighty things He did in the past. He is as mighty today and wants to work powerfully in your life.

You can be certain that His love for you will always remain sure and that He will honour your faith in His word.

YOU LIVE IN CHRIST JESUS, WHO IS ALWAYS THE SAME, CONSTANT IN HIS LOVE FOR YOU, AND ALWAYS FAITHFUL TO HIS WORD.

15

THE RESULTS OF FAITH

The Son of Man must be lifted up, that everyone who believes may have eternal life in him (John 3:14–15).

Jesus had to die in order that sinners could be reconciled with God. Because you have put your faith in Him and in what He did for you on the cross, you "have eternal life in him". You did not deserve that; you could do nothing to achieve it. *God has given you eternal life as a gift* – not because of what you are, but because of who Jesus is; not because of what you have done, but because of what He has done for you. Your eternal life is *in Him*.

For God so loved the world that he gave his one and only Son, that whoever believes in him shall not perish but have eternal life (v. 16).

You are that valuable to God! You need not fear eternal death and separation from God, because you belong to Him. His gift of eternal life is yours already. But remember that God sent His Son out of love for the world and everyone in it. Use the opportunities you are given to share with others the good news of the life that is available in Jesus.

THROUGH FAITH IN JESUS YOU WILL NOT PERISH ETERNALLY. THROUGH FAITH IN JESUS, GOD HAS GIVEN YOU ETERNAL LIFE.

RIGHTEOUSNESS BY FAITH

This righteousness from God comes through faith in Jesus Christ to all who believe (Rom. 3:22).

The only way to righteousness before God, being made

acceptable to Him, is faith in Jesus Christ. All who believe in Him and the work of His cross are made righteous in God's sight. *No longer do you need to think of yourself as an unacceptable, spiritual reject.* You would not be counted worthy before Him if it was not for Jesus – God declares His love for you because of Him. In that love you have placed your faith. That is all you could do, or had to do, to obtain "this righteousness from God".

YOU HAVE BEEN MADE RIGHTEOUS BEFORE GOD, THROUGH YOUR FAITH IN JESUS CHRIST.

FOUND IN HIM

I consider everything a loss compared to the surpassing greatness of knowing Christ Jesus my Lord, for whose sake I have lost all things. I consider them rubbish, that I may gain Christ and be found in him, not having a righteousness of my own that comes from the law, but that which is through faith in Christ – the righteousness that comes from God and is by faith (Phil. 3:8–9).

Paul speaks of himself like the man in the parable of Jesus: "The kingdom of heaven is like treasure hidden in a field. When a man found it, he hid it again, and then in his joy went and sold all he had and bought that field" (Matt. 13:44). It is worth losing everything that the world counts dear or that the flesh craves, for "the surpassing greatness of knowing Christ Jesus my Lord!" He is only to be known through faith in Jesus – not through "a righteousness of my own that comes from the law", by trying to please God by good works.

But it is not only to gain Christ that concerns Paul; he desires to be 'found in him'. Now that you have been drawn into the life of Jesus, *God wants you to live in Him by faithful obedience to the leading of His Holy Spirit in your life.* And having been found faithful "somehow to attain to the resurrection from the dead" (v.11).

YOU ARE MADE RIGHTEOUS, NOT BY GOOD WORKS, BUT BY FAITH IN CHRIST.

The Results of Faith

JUSTIFIED THROUGH FAITH

> Therefore, since we have been justified through faith, we have peace with God through our Lord Jesus Christ, through whom we have gained access by faith into this grace in which we now stand (Rom. 5:1–2).

You 'have been justified' before God through your faith in Jesus. That means that *you are completely forgiven by Him. He declares you innocent*, even of those things of which you were guilty, because your guilt is washed away by the blood of Jesus.

Clearly this is a work of His grace. Nobody can deserve to be declared innocent if he is really guilty of the offence. God overlooks the guilt because your punishment has been suffered by Jesus. Now you can have peace with God 'through our Lord Jesus Christ'. There is no peace with God apart from Him. You now stand in His grace; He continues to pour into your life the gifts of His love and goodness although, of yourself, you deserve nothing.

THROUGH FAITH IN JESUS, YOU HAVE BEEN JUSTIFIED AND ARE DECLARED INNOCENT BY GOD.

THROUGH FAITH IN JESUS, YOU HAVE PEACE WITH GOD.

THROUGH FAITH IN JESUS, YOU NOW STAND IN GOD'S GRACE.

REDEMPTION

> In him we have redemption through his blood, the forgiveness of sins, in accordance with the riches of God's grace that he lavished on us with all wisdom and understanding (Eph. 1:7–8).

Jesus has redeemed you; He has paid the price for you with His own life. That is what it cost to bring you out of darkness and into His light, that you might become His child. In this He has lavished His grace on you and given you His wisdom and understanding. Before you were alive in the Spirit you could not understand the necessity for the cross; now you cannot stop being thankful to God for all that He did there. What seemed unnecessary foolishness is now seen to be the wisdom of God.

He has not declared His love for you grudgingly; *He has lavished the riches of His grace on you*. He wants you to continue to live in His grace, looking to Him to give to you abundantly, although you deserve nothing. He opens the eyes of your spiritual understanding that you may know that you live 'in Christ Jesus' and He in you.

JESUS HAS PAID THE PRICE FOR YOU; YOU HAVE BEEN REDEEMED BY HIM; YOU HAVE FORGIVENESS OF SINS THROUGH HIS BLOOD; GOD HAS LAVISHED THE RICHES OF HIS GRACE ON YOU.

INCLUDED IN CHRIST

And you also were included in Christ when you heard the word of truth, the gospel of your salvation. Having believed, you were marked in him with a seal, the promised Holy Spirit, who is a deposit guaranteeing our inheritance until the redemption of those who are God's possession – to the praise of his glory (Eph. 1:13–14).

When you responded with faith to the gospel, you were incorporated into Christ. Subsequently, *you have been sealed with the Holy Spirit*; God has filled you to overflowing with Himself, to lead you to the fulfilment of that purpose that He has for you, when you will see Him face to face and know your unity with Him for ever. God will accomplish that for His own sake – "to the praise of his glory".

YOU HAVE BEEN INCLUDED IN CHRIST.
YOU HAVE BELIEVED THE WORD OF TRUTH.
YOU HAVE BEEN SEALED WITH THE HOLY SPIRIT.

MADE ALIVE WITH CHRIST

But because of his great love for us, God who is rich in mercy, made us alive with Christ even when we were dead in transgressions – it is by grace you have been saved (Eph. 2:4–5).

Before you believed, you were spiritually dead, alienated from God, "dead in transgressions". *God has brought you to life with Jesus "because of His great love" for you,*

The Results of Faith

because He is 'rich in mercy' and through the wonder of His grace. You have been saved from sin, from death, from Satan, from being bound by the law of sin and death. Jesus has fulfilled the purpose of His coming in you: "I have come that they may have life, and have it to the full" (John 10:10).

GOD HAS SHOWN HIS GREAT LOVE FOR YOU;
GOD IS RICH IN MERCY TOWARDS YOU;
GOD HAS MADE YOU 'ALIVE WITH CHRIST';
YOU HAVE BEEN SAVED BY HIS GRACE.

BORN OF GOD:

Everyone who believes that Jesus is the Christ is born of God (1 John 5:1).

When you put your faith in the Lord Jesus, you were 'born of God'; you became a child of God. *He is now your Father and Jesus is not ashamed to call you His 'brother'.*

YOU ARE BORN OF GOD.

SALVATION OF YOUR SOUL

Though you have not seen him, you love him; and even though you do not see him now, you believe in him and are filled with an inexpressible and glorious joy, for you are receiving the goal of your faith, the salvation of your souls (1 Pet. 1:8–9).

You are one of the blessed ones who have believed in the risen Jesus, even though you have not see Him. The knowledge that through Him you are loved, accepted and approved of by God will inevitably fill you with "an inexpressible and glorious joy". And you can know that *you are receiving the goal of your faith; the salvation of your soul.* In His love, your heavenly Father will continue to discipline you, to refine and prune you. He will bring to completion that good work that He has begun in you.

YOU BELIEVE IN HIM AND ARE FILLED WITH AN INEXPRESSIBLE AND GLORIOUS JOY.
YOU ARE RECEIVING THE GOAL OF YOUR FAITH, THE SALVATION OF YOUR SOUL.

16

CHOSEN TO BE IN GOD

IN GOD

> We know that we live in him and he in us, because he has given us of his Spirit (1 John 4:13).
> If anyone acknowledges that Jesus is the Son of God, God lives in him and he in God (1 John 4:15).

To live 'in Christ Jesus' is to live in God. The gift of the Holy Spirit is evidence that you live in Him and that He lives in you. Your flesh could not live in God. That was unacceptable to Him and had to be put to death. *As a new creature you live in Him.*

You acknowledge that Jesus is the Son of God. That means more than assenting to a belief. To acknowledge means that you speak out or declare the truth. You need to proclaim that Jesus is the Son of God, not only by what you say, but also by what you are and the things you do. It needs to be seen that your life is submitted to the authority of Jesus. You believe He is Lord and the Son of God and you are ready to acknowledge His Lordship over your life.

YOU LIVE IN GOD.
GOD LIVES IN YOU.

'IN CHRIST'

> On that day you will realise that I am in my Father, and you are in me, and I am in you (John 14:20).

Jesus is speaking at the Last Supper and has just given the disciples the promise that, when He returns to the Father, He will ask Him to give them the gift of the Holy Spirit. When the Spirit comes upon you, you know that Jesus lives in you; He lives in you by the power of His Spirit. You are also to know that *you are in Jesus*. It is the part of the ministry of the Holy Spirit in your life to declare that truth to your heart. *You are in Jesus*. He alone can show you the wonderful implications of that great truth. And He will do so.

YOU ARE IN JESUS.
JESUS IS IN YOU.

THE TRUE VINE

> I am the vine; you are the branches. If a man remains in me and I in him, he will bear much fruit; apart from me you can do nothing (John 15:5).

Jesus is the True Vine. You are a branch of that Vine. You belong to Him. You are part of Him. *God has placed you in His Son so that you will bear much fruit.* You cannot produce that fruit yourself. It comes by abiding in the Vine, remaining, or living continuously, in Jesus. "No branch can bear fruit by itself; it must remain in the vine. Neither can you bear fruit unless you remain in me" (John 15:4).

Jesus is saying to you: "Go on living where my Father has put you – in me; and I will continue to live in you." To be separated from the Vine would render you useless: "If anyone does not remain in me, he is like a branch that is thrown away and withers." Anything you do apart from Jesus is of no value to God.

To remain in Jesus produces very different results: "If you remain in me and my words remain in you, ask whatever you wish, and it will be given you. This is to my Father's glory, that you bear much fruit, showing yourselves to be my disciples" (vv. 7–8).

Notice that Jesus stresses the importance of His words living in you. You cannot produce your own fruit; so do not try. The fruit is produced by the 'sap' of the Holy Spirit that flows through every branch of the Vine; God is working in you and through you. And that fruitfulness is manifested in answered prayer, which is the result of an abiding trust and dependence upon the One in whom you live. He says to you: "Remain in me, and I will remain in you" (v. 4).

YOU ARE A BRANCH OF THE TRUE VINE.

APART FROM JESUS YOU CAN DO NOTHING.
IF YOU REMAIN IN HIM, YOU WILL BEAR MUCH FRUIT.

A NEW CREATION

> Therefore, if anyone is in Christ, he is a new creation; the old has gone, the new has come! (2 Cor. 5:17).

Because you are in Christ you are a new creation. The old flesh could not have access to God because it was under condemnation of death, owing to its inherent sinfulness and selfishness. Now the old has gone and the new nature, the new life, the new creation has come. *Now you are made acceptable to God and you can stand in His presence and actually live in Him.* You are not the same person as you were before you put your faith in Jesus. You are not the person you were when you were born. You are a new creation. Your new life is to be lived on completely different principles from the old.

> All this is from God, who reconciled us to himself through Christ and gave us the ministry of reconciliation: that God was reconciling the world to himself in Christ, not counting men's sins against them. And he has committed to us the message of reconciliation (2 Cor. 5:18–19).

Apart from Him, you have no standing before God, and can make no claims upon Him. God has reconciled you to Himself through Jesus. He has accomplished that reconciliation. He wants you to do more than rejoice in your own personal salvation. To those who have been reconciled with Him, he gives a share in that ministry of reconciliation: to share with all men everywhere, that Jesus has made possible their reconciliation to God. All those who come to Him through Jesus, pleading not their own cause, but the power of His blood, will know the forgiveness of God. He will not count their sins against them, but will forgive them and welcome them into fellowship with Himself that they may also know what it is to live in Christ.

YOU ARE A NEW CREATION.
THE OLD LIFE HAS GONE; THE NEW LIFE HAS COME

FULNESS IN CHRIST

> For in Christ all the fulness of the Deity lives in bodily form, and you have been given fulness in Christ, who is the head over every power and authority (Col. 2:9–10).

Jesus is God become man, taking human nature, to enable you to share in His divine nature. *In Jesus, you have been given the fulness of God's life.* You will only know and reflect that life imperfectly on earth, but will manifest it perfectly in the life to come. That is why you do not need to fear physical death. Not only will you be able to enjoy the Lord without the temptations of the world, the flesh and the devil; you will also be able to reflect Jesus perfectly for the glory of the Father.

However, you have that fulness of life. That is your inheritance that God wants you to enjoy – His life, His love and joy and peace. He wants you to be constantly drawing on His inexhaustible supply of riches, because you are His child, living in Him. There is nothing He has that He desires to withhold from you.

He is the head over every spiritual power and authority that would seek to steal that life from you or prevent you from living in the power of Jesus. He that is in you is greater than he that is in the world!

YOU HAVE BEEN GIVEN FULNESS OF LIFE IN CHRIST.

ENRICHED IN EVERY WAY

> I always thank God for you because of his grace given you in Christ Jesus. For in him you have been enriched in every way – in all your speaking and in all your knowledge – because our testimony about Christ was confirmed in you (1 Cor. 1:4–6).

God's grace has been given to you in Christ Jesus, in whom you live. *In Him you have been enriched in every way.* By His grace God has blessed *you* in Christ with every spiritual blessing in the heavenlies. Now that you are alive in the Spirit, God enriches you with wisdom and understanding of His ways, knowledge that is beyond the unspiritual man. He enriches you in every way with your speaking, that you may build up others, encouraging them by speaking words of faith and love and truth, and no longer giving voice to negative reactions of fear and doubt. God has enriched you in every way; so make full use of those riches.

YOU HAVE BEEN GIVEN GOD'S GRACE IN CHRIST JESUS.

YOU HAVE BEEN ENRICHED IN EVERY WAY IN HIM.

EVERY SPIRITUAL BLESSING

Blessed be the God and Father of our Lord Jesus Christ, who has blessed us in Christ with every spiritual blessing in the heavenly places (Eph. 1:3 R.S.V.).

Nothing hinders faith more than the failure to appreciate who you are, now that God has made you His child. Not that you have any rights of your own. You are a son of God because of what He has done for you in Christ. His Father has become your Father; His inheritance has become your inheritance.

By God's grace He has forgiven you and accepted you in His love. More than that, He has given you in Christ every blessing in heaven. He intends you to appropriate those blessings; He desires to see them effective in your experience.

All these blessings that heaven has are available only in Christ. That is where you are; that is where God has put you so that you can enjoy the full inheritance of your adoption as a son of God.

And notice that the scripture teaches clearly that God our Father *has blessed us* in Christ with every spiritual blessing in heaven. It is not a promise of what God says He will do, but a bold statement of what He has done, of what He has already accomplished. *Whatever God has to give is yours already in Christ.* Your faith can reach into the heavenlies and enable you to appropriate more and more of that inheritance while here on earth. What you do not possess now will be fully yours in the life to come.

Those spiritual blessings begin with your righteousness, and the acceptance by God that you are made holy before Him, are clothed with Jesus, have received His Spirit and

Chosen to be in God

are promised that He will meet your every need. And God will continue to bless you to bring about the fulfilment of His purpose: "We know that when he appears, we shall be like him, for we shall see him as he is" (1 John 3:2).

The Christian life is a continual entering into what God has already done for you in Jesus, and what He makes available to you through Him. It is easy to profess a faith in the Lord Jesus Christ and yet still not enter into the full potential of all that God gives you in Him. If you understand the position that you have before God in Christ, your heart will be filled with praise. If you live in the inheritance that is yours in Christ, you will be giving expression to that praise continually.

To be living in Christ Jesus is in itself sufficient cause for praise, rejoicing and thanksgiving. To begin to understand the riches and privileges that this fact gives to the believer means that he cannot hope to find words to express the joy and thankfulness of his heart. "Praise be to the God and Father of our Lord Jesus Christ . . ."

GOD HAS BLESSED YOU IN CHRIST WITH EVERY SPIRITUAL BLESSING IN THE HEAVENLY PLACES.

CHOSEN

For he chose us in him before the creation of the world to be holy and blameless in his sight (Eph. 1:4).

God has chosen you. He wanted you for Himself, to be His child. He chose you 'before the creation of the world'. That is something that your mind will not be able to understand. You can only rejoice that it has always been God's purpose that you should belong to Him. You were chosen "in accordance with his pleasure and will" (v. 5).

Jesus told His disciples: "You did not choose me, but I chose you" (John 15:16). When you believed the gospel, you were responding to the initiative that God had taken in your life. When you came to repentance, you were responding to the conviction of sin that His Spirit had made you aware of. When you were filled with the Spirit you were responding to the promise of God and to the purpose that He had for you. Throughout, He did not interfere with your free will. He waited for you to respond to what He wanted for you.

He has chosen you to be holy and blameless before Him. That could only be accomplished through Jesus. He has chosen you in Him. It is only in Him that you can appear holy and blameless before God. It is only in Him that you can live in holiness. It is only in Him that you will finally be presented holy and spotless before Him. He has chosen you in love:

> In love he predestined us to be adopted as his sons through Jesus Christ, in accordance with his pleasure and will – to the praise of his glorious grace, which he has freely given us in the One he loves (Eph. 1:5–6).

It is by His pleasure and will that you have been chosen – not through any merit of your own. He has chosen you "to the praise of his glorious grace". It is an act of that glorious grace that you belong to Him. He has given you that grace freely, and you now live 'in the One he loves'.

GOD HAS CHOSEN YOU.

HE HAS CHOSEN YOU IN LOVE.

HE HAS CHOSEN YOU "IN ACCORDANCE WITH HIS PLEASURE AND WILL".

HE HAS CHOSEN YOU THROUGH HIS GLORIOUS GRACE, WHICH HE HAS FREELY GIVEN YOU.

HE HAS CHOSEN YOU TO BE HOLY AND BLAMELESS IN HIS SIGHT.

RAISED WITH CHRIST

> And God raised us up with Christ and seated us with him in the heavenly realms in Christ Jesus, in order that in the coming ages he might show the incomparable riches of his grace expressed in his kindness to us in Christ Jesus (Eph. 2:6–7).

That is where you are in Christ: seated with Him in the heavenly realms. Because you have died with Him, you are also raised with Him. You already belong to heaven, to the Kingdom of God; you are a citizen of heaven. *You are already part of His victory, of His triumphal and eternal reign*. You cannot understand fully what it means to be seated 'with him in the heavenly realms in Christ Jesus'. You can only rejoice in the truth of it.

In the coming ages this truth will be seen by all, the evidence of the immense grace of God, that He should call and choose men and women who were disobedient, rebellious, selfish and sinful, and make them His sons and inheritors of His everlasting Kingdom. Instead of dealing with you in His wrath, as you deserve, He has dealt with you in His kindness, supremely expressed in all that He has done through Jesus.

> For it is by grace you have been saved, through faith – and this is not from yourselves, it is the gift of God – not by works, so that no one can boast (Eph. 2:8–9).

Even the faith that has enabled you to trust in the death and resurrection of Jesus is a gift from God. You cannot even boast that you have any faith of your own. God will not allow that faith to be regarded as a good work that enabled you to come into the Kingdom of God. He will not allow anyone to say: "It was by *my faith* that I have been saved from sin and death, and belong to God." No, it is only by His grace and through the faith He gives by that grace.

> For we are God's workmanship, created in Christ Jesus to do good works, which God prepared in advance for us to do (v. 10).

You are part of the new creation that is His handiwork. You are 'created in Christ Jesus', and God has a particular purpose that He has planned for your life. You cannot even claim the credit for the good works that you do in the power of the Spirit. God has already prepared them in advance for you. He intends you to be fruitful. There is nothing for which you can take credit, which is why life 'in Christ' is so totally different from life in the world, where men seek honour, recognition and praise from one another. In Christ all the glory belongs to Him.

GOD HAS RAISED YOU UP WITH CHRIST.

HE HAS SEATED YOU WITH HIM IN THE HEAVENLY REALMS 'IN CHRIST JESUS'.
HE HAS DEALT KINDLY WITH YOU TO SHOW THE EXTENT OF HIS GRACE.
GOD HAS GIVEN YOU FAITH.
YOU ARE HIS WORKMANSHIP.
YOU ARE CREATED 'IN CHRIST JESUS' TO DO GOOD WORKS, WHICH GOD HAS PREPARED FOR YOU.

17

MADE HOLY

THE WILL OF GOD

He said, "Here I am, I have come to do your will." . . .
And by that will, we have been made holy through the sacrifice of the body of Jesus Christ once for all (Heb. 10:9–10).

When God sent His Son, it was His will to make you holy "through the sacrifice of the body of Jesus Christ once for all". Jesus came to do His Father's will – and accomplished it. By that will, you have been made holy.

The word 'holy' means 'set apart'. A holy person is one who is 'set apart' for God. Whatever is 'set apart' for Him must be pure and righteous. And so the word 'holy' also comes to mean 'pure'.

You have been made pure and righteous before God through the sacrifice of Jesus. Now you belong to Him. *He has chosen you to be holy, one of His 'set-apart' children.* Your life is set apart to be lived in loving obedience to Him, for His praise and glory.

You cannot achieve a state of holiness by any amount of self-effort. Through Jesus, you have already been made

Made Holy

holy. God wants you to live out your life in that holiness.

YOU HAVE BEEN MADE HOLY THROUGH THE SACRIFICE OF JESUS.

YOU HAVE BEEN 'SET APART' FOR GOD.

YOU HAVE BEEN MADE PURE AND RIGHTEOUS THROUGH JESUS.

MADE PERFECT FOR EVER

By one sacrifice he has made perfect for ever those who are being made holy (Heb. 10:14).

That is the glorious paradox. By the one, perfect sacrifice of Jesus we have been made perfect and acceptable to God. By the continuing work of His cross and His Spirit we are being 'made holy'.

What is true for us 'in the Spirit' has to be worked out in our present lives through the soul and body. Your new nature in Christ is perfect and holy already. As your soul responds to that new nature and allows it to be expressed in your life, so you will manifest that perfection and holiness. The more your soul and body come under the direction, the influence and authority of the Holy Spirit, the more that holiness will be seen through you. However, if your soul and body operate independently of the Spirit, then they will reflect the weakness and imperfections of your natural being.

Realise that *God is encouraging you to live in the power of the new nature that He has given you in Christ*. It is His purpose "to present you holy in his sight, without blemish and free from accusation" (Col. 1:22). This He will do "if you continue in your faith, established and firm, not moved from the hope held out in the gospel" (v. 23).

YOU HAVE BEEN MADE PERFECT FOR EVER.

YOUR SOUL IS BEING MADE HOLY.

PERFECT IN CHRIST

We proclaim him, admonishing and teaching everyone with all wisdom, so that we may present everyone perfect in Christ (Col. 1:28).

It is Jesus Himself who is to be proclaimed for He is the way to the Father. Only in Him can men be presented perfect before God through the work of His cross. *You have been given to Jesus and placed in Him by the Father, that He might present you back to Him "holy and blameless in His sight"*.

And what is true of the spirit, the Lord is now working out in your soul, changing you from one degree of glory to another, so that you manifest more of His perfection. He does not leave you as a spiritual infant, but leads you on in His ways so that you may be presented 'mature in Christ'.

It was to this end that Paul worked in his ministry to the churches. The great commission that Jesus gave to His Church was to go and make disciples of all nations – not simply converts, but those who would follow faithfully in the way of Jesus, the way of holiness, living a life 'set apart' for God. This is the only wise course for the Christian, for, if he tries to live independently of the Spirit, he will only grieve the Lord and will miss many of the riches God intends for him.

YOU WILL BE PRESENTED PERFECT IN CHRIST.

WASHED, SANCTIFIED, JUSTIFIED

But you were washed, you were sanctified, you were justified in the name of the Lord Jesus Christ and by the Spirit of our God (1 Cor. 6:11).

Another translation reads: "*But you have been purified from sin; you have been dedicated to God; you have been put right with God by the Lord Jesus Christ and by the Spirit of our God*" (G.N.B.). Notice the past tense; all this has already been accomplished by Jesus and the Holy Spirit. Paul is telling the Corinthians to live in the truth and power of what God has made them, and not to give way to their own desires.

YOU HAVE BEEN WASHED – PURIFIED FROM SIN.

YOU HAVE BEEN SANCTIFIED, MADE HOLY, SET APART FOR GOD AND DEDICATED TO HIM.

YOU WERE JUSTIFIED, PUT RIGHT WITH GOD.

OUR RIGHTEOUSNESS, HOLINESS AND REDEMPTION

> But God has brought you into union with Christ Jesus, and God has made Christ to be our wisdom. By him we are put right with God; we become God's holy people and are set free (1 Cor. 1:30 G.N.B.).

As a new creature, Jesus is your wisdom. The world does not understand Him and considers that faith in Him is foolishness. But you know that through the 'foolishness' of the cross you have been put right with God. You have been made one of God's holy, set-apart people. He has set you free from what you were in the old life, alienated from God, bound by sin and under judgment of death. Now you are made one with God through Jesus, through His death and through His risen life in which you now share. You can affirm it again and again. *You are set free by all that Jesus has done for you.* That is the truth – the truth that sets you free.

You did nothing to bring yourself into union with Jesus. God Himself did that; it was His purpose for you. That is a purpose you share with every other person who is 'in Christ'. What is true of you is true of every other person to whom God has given this rich inheritance. Remember that, especially when you are tempted to look at the faults of others with criticism. They do not manifest their new nature perfectly as yet; neither do you.

GOD HAS BROUGHT YOU INTO UNION WITH CHRIST JESUS.

JESUS IS YOUR WISDOM.

YOU ARE PUT RIGHT WITH GOD BY HIM.

YOU ARE ONE OF GOD'S HOLY PEOPLE.

YOU ARE SET FREE.

SANCTIFIED

> To the church of God in Corinth, to those sanctified in Christ Jesus and called to be holy, together with all those everywhere, who call on the name of our Lord Jesus Christ – their Lord and ours (1 Cor. 1:2).

Christians are "those sanctified in Christ Jesus and called to be holy". That is the common status and common calling of all Christians everywhere. God calls every believer 'to be holy'. God calls you to be holy. He does not want you to rejoice in what God has done for you without also allowing His purpose to be worked out in you. To live a life that is set apart for God and dedicated to Him means that you have yielded any right that you thought you ever had to live your own life in your own way. *It is now His life to be lived in His way*, that you might manifest His love and continue to receive His riches that He gives you by His grace. As He has made you clean in His sight so He wants to see you living with a clean heart. Your motive is to praise Him in thought, word and action.

YOU ARE SANCTIFIED IN CHRIST.
YOU ARE CALLED TO BE HOLY.

GOD'S HOLY NATION

But you are a chosen people, a royal priesthood, a holy nation, a people belonging to God, that you may declare the praises of him who called you out of darkness into his wonderful light. Once you were not a people, but now you are the people of God; once you had not received mercy, but now you have received mercy (1 Pet. 2:9–10).

Together with all others 'in Christ Jesus' you share this common heritage. You are one of His chosen people. You are part of the royal priesthood; you belong to the King of Heaven, and your life is to be offered to God in Him as a sacrifice of praise and thanksgiving. You are part of God's "holy nation, a people belonging to God. You have been brought out of darkness into His wonderful light." Once you were separated from God and did not belong to Him. Now you are numbered among those that He claims as His children. You have received God's mercy. *He has forgiven you for what you were and has empowered you to be what He wants you to be*: not in isolated Christian rejoicing in your salvation, but part of His body on earth, called to continue the ministry of Jesus in the world.

Made Holy

TOGETHER WITH OTHER CHRISTIANS
   YOU ARE A CHOSEN PEOPLE,
   A ROYAL PRIESTHOOD,
   A HOLY NATION,
   A PEOPLE BELONGING TO GOD.
YOU LIVE IN HIS WONDERFUL LIGHT.
YOU HAVE RECEIVED MERCY.

GOD'S BUILDING

In him the whole building is joined together and rises to become a holy temple in the Lord. And in him you too are being built together to become a dwelling in which God lives by his Spirit (Eph. 2:21–22).

You are one of the living stones that together comprise "a holy temple in the Lord". *To belong to Christ is to belong to the others who are in Him*, part of a body of people built together, in whom God lives by the power of His Spirit.

This temple is 'holy', set apart and consecrated to Him; a holy people concerned to do His will. A people of praise and worship. A people among whom God lives, and in Whom they live. "You are no longer foreigners and aliens, but fellow-citizens with God's people and members of God's household" (Eph. 2:19).

Realise the immense privilege of that – and the responsibilities too. You are responsible to the Lord, to love Him and obey Him. You are responsible to the other 'living stones', for it is only together that God can build the temple of His Presence. Do not grasp at the joy of belonging to God without facing the implications of that great privilege. You cannot choose whether to have these responsibilities or not. They are yours already, by virtue of the fact that you are 'in Christ Jesus'.

WITH OTHER CHRISTIANS
   YOU ARE A HOLY TEMPLE IN THE LORD,
   YOU ARE JOINED TOGETHER WITH THEM,
   YOU ARE A DWELLING IN WHICH GOD LIVES BY HIS SPIRIT,
   YOU ARE GOD'S HOUSEHOLD,
   YOU ARE GOD'S PEOPLE, FELLOW-CITIZENS OF HIS KINGDOM.

ONE BODY

> Just as each of us has one body with many members, and these members do not all have the same function, so in Christ we who are many form one body, and each member belongs to all the others (Rom. 12:4–5).

God does not see His children as independent believers. He sees all those who are in Christ as one body. Because each belongs to Him, they each belong to one another. As they are committed to love Him, so they are committed to love one another. The Church is, therefore, those who are truly in Christ, not those belonging to a human institution or structure. They are to live and work together like the limbs and organs of a human body, each with its distinctive function and willingness to be dependent upon the other parts.

You are part of that body, by virtue of the fact that you belong to Christ and live in Him. You not only belong to Him; you also "belong to all the others" who are in Him, the household of faith, those who together are to love and serve the Lord.

There is only one body of Christ. The institutional church may be divided into several denominations, but there is only one true Church – all those who live 'in Christ Jesus'. All who are in Him are part of that one body, and no structural or doctrinal disunity can destroy that essential unity that they have in Christ. "There is one body and one Spirit" (Eph. 4:4).

Within His body, the Lord has a specific function for you: "We have different gifts, according to the grace given us" (Rom. 12:6). His purpose is that all exercise the ministries that He gives them "so that the body of Christ may be built up until we all reach unity in the faith and in the knowledge of the Son of God and become mature, attaining to the whole measure of the fulness of Christ" (Eph. 4.12–13).

YOU ARE A MEMBER OF THE ONE BODY OF CHRIST.

YOU HAVE A SPECIFIC FUNCTION WITHIN THAT BODY.

YOU BELONG TO ALL THE OTHER MEMBERS AND THEY BELONG TO YOU.

18

FAITHFUL SONS

SONS OF GOD THROUGH FAITH

You are all sons of God through faith in Christ Jesus, for all of you who were baptised into Christ have been clothed with Christ (Gal. 3:26–27).

Through faith in what He has done for you through Jesus, God not only accepts you, *He also makes you His Son. You are an inheritor with Jesus of all that He has*. Your baptism into Christ signified that you have died and lay buried with him. The old life of sin and self has been crucified so that you do not need to live in that any longer. Now you have been clothed with Christ, with His life and love and power.

There is neither Jew nor Greek, slave nor free, male nor female, for you are all one in Christ Jesus (v. 28).

God recognises His own children, all who are in Christ, without distinction of race or sex. What separates His children from the rest of humanity is their faith in Jesus, and what makes them different is the life and power of the Spirit who lives in them. It is the Spirit that would keep them in fellowship with the Father and His Son, and would draw them into closer fellowship and unity with one another.

YOU ARE A SON OF GOD THROUGH FAITH IN JESUS.
YOU HAVE BEEN 'CLOTHED WITH CHRIST'.

HEIRS

So you are no longer a slave, but a son; and since you are a son, God has made you also an heir (Gal. 4:7).

Because you are a son of God, He wants you to live like a son, not a slave. A slave is ordered by his master and is compelled to obey. A loving son is obedient to his father, but is not under compulsion. The Lord looks for loving submission to His will. He does not order you about like a slave; He leads and guides you as a son. He does not punish you in anger, as a slave might be punished; He disciplines you in love because He is your Father.

You are an heir with Jesus of everything that the Father has; He wants you to enjoy your inheritance now, "every spiritual blessing in the heavenly places". And He wants you to know that, with Jesus, you are an heir of eternal life.

YOU ARE NO LONGER A SLAVE, BUT A SON OF GOD.

YOU ARE AN HEIR OF HIS.

LOVE OF THE BRETHREN

We know that we have passed from death to life, because we love our brothers (1 John 3:14).

To be a son of God means that you are responsible to your Father, to love Him with all your heart, mind, soul and strength. To be a son is also to recognise your responsibility to love the others who are sons and who live with you 'in Christ Jesus'. Your love for them is the evidence that you "have passed from death to life", from the death of independence and selfishness to the life of love in Christ. You are eager, then, to see the fulfilment of the new command that Jesus gave: "Love each other as I have loved you" (John 15:12).

And you recognise that neither love for God nor your brother is possible with the weak resources of your human love. But God has put His Spirit of love within you to enable you to love with His love.

YOU HAVE PASSED FROM DEATH TO LIFE.

YOU HAVE THE SPIRIT OF LOVE TO ENABLE YOU TO LOVE YOUR BROTHERS.

LIVE AS A SON

Your attitude should be the same as that of Christ Jesus (Phil. 2:5).

Faithful Sons

To live as a son of God means that "your attitude should be the same as that of Christ Jesus." He said: "By myself I can do nothing" (John 5:30). The same is true of you; by yourself you can do nothing of any value for God.

Jesus said: "My food is to do the will of him who sent me and to finish his work" (John 4:34). That is your food too, to do the will of God and fulfil the purpose God has for you. The work of God is this: "to believe in the one he has sent" (John 6:29). *You can only fulfil God's purpose for your life by faith in Jesus.*

Jesus said: "If I glorify myself, my glory means nothing" (John 8:54). The same is true for you. If you live to glorify yourself, what you do means nothing. Like Jesus, you live your new life as a son of God, to glorify your heavenly Father.

Jesus said: "Whoever serves me must follow me; and where I am my servant also will be. My Father will honour the one who serves me" (John 12:26). You are not a servant who is forced to obey, but a son who loves to serve. "I no longer call you servants, because a servant does not know his master's business. Instead, I have called you friends, for everything that I learned from my Father I have made known to you" (John 15:15).

If you desire to be an obedient son, God will lead you and will teach you His will. He will regard you as His friend to whom He can reveal Himself and the wonder of His love.

APART FROM JESUS YOU CAN DO NOTHING.

YOUR FOOD IS TO DO THE WILL OF GOD.

YOUR WORK IS TO LIVE BY FAITH IN JESUS.

YOU LIVE AS A SON OF GOD TO GLORIFY YOUR HEAVENLY FATHER.

QUALITY OF OUR LIFE IN JESUS

His divine power has given us everything we need for life and godliness through our knowledge of him who called us by his own glory and goodness (2 Pet. 1:3).

Through your knowledge of God and what He has done for you, you have been given everything you need to live as a son of God, a citizen of the Kingdom of heaven. *He has*

given you everything you need to live your life for His glory.
He has enabled you by 'His divine power'. You have everything you need for 'godliness', a life that reflects the love and power of God. It is for this that He has called you, "by his own glory and goodness". Whatever the Lord asks of you, He enables you to do in His power. To live as a son involves knowing that you can trust Him to provide for you.

YOU HAVE EVERYTHING YOU NEED FOR LIFE AND GODLINESS BY HIS DIVINE POWER.

YOU HAVE BEEN CALLED BY GOD "BY HIS OWN GLORY AND GOODNESS".

Through these he has given us his very great and precious promises, so that through them you may participate in the divine nature and escape the corruption in the world caused by evil desires (2 Pet. 1:4).

To live in Christ is to "participate in the divine nature", to live in God. As you live in the power of the new nature He has given you, so you reckon yourself dead to the old life, together with its selfish and evil desires, which cause "the corruption of the world". Instead of being part of that corruption you live in Christ, to manifest His goodness and love. As you live in His truth you have nothing to hide in the dark. The world is full of intrigue, whereas those who live in Jesus can afford to be open and honest at all times. So turn away from everything that belongs to the old, and embrace the new life you have in Him. The desires to please yourself will still be there, but you no longer have to yield to them.

The way in which you live out your participation in the divine nature is through "his very great and precious promises". God has chosen to work in the lives of His children through making many promises. He is the God of promise. What He promises, He will do, but those promises are to be believed. As you believe God's words, so you will see the fulfilment of what those words promise. *It is by believing these promises that you are able to share in God's life and being*; it is by exercising that faith that "you escape the corruption in the world caused by evil desires".

GOD HAS GIVEN YOU "HIS VERY GREAT AND PRECIOUS PROMISES", YOU PARTICIPATE IN THE DIVINE NATURE AS YOU BELIEVE

Faithful Sons

THOSE PROMISES. YOU ESCAPE THE CORRUPTION OF THE WORLD AND HAVE THE VICTORY OVER EVIL DESIRES AS YOU CONTINUE TO PUT YOUR FAITH IN JESUS.

> For this reason, make every effort to add to your faith goodness; and to goodness, knowledge; and to knowledge, self-control; and to self-control, perseverance; and to perseverance, godliness; and to godliness, brotherly kindness; and to brotherly kindness, love (2 Pet. 1:5–7).

Here is a portrait of the man who lives 'in Christ', who sets his mind on the things of the Spirit; who is concerned to live in the power of His new nature. Notice that the portrait begins with faith and ends in love. Without faith you cannot begin to please God, and everything He does in you is to enable you to live more fully in His love.

These are the marks of the man of the Spirit:

He has a firm faith in the Lord Jesus, that will not be shaken by circumstances, because He lives by the facts of what God has done for him and has made him in Christ.

He is concerned to show the goodness of God in the person he is and the things he does.

He is increasing in his knowledge of God and His purposes as he allows Him to reveal His word, and as he shares that word with others.

He uses constantly that fruit of the Spirit which is self-control, so that he will give no place to the desires of the old sinful nature and will resist temptation to indulge himself.

He will persevere in his dependence and trust in the Lord, even when everything seems difficult and contrary. He will not be deterred by opposition of any kind from fulfilling what he knows to be the call of God on his life.

He manifests godliness, through the work of the Holy Spirit in him: love, joy, peace, patience, kindness, goodness, faithfulness, gentleness and self-control.

His love for God is shown in His love for others, treating them in the way that God has treated him, with forgiveness, graciousness, mercy and generosity.

Above all, he is a man who is seen to love God and will not allow anybody or anything to shake him from the purposes of God.

> For if you possess these qualities in increasing measure, they will keep you from being ineffective and unproductive in your knowledge of our Lord Jesus Christ (2 Pet. 1:8).

Do not be deterred because you feel that you do not measure up to this portrait. You will possess these qualities 'in increasing measure'. The Lord will refine your soul of the self-interest with which it has been conditioned in the past, and enable more of Jesus to be seen in you. You will become increasingly aware of those things that do not glorify Him. That will spur you on to seek Him further, and welcome His pruning to make you 'more fruitful still'. For it is to be fruitful that the Lord has brought you to a knowledge of Himself and placed you in His Son. The promise of this verse is that, as you seek to live in the power of your new life in Christ, you need not fear being ineffective and unproductive for God.

YOU WILL POSSESS THE QUALITIES OF GOD'S LIFE IN INCREASING MEASURE.

YOU WILL NOT BE INEFFECTIVE AND UNPRODUCTIVE, BUT FRUITFUL.

LIGHT IN THE LORD

> For you were once darkness, but now you are light in the Lord (Eph. 5:8).

Faithful Sons

Through Jesus, you have been transferred from the kingdom of darkness into His own Kingdom of light (Col. 1:13). Because you live in Jesus you can bring His light into the darkness of the world. You are no longer part of that darkness yourself. Now you can share the light of Jesus with others around you who are still in darkness.

Jesus is 'the light of the world' (John 8:12). To those who believe in Him, He says: "You are the light of the world. A city on a hill cannot be hidden. Neither do people light a lamp and put it under a bowl. Instead they put it on its stand, and it gives light to everyone in the house. In the same way, let your light shine before men, that they may see your good deeds and praise your Father in heaven" (Matt. 5:14–16).

Jesus also said: "Everyone who does evil hates the light, and will not come into the light for fear that his deeds will be exposed. But whoever lives by the truth comes into the light, so that it may be seen plainly that what he has done has been done through God" (John 3:20–21).

Paul reminds the Ephesians: "you are light in the Lord." That is true of you as well; you are light in the Lord; you live in Him who is light. In Him there is no darkness, and wherever His light shines darkness disappears. No darkness can withstand the light of Jesus. So Paul continues:

> Live as children of light (for the fruit of the light consists in all goodness, righteousness and truth) and find out what pleases the Lord. Have nothing to do with the fruitless deeds of darkness, but rather expose them (Eph. 5:8–11).

As one who lives in Christ, the light of the world, you are to turn away from "the fruitless deeds of darkness" so that you may be free to do what pleases the Lord. Again and again God says to you through the words of scripture: "Remember who you are, now that you belong to me and are my child; live as one who would be like His Father."

YOU ARE LIGHT IN THE LORD.

YOU ARE TO HAVE NOTHING TO DO "WITH THE FRUITLESS DEEDS OF DARKNESS".

YOU ARE LIGHT FOR THE WORLD.
YOU ARE TO LET YOUR LIGHT SHINE BEFORE MEN.

PUT SIN TO DEATH

Put to death, therefore, whatever belongs to your earthly nature: sexual immorality, impurity, lust, evil desires and greed, which is idolatry. Because of these, the wrath of God is coming. You used to walk in these ways in the life you once lived. But now you must rid yourselves of all such things as these: anger, rage, malice, slander and filthy language from your lips. Do not lie to each other, since you have taken off your old self with its practices and have put on the new self, which is being renewed in knowledge in the image of its Creator (Col. 3:5–10).

First, "you have taken off your old self with its practices." Second, you have "put on the new self, which is being renewed in knowledge in the image of its Creator". Third, you are to "put to death, therefore, whatever belongs to your earthly nature".

The old self has to be taken off before the new self can be put on. That new self is "being renewed in knowledge". As you learn and understand more of what God has done for you and what He has made you, so you can reflect more of Him. You become more like Him as you follow Him faithfully, living in the truth of His word.

But you can only live in the power of the new if you constantly reckon the old nature as dead and if you 'put to death' those desires that appeal to 'your earthly nature'. You are now a citizen of the Kingdom of heaven and are to live accordingly. Notice the wide range of examples that Paul gives of those things that belong to the earthly nature. Be thankful that God extends His forgiveness, not condemnation, when you fail to live in the power of the new life.

"YOU HAVE TAKEN OFF YOUR OLD SELF WITH ITS PRACTICES."

"YOU HAVE PUT ON THE NEW SELF."

YOU ARE GROWING IN THE IMAGE OF YOUR CREATOR.

YOU ARE TO PUT TO DEATH WHATEVER BELONGS TO YOUR
EARTHLY NATURE.

FORGIVENESS

If we confess our sins, he is faithful and just and will
forgive us our sins and purify us from all unrighteousness
(1 John 1:9). But if anybody does sin, we have one who
speaks to the Father in our defence – Jesus Christ, the
Righteous One. He is the atoning sacrifice for our sins,
and not only for ours but also for the sins of the whole
world (1 John 2:1–2).

Because you "are being made holy", God knows that
there will be times when you will not live up to the
perfection you have in Jesus. *When you confess your sins,
God is ready to forgive you and restore you to that state of
perfection and righteousness before Him. When you sin, you
have one who speaks to the Father in your defence – "Jesus
Christ, the Righteous One"*. He does that because He shed
His blood on your behalf. He is ready to speak on behalf of
all those who come to the Father through Him. He continually intercedes for those who are His 'brothers', the
sons of God.

GOD WILL FORGIVE YOUR SINS AND PURIFY YOU FROM ALL
UNRIGHTEOUSNESS, WHEN YOU CONFESS YOUR SINS TO HIM.
JESUS, THE RIGHTEOUS ONE, SPEAKS TO THE FATHER IN YOUR
DEFENCE.

'NO' TO TEMPTATION

For the grace of God that brings salvation has appeared
to all men. It teaches us to say 'No' to ungodliness and
worldly passions, and to live self-controlled, upright and
godly lives in this present age, while we wait for the
blessed hope – the glorious appearing of our great God
and Saviour, Jesus Christ, who gave himself for us to
redeem us from all wickedness and to purify for himself a
people that are his very own, eager to do what is good
(Titus 2:11–14).

God does not ask you to fight temptation on your own.

His word tells you to reckon yourself dead to the old, to put to death your earthly desires, and to say 'No' to ungodliness and worldly passions. Even in that, He does not leave you on your own, but makes His grace available to you. It is by that free gift of God that He has brought you salvation, *and it is by His continuing grace that you are to live out that salvation in your life*. It is by dependence upon the power of His grace that you are to live a "self-controlled, upright and godly" life.

You are a part of the reason why Jesus gave Himself. He has redeemed you from all wickedness; you are one of the people He is purifying for Himself: you are "his very own" and He wants you to be "eager to do what is good".

GOD GIVES YOU HIS GRACE TO RESIST TEMPTATION.

YOU CAN SAY 'NO' TO UNGODLINESS AND WORLDLY PASSIONS.

GOD GIVES YOU HIS GRACE TO LIVE A SELF-CONTROLLED, UPRIGHT AND GODLY LIFE.

HE HAS REDEEMED YOU FROM ALL WICKEDNESS.

YOU ARE ONE OF HIS OWN PEOPLE, WHOM HE IS PURIFYING.

YOU ARE TO BE EAGER TO DO WHAT IS GOOD.

HELP IN TEMPTATION

Because he himself suffered when he was tempted, he is able to help those who are being tempted (Heb. 2:18). Therefore, since we have a great high priest who has gone through the heavens, Jesus the Son of God, let us hold firmly to the faith we profess. For we do not have a high priest who is unable to sympathise with our weaknesses, but we have one who has been tempted in every way, just as we are – yet was without sin. Let us then approach the throne of grace with confidence, so that we may receive mercy and find grace to help us in our time of need (Heb. 4:14–16).

Jesus is able to help you when you are being tempted. Turn to Him for that help. This applies not only to your Christian behaviour, but to your faith as well. "Hold firmly to the faith" you profess when tempted to doubt or despair. Jesus has shared your weakness, and resisted every temptation to doubt! Because you have direct access to the Father through Him, you can call upon God's mercy and grace at any time of need. *Approach Him with confidence, knowing that it is His intention and desire to help you.* It is the throne of grace that you approach. By His grace God gives freely to those who deserve nothing. Do not let any sense of unworthiness deter you from coming boldly before Him. For you live in Him and He lives in you – and He resisted every temptation, even that of doubt. He wants to help you.

Nothing is more important than being honest with God. There is no point in trying to hide your doubts from Him. When you are aware of doubt persisting, bring that doubt to Him in prayer, ask for His forgiveness and for the Holy Spirit to give you the faith that you need. Because He forgives your doubt when it is confessed to Him, your confidence before Him will be restored.

JESUS IS ABLE TO HELP YOU RESIST TEMPTATION.

YOU ARE TO HOLD FIRMLY TO YOUR FAITH.

YOU ARE TO APPROACH THE THRONE OF GRACE WITH CONFIDENCE.

YOU WILL RECEIVE MERCY AND GRACE TO HELP YOU IN YOUR TIME OF NEED.

NO ANXIETY

Cast all your anxiety on him because he cares for you (1 Pet. 5:7).

Any loving father wants to relieve his children of anxiety. You are to cast *all* your anxiety on your heavenly Father "because he cares for you". Jesus says: "Do not worry about tomorrow, for tomorrow will worry about itself" (Matt. 6:34). He says: "I tell you, do not worry about your life" (Matt. 6:25). If you "seek first his kingdom and his righteousness", then God will supply whatever needs you have (v. 33).

Anxiety can stifle the spiritual life of Christians. It is an indication that they are not trusting the Lord, at least for those areas of their lives about which they are anxious. Anxiety is a natural reaction to trouble; as soon as you are anxious obey this scripture. It is disobedience to carry the weight of anxiety yourself. *Believe that God will not only carry the burden, but will also move in the situation to supply your need.*

YOU ARE TO CAST ALL YOUR ANXIETY ON GOD.

HE CARES FOR YOU.

SET YOUR HEARTS AND MINDS ON THINGS ABOVE

Since, then, you have been raised with Christ, set your hearts on things above, where Christ is seated at the right hand of God. Set your minds on things above, not on earthly things (Col. 3:1–2).

Your mind is part of your soul. It can either come under the influence and direction of the Spirit, or it can be set upon earthly things, the things of the flesh. Therefore, it plays a crucial part in determining whether you will walk in the Spirit, obeying the Lord, or whether you will pursue your own course, because you have been considering your own desires, weakness, failure, temptation, fears or doubts.

Those who live according to the sinful nature have their minds set on what that nature desires; but those who live in accordance with the Spirit have their minds set on what the Spirit desires. The mind of sinful man is death, but the mind controlled by the Spirit is life and peace (Rom. 8:5–6).

Paul says your mind will need to be *set* on things above, on what the Spirit desires. Be determined to pursue that course. That is where your whole concentration will have to lie. *You are going to live in the power of your new nature and not allow yourself to be dragged back into sin.*

Your mind may often be assailed by unholy, critical and unloving thoughts. Every time that happens, do not dwell upon those thoughts, and do not feel condemned for having them. Turn away from them immediately and fix your thoughts on things above. The easiest way to do that is to

Faithful Sons

praise the Lord, pray to Him, or begin to speak His word to yourself.

If your desire is to love and please the Lord, set your heart on things above. As with your mind so with your heart. Let it be set on pleasing the Lord and obeying Him. Do not allow your mind to lure your heart into desiring what the sinful nature desires, or your will may be weakened and you will then yield to temptation.

Your heart and mind are to be set on things above, because "you have been raised with Christ". You live in Him; you have been raised to a new life; you belong to His Kingdom and you are to live His Kingdom life for His praise and glory.

YOU HAVE BEEN RAISED WITH CHRIST.
YOU ARE TO SET YOUR HEART ON HEAVEN.
YOU ARE TO SET YOUR MIND ON THINGS ABOVE.

DEAD TO SIN

We died to sin: how can we live in it any longer? (Rom. 6:2).

You have died to the old life of sin. Although you have died, sin has not. Sin itself still exists and the temptation to sin will always be with you in this life. Even Jesus was not immune from temptation. *You no longer need to sin by yielding to temptation.* Sin is no longer the guiding principle of your life. Do not continue in any deliberate disobedience to the Lord, therefore. And do not set your mind on temptation and the things that cause you to sin. Avoid putting yourself in situations where the 'flesh' would be stirred to any activity. And do not fall into the subtle sin of trying to serve God in your own way in your own strength.

YOU DIED TO SIN.
YOU DO NOT HAVE TO CONTINUE TO SIN.

DO EVERYTHING IN THE NAME OF JESUS

And whatever you do, whether in word or deed, do it all in the name of the Lord Jesus, giving thanks to God the Father through him (Col. 3:17).

Recognising that you have died to sin deals with the negative. This is what God is positively asking of you: *whatever you do in word or action, do everything, "in the name of the Lord Jesus"*. In scripture the name denotes the person. To speak or act in the name of Jesus means that you say or do what He would say or do in that situation. You speak or act on His behalf.

As you do this, you are to give thanks "to God the Father through him". Jesus lived for the glory of the Father. So do you if you live out your life in Him faithfully, and act truly in the name of Jesus. Through Him God makes available to you all that He made available to Jesus. He does not leave you to flounder on your own. You can be thankful that you have the resources of heaven available to you.

And it is through Jesus that you have that direct access to the Father. You can praise and thank Him with the loving obedience of your life, as well as with your mouth. "Give thanks in all circumstances, for this is God's will for you in Christ Jesus" (1 Thess. 5:18).

Whenever you are uncertain as to whether you should say or do a particular thing, it is good to ask yourself: "Can I do this in the name of the Lord Jesus?" If the answer is "Yes", then do it; if the answer is "No" – don't do it.

YOU ARE TO SPEAK AS JESUS WOULD SPEAK – IN HIS NAME.

YOU ARE TO DO WHAT JESUS WOULD DO – IN HIS NAME.

YOU HAVE ALL THE RESOURCES OF HEAVEN AVAILABLE TO YOU.

YOU ARE TO GIVE THANKS IN ALL CIRCUMSTANCES, FOR THIS IS GOD'S WILL FOR YOU.

WITH ALL YOUR HEART

Whatever you do, work at it with all your heart, as working for the Lord, not for men, since you know that you will receive an inheritance from the Lord as a reward. It is the Lord Christ you are serving (Col. 3:23–24).

If you do everything in the name of Jesus, you "work at it with all your heart, as working for the Lord, not for men". Jesus did everything from His heart for the glory of His

Faithful Sons

Father, and that needs to be your motivation as well. Notice that this applies to whatever you do. You have the promise of "an inheritance from the Lord as a reward". That is not a motive for working for the Lord with all your heart; it is the reward that awaits you if you do. Your true motive is the joy and privilege of serving the Lord Christ.

WHATEVER YOU DO YOU ARE TO DO WITH YOUR HEART AS WORKING FOR THE LORD.

YOU WILL RECEIVE AN INHERITANCE FROM THE LORD AS A REWARD.

YOU ARE SERVING THE LORD CHRIST.

EQUIPPED BY GOD

May the God of peace, who through the blood of the eternal covenant brought back from the dead our Lord Jesus, that great Shepherd of the sheep, equip you with everything good for doing his will, and may he work in us what is pleasing to him, through Jesus Christ, to whom be glory for ever and ever. Amen. (Heb. 13:20–21).

The writer to the Hebrews prays that the Lord Jesus may "equip you with everything good for doing his will". God is willing to answer this prayer because He wants you to speak and to do in the name of Jesus those things that are His will for you. The prayer continues that Jesus may work in you what is pleasing to the Father. Everything that you do of value to the Lord will be His work in you, and all the glory will belong to Him.

GOD WANTS TO EQUIP YOU WITH EVERYTHING GOOD FOR DOING HIS WILL.

HE WANTS TO WORK IN YOU WHAT IS PLEASING TO HIM.

HE WILL DO THIS THROUGH JESUS, TO WHOM ALL THE GLORY WILL BELONG.

LIVING AS JESUS DID

But if anyone obeys his word, God's love is truly made complete in him. This is how we know we are in him: whoever claims to live in him must walk as Jesus did (1 John 2:5–6).

You can rejoice to live 'in Christ Jesus' by God's gracious act. John reminds you of the responsibility of that great fact. If you claim to live in Him, then you must "walk as Jesus did". That seems an awesome task; so you need to be reminded quickly that God has given you the power of His Spirit to enable you to do just that. And whenever you fail to reflect Jesus, you have the continuing grace of His forgiveness to restore you.

There is no point in saying you live in Christ, while at the same time living a life of self-indulgence, fulfilling your desires and being disobedient to His will, caring little for His word.

Why do you fail to walk as Jesus did? Because of the strong self-conditioned soul life of yours that still wants to act independently of God. If you look at the life of Jesus, you see that He was free of excesses. There was the right balance between prayer and activity, feasting and fasting, giving and receiving, talking and silence. *Any excesses in your life are a danger-signal because they are an indication that the soul is running its own course, and is not properly submitted to the Spirit.* Allow God to deal with those excesses, and allow His Spirit to lead you into a well-balanced life that is evidence of walking with Jesus.

God's love will only be 'made complete' in you by your obeying His word. It is that word that sets you free to love, tells you who to love and shows you how to love.

YOU ARE TO WALK AS JESUS DID BECAUSE YOU LIVE IN HIM.
GOD'S LOVE IS MADE COMPLETE IN YOU THROUGH OBEDIENCE TO HIS WORD.

19

LIVING IN OBEDIENCE

CONTINUE IN HIM

> The anointing you received from him remains in you, and you do not need anyone to teach you. But as his anointing teaches you about all things and as that anointing is real, not counterfeit – just as it has taught you, remain him him (1 John 2.27).

You have received the anointing of God's Holy Spirit. He is your Teacher, 'the Spirit of truth', who will guide you into all truth. He will teach you everything; Jesus promises that. And what does the Holy Spirit teach you? *"Remain in him."* Live in Jesus. Keep walking in His way, looking to Him who is the author and perfector of your faith – not looking back, or down, or in, but up to Him. And the outcome?

> And now, dear children, continue in him, so that when he appears we may be confident and unashamed before him at his coming (1 John 2:28).

You have been made righteous that you might live in righteousness. You have been made holy that you might live in holiness. You have been given His Spirit that you might live in His love and power. You have been crucified with Christ, so that it is no longer you who live, but Christ who lives in you.

As you live in His righteousness and holiness, by His Spirit and Presence within you, so you "may be confident and unashamed before him at his coming". The blood of Jesus washes your shame away because He has accepted and forgiven you.

> How great is the love the Father has lavished on us, that we should be called children of God! And that is what we are!... Dear friends, now we are children of God, and what we will be has not yet been made known. But we know that when he appears, we shall be like him, for we shall see him as he is (1 John 3:1-2).

That is the glorious promise of what you shall be. You cannot imagine what it will be like, but when the Day of the Lord comes you shall be like Him. All those things about your soul that you know dishonour him shall be swept away. You shall be like Him, because you "shall see him as he is". Somehow that moment will complete the work of perfection that God has planned for you.

GOD'S ANOINTING REMAINS IN YOU.

HIS SPIRIT WILL TEACH YOU.

YOU ARE TO REMAIN IN THE SPIRIT, LIVING 'IN CHRIST JESUS'.

THE FATHER HAS LAVISHED HIS LOVE UPON YOU BY MAKING YOU HIS CHILD.

YOU WILL BE CONFIDENT AND UNASHAMED BEFORE JESUS AT HIS COMING.

WHEN HE APPEARS, YOU SHALL BE LIKE HIM, FOR YOU SHALL SEE HIM AS HE IS.

PURIFY YOURSELF

> Everyone who has this hope in him purifies himself, just as he is pure (1 John 3:3).

Because you shall be like Him does not mean that you are to care little about how much of Him can be seen in your life now. Far from it. Because He is pure, you are to seek purity of heart and motive now, purity of mind and thought, purity of desire and affection, purity of life and action, living the holy life of God's holy people in the power of His Holy Spirit.

> You know that he appeared so that he might take away our sins. And in him is no sin. No one who lives in him keeps on sinning. No one who continues to sin has either seen him or known him (1 John 3:5-6).

Living in Obedience

There is no sin in Jesus, for sin is whatever opposes God. If you live in Him you live in the sinless one. It would be totally inconsistent, therefore, to persist in your sinful ways, opposing God in your life. Those who claim faith in Jesus, but do not demonstrate a life that is lived for Him, do not truly know or love Him. The power of sin no longer grips your life. Even though you can still sin, you no longer have to.

Dear children, do not let anyone lead you astray. He who does what is right is righteous, just as he is righteous. He who does what is sinful is of the devil, because the devil has been sinning from the beginning. The reason the Son of God appeared was to destroy the devil's work. No one who is born of God will continue to sin, because God's seed remains in him; he cannot go on sinning, because he has been born of God (1 John 3:7-9).

God has made you righteous, and now you can do what is right in His sight. You are no longer a child of the devil, in rebellion against the Lord. You no longer need to persist in sin. *Jesus has destroyed the devil's work and delivered you from the power of sin.* God lives in you by the power of His Spirit and He will guide you into truth and life and peace, not sin. If you follow His leading in your life you will not persist in your sins.

This does not mean that you will never sin again, but if you desire to glorify God, then you will not willingly or wilfully persist in disobedience. When God points out your fault you will come readily to Him in repentance, praising Him again for the power of the blood of His Son.

YOU ARE TO PURIFY YOURSELF, AS HE IS PURE.

YOU ARE NOT TO KEEP ON SINNING, PERSISTING WILFULLY IN DISOBEDIENCE.

YOU ARE NOT TO PERSIST IN THOSE SINS, BECAUSE YOU ARE BORN OF GOD.

LIVING IN OBEDIENCE

> Those who obey his commands live in him, and he in them. And this is how we know that he lives in us: we know it by the Spirit he gave us (1 John 3:24).

God has given you His Spirit to lead you in a life of obedience. As Jesus submitted totally to the will of His Father, so all those who live in Him are to do likewise. You can only obey if you are prepared to wait upon the Lord, to learn how to listen to Him in His word and through prayer. The Spirit is given to declare God's word to you. That means that He will teach you what the scriptures mean, and will bring them to life for you. But more than that, the Spirit will speak the right word to you at the right time. That will be God's word to you for that situation at that time – His prophetic word. He will do that through the scriptures and through the prophetic gifts of the Spirit. Time and time again the Spirit will direct you to the relevant scriptures, calling them to your mind as you pray, or even in the middle of the situation where you need to know His word to you.

Having heard the Lord, obey Him!

BECAUSE YOU LIVE IN JESUS, YOU ARE TO OBEY HIM.

HE HAS GIVEN YOU HIS SPIRIT TO SPEAK TO YOU AND LEAD YOU IN OBEDIENCE.

LOVING OBEDIENCE

> If anyone loves me, he will obey my teaching. My Father will love him, and we will come to him and make our home with him (John 14:23).

The commands of the Lord are not burdens that He lays upon us: they are not to be compared with the intricate niceties of the law which it was impossible to obey. The commands of the new covenant flow from God's love for you, and from the response to that love that He asks from you.

If you love the Lord you will live close to His word, not because you regard the Bible as a rule-book, but because you know that His words are 'spirit and life'. If you love the Lord you will want to see things as He sees them, understand them as He understands them, do what He wants you to do, say what He wants you to speak. Remember that the scriptures give you the revelation of who God is, what He has done for you in Jesus, who you are now that you belong to Him, and what He promises you as one who lives 'in Christ Jesus'.

To disregard His word is to disregard the Lord – and that is not an indication of love for Him. As your love for God continues to increase, so will your love for His word. *To love the word of God means that you love to do it*, not simply study it!

The wonderful promise is that the Father and the Son will make their home with the one who keeps His word. Let that be true for you; that you are not trying to obey God as a good work, but you know the Father and Son have come to live in fellowship with you to lead you and enable the fulfilment of your heart's desire: to please Him by obeying Him.

YOU ARE TO EXPRESS YOUR LOVE FOR GOD BY OBEYING HIS WORD.
AS YOU DO THAT, THE FATHER AND SON COME TO YOU AND MAKE THEIR HOME WITH YOU.

ABIDE IN LOVE

As the Father has loved me, so have I loved you. Now remain in my love. If you obey my commands you will remain in my love, just as I have obeyed my Father's commands and remain in his love. I have told you this so that my joy may be in you and that your joy may be complete (John 15:9–11).

You are to live continually in the Lord's love. *Jesus loves you as the Father loved Him – perfectly*. It is in that love that you are to live. You will remain in that love by obeying what God asks of you. Disobedience spoils the unity of love between the Father and His child, and unity is only restored through forgiveness. Jesus maintained His unity with His Father by obeying His commands. It was through that obedience that He could "remain in his love".

If Jesus needed to be obedient to maintain His relationship with the Father and remain in His love, then so will you need to obey Him. Remember that obedience is not a burden, but leads to joy. You will know the joy, as well as the love and peace of God, as you seek to obey Him and refuse to follow your own course.

YOU ARE TO REMAIN IN THE LOVE OF JESUS.
YOU ARE TO OBEY THE COMMANDS OF JESUS AND THEN YOU WILL REMAIN IN HIS LOVE.
AS YOU OBEY THE LORD, YOUR JOY WILL BE FULL.

PROMISE

If you remain in me and my words remain in you, ask whatever you wish, and it will be given you. This is to my Father's glory, that you bear much fruit, showing yourselves to be my disciples (John 15:7–8).

This is the Lord's promise to you if you live in Him and allow His words to live in you: "Ask whatever you wish, and it will be given you." God makes such a promise for His own glory. He desires to be glorified by your bearing much fruit. That will only happen if you are a praying person. You will not be fruitful on your own; that will happen only through prayerful dependence on the Lord. Pray with faith, believing His word to you. As a disciple, *God wants to show His love for you by answering your prayers*. But realise the context in which Jesus makes this promise. God is ready to answer prayer that comes from a life lived in Him, prayer that comes from His child in whom His words are lived.

YOU ARE TO LIVE IN JESUS.
YOU ARE TO ALLOW HIS WORDS TO LIVE IN YOU.
YOU ARE TO BEAR MUCH FRUIT.
GOD WILL ANSWER YOUR PRAYERS TO ENABLE THAT FRUITFULNESS.

WARNING

If anyone does not remain in me, he is like a branch that is thrown away and withers; such branches are picked up, thrown into the fire and burned (John 15:6).

Living in Obedience

You have heard the promise of Jesus; now heed his warning:

> Anyone who runs ahead and does not continue in the teaching of Christ does not have God; whoever continues in the teaching has both the Father and the Son (2 John 9).

You are not to run ahead of the Lord. You can follow Him, live in Him, walk with Him, but not run ahead of Him. It is possible to run ahead with your own ideas and enthusiasms, even for the Lord's work. It is easy, having discerned His purpose, to rush to achieve that purpose by your own efforts in your own way.

Do not allow the enemy to deceive you into taking the world's burdens upon your shoulders, or imagining that you can meet the needs of all the demanding people around you.

Beware of your own opinions and ideas. If they conflict with the revelation of God's word, they are wrong. Anyone who "does not continue in the teaching of Christ does not have God". You have the teaching of Jesus. *Live in His word and you have both the Father and the Son.*

YOU ARE TO CONTINUE IN THE TEACHING OF CHRIST.
AS YOU DO SO, YOU HAVE BOTH THE FATHER AND SON.

FAITH AND LOVE

> What you heard from me, keep as the pattern of sound teaching, with faith and love in Christ Jesus (2 Tim. 1:13).

This is Paul's own way of saying to Timothy: continue in the word of truth, the word that will set people free. That word is to be lived and proclaimed with faith and love. The word is of no use to you unless you believe it and so receive from God the life of which that word speaks. As you live with faith in God, so you can encourage others to put their trust in Him and know that "heaven and earth will pass away", but His words will never pass away.

And that faith is perfected in love. *Your faith in God and in His word comes out of your love for Him.* And that love is a response to the love that He has for you. That faith and love are an essential part of your inheritance 'in Christ Jesus'.

Remember that it is "the holy scriptures, which are able to make you wise for salvation through faith in Christ Jesus" (2 Tim. 3:15).

YOU ARE TO KEEP TO THE "PATTERN OF SOUND TEACHING, WITH FAITH AND LOVE IN CHRIST JESUS".

KNOWLEDGE AND INSIGHT

> And this is my prayer: that your love may abound more and more in knowledge and depth of insight, so that you may be able to discern what is best and may be pure and blameless until the day of Christ, filled with the fruit of righteousness that comes through Jesus Christ – to the glory and praise of God (Phil. 1:9–11).

The fruit of righteousness, the fruit of being accepted by God, is that you may live a life that is pure and blameless. That can only happen if your love for God abounds more and more. *Obedience comes out of love for Him* – not out of trying to fight your desires to be disobedient. Out of your growing relationship of love for the Lord, you will "abound more and more in knowledge and depth of insight" into what is best, into His will and purpose. Out of that same love will come the motivation to do what is best. That is the fruit of righteousness: doing what the Lord considers best. And when you fail to do that, He makes His forgiveness available to you. He wants to keep you "pure and blameless until the day of Christ", when He returns in majesty and power.

MAY YOUR LOVE ABOUND MORE AND MORE, THEN

YOU WILL KNOW WHAT IS BEST,

YOU WILL BE KEPT PURE AND BLAMELESS UNTIL THE DAY OF CHRIST,

YOU WILL BE FILLED WITH THE FRUIT OF RIGHTEOUSNESS THROUGH JESUS.

CONTINUE IN HIM

> So then, just as you received Christ Jesus as Lord, continue to live in him, rooted and built up in him, strengthened in the faith as you were taught, and overflowing with thankfulness (Col. 2:6–7).

You will live in the power of your new nature only if you keep your eyes on the faith taught in God's word. Faith comes from hearing God speak His word to your heart. Look at yourself, look at the problems around you, and faith begins to dwindle. *Look at the Lord and His word in the midst of the situation and He will give you faith to trust Him to carry you through the difficulty*. It is the word brought to your heart by the Holy Spirit that will enable you to be "built up in him". You received Him by faith; continue to live in him by faith, "overflowing with thankfulness", for He holds you faithfully in His love.

YOU ARE TO CONTINUE TO LIVE IN JESUS BY FAITH,

YOU WILL BE ROOTED AND BUILT UP IN HIM, BY HIS WORD AND SPIRIT.

YOU WILL BE STRENGTHENED IN FAITH AS YOU LIVE 'IN HIM'.

YOU CAN OVERFLOW WITH THANKFULNESS FOR HIS FAITHFUL LOVE FOR YOU.

20

STAND FIRM IN VICTORY

WEAK, YET POWERFUL

> For to be sure, he was crucified in weakness, yet he lives by God's power. Likewise we are weak in him, yet by God's power we will live with him to serve you (2 Cor. 13:4).

Whenever you look at yourself you will always be able to see how weak you are, how totally incapable of pleasing God in your own strength or by your own efforts. When you look inside yourself, you will see selfishness, self-concern and self-love. You will realise that there are many ways in which you do not want to please God, but desire to maintain control over your own affairs.

All this demonstrates how unprofitable it is to keep our eyes on ourselves. God has put us 'in Him' so that "by God's power we will live with him to serve you."

You will always remain weak of yourself. God will not strengthen that weakness lest you continue to depend upon yourself. *He will teach you that, of yourself, you are utterly weak; yet by God's power, by dependence upon Him, all things become possible for you.* Although you need to be aware of your weakness, your concentration needs to be upon His strength and His enabling.

Notice why it is God's purpose that we should live with Him: to serve. God does not give us His presence or His power for our self-indulgent pleasure, but for service. To attempt to serve without His presence and power ends in fruitless futility. To have Him and not be fruitful is similarly futile. God's intention is for you to live in His power, so that He can flow through your life and make you fruitful in His service.

In this you will be like Jesus, for "he was crucified in weakness, yet he lives by God's power." It is no longer necessary to contemplate your own weakness; now you can live in the power of your new nature.

YOU ARE WEAK IN HIM.

YET BY GOD'S POWER YOU WILL LIVE WITH HIM TO SERVE HIM.

SUBMIT AND RESIST

> Submit yourselves, then, to God. Resist the devil, and he will flee from you. Come near to God and he will come near to you (James 4:7–8).

You are to submit yourself to God: not the old life of weakness, for that has already been offered to Him. You are to submit yourself as a new creature with new life. Stand

Stand firm in Victory

firm against the devil; resist all his efforts to persuade you to concentrate on your weakness and inadequacy. *Knowing full well your own weakness, you can throw yourself in complete dependence on the Lord, and not be rendered ineffective by a sense of total inadequacy.*

If you resist the devil's temptations to please self and depend upon self, he will flee from you. That is God's promise that you will find to be true. The enemy will attack again, but he will have to flee again if you continue to resist him.

Whenever you are being subjected to temptation, turn to the Lord in praise; draw near to God, for Satan has no place in the courts of praise. And as you draw near to the Lord in worship, so He "will come near to you". *You will know that you do not have to resist the devil with your own weakness, but in His strength.*

YOU ARE TO SUBMIT YOURSELF TO GOD.

YOU ARE TO RESIST THE DEVIL – AND HE WILL FLEE FROM YOU.

YOU ARE TO COME NEAR TO GOD – AND HE WILL COME NEAR TO YOU.

FREEDOM

It is for freedom that Christ has set us free. Stand firm, then, and do not let yourselves be burdened again by a yoke of slavery (Gal. 5:1).

Jesus has set you free that you might live in freedom. He has set you free from slavery to sin, to fear and disobedience. You no longer need to live like that. Jesus has set you free to live in freedom, not to slip back into bondage.

Again the scripture tells you to 'stand firm'. Stand firm in that new life God has given you, calling upon all the resources of His Spirit that He has made available to you.

Freedom does not mean that you have the licence to do as you wish. You are free to do the will of the Lord and to please Him. Neither does it mean that you are to live an undisciplined life. *A life that is submitted to God is willing to be disciplined, or discipled, by Him.* He will lead and guide; He will correct in love; He will inspire and enable.

Sin produces a yoke of slavery; you are now yoked to Jesus. Allow Him to guide you, for He will never lead you into sin.

YOU HAVE BEEN SET FREE BY JESUS.
YOU ARE TO LIVE IN FREEDOM.
YOU ARE TO STAND FIRM AGAINST SIN.
YOU ARE YOKED WITH JESUS – NOT SIN.

STAND FIRM

Now it is God who makes both us and you stand firm in Christ. He anointed us, set his seal of ownership on us, and put his Spirit in our hearts as a deposit, guaranteeing what is to come (2 Cor. 1:21–22).

You cannot stand firm by yourself: you are too weak. It is God Himself who makes you "stand firm in Christ". How does He do this?

He has anointed you with His Spirit, the fulness of His power. He has "set his seal of ownership upon you". The very fact that God lives in you by the power of His Spirit is the demonstration of the truth that he has accepted you and made you His own. Never lose sight of that fact, especially when you are faced by contrary and difficult circumstances.

It is the Spirit who will inspire faith within you to believe the promises of God, that you may continue to enter into all those good things that God has prepared for you. He does not want you to slip away from Him. He gives you His Spirit to make you "stand firm in Christ". The Holy Spirit is the first instalment of what God has planned for you – to be reigning with Him eternally in glory. He in you and you in Him.

You cannot stand firm in yourself. *You are to stand firm in Christ, where God has put you and where you belong.*

GOD MAKES YOU STAND FIRM IN CHRIST.
HE HAS ANOINTED YOU WITH HIS HOLY SPIRIT.
HE HAS SET HIS SEAL OF OWNERSHIP ON YOU.
HE HAS PUT HIS SPIRIT IN YOUR HEART.

HE WILL INSPIRE FAITH IN YOU; YOU ARE GUARANTEED "WHAT IS TO COME".

STRONG IN GRACE

You then, my son, be strong in the grace that is in Christ Jesus (2 Tim. 2:1).

Never doubt the grace of God and His willingness to deal graciously with you. It is the work of His grace that He has forgiven you, that He has accepted you, that He has loved you, that He has made you His child, that He has given you the gift of His Holy Spirit, that you live 'in Christ Jesus'. If God has already done all that in His love and grace, He is ready to continue to give of His riches to you. Never be put off by thoughts of your own unworthiness. *God has accepted you and given you direct access to Himself, that you may be bold in your asking, knowing the immensity of His grace.* Like Timothy, you need to "be strong in the grace that is in Christ Jesus".

Never be put off by awareness of your own weakness. *Weak though you are, you live in Christ Jesus and God has made available to you through Him the abundance of His grace.* You deserve nothing; yet He gives you "every spiritual blessing in Christ".

YOU ARE TO "BE STRONG IN THE GRACE THAT IS IN CHRIST JESUS".

YOU ARE TO BELIEVE GOD'S WILLINGNESS TO GIVE HIS RICHES TO YOU, DESPITE YOUR OWN UNWORTHINESS AND WEAKNESS.

BE STRONG IN THE LORD

Finally, be strong in the Lord and in his mighty power (Eph. 6:10).

You cannot be strong in yourself. You *can* "be strong in the Lord and in his mighty power". That means that you are to be strong in your dependence upon Him and in your looking to the resources of 'his mighty power' to be at work for you in one situation after another. You can "put on the full armour of God so that you can take your stand against the devil's schemes" (v. 11).

You need to be strong in His mighty power because your "struggle is not against flesh and blood, but against the rulers, against the authorities, against the powers of this dark world and against the spiritual forces of evil in the heavenly realms" (v. 12). It is these powers that are responsible for stirring up opposition, strife and rebellion against God. "Therefore put on the full armour of God, so that when the day of evil comes, you may be able to stand your ground, and after you have done everything, to stand" (v. 13).

You are to stand firm in the armour that God has provided for you. The belt of *truth*, the breastplate of *righteousness*; your feet fitted with the readiness that comes from the gospel of *peace*. You are to take "the shield of *faith*", which will enable you to emerge victorious from everything that the enemy would throw against you. You have the helmet of *salvation* and the sword of the *Spirit*, which is the *word* of God.

And you are to "pray in the Spirit on all occasions with all kinds of prayers and requests" (v. 18). Even what you could never accomplish, the Spirit is able to do through you. Do not depend upon your own wisdom in prayer. The Spirit always knows how to pray, even when you do not; He knows what to pray against and how to pray for you in every situation. Learn, therefore, to let the Spirit of God pray through you in the prayer language that He gives you.

Let your strength be in Him, not yourself; in His resources, not your own.

YOU ARE TO BE STRONG IN THE LORD.

YOU ARE TO BE STRONG IN HIS MIGHTY POWER.

YOU ARE TO PUT ON THE FULL ARMOUR OF GOD.

YOU ARE TO PRAY IN THE SPIRIT ON ALL OCCASIONS.

PEACE AND VICTORY

I have told you these things, so that in me you may have peace. In this world you will have trouble. But take heart! I have overcome the world! (John 16:33).

It is inevitable that those who are faithful to Jesus will encounter opposition, misunderstanding, rejection and even persecution. Jesus said as much. Yet in the midst of difficulties and opposition. you have His peace within you. *You have the victory of Jesus over everything that the world or "the spiritual forces of evil" bring against you.* There is no need to live in fear, therefore. As you stand firm you will see that Jesus really does reign in this world, that He will answer your prayers and change circumstances to fulfil His promise to you.

Remember it is not with your human weakness that you will prevail. In your weakness trust in the might of Jesus and see Him prevail, for He has "overcome the world".

IN THIS WORLD YOU WILL HAVE TROUBLE.
YOU LIVE IN JESUS WHO HAS OVERCOME THE WORLD.

MORE THAN CONQUERORS

No, in all these things we are more than conquerors through him who loved us (Rom. 8:37).

What kind of difficulty and opposition could you encounter? "Who shall separate us from the love of Christ? Shall trouble of hardship or persecution or famine or nakedness or danger or sword?" (Rom. 8:35). That is a comprehensive list. Paul's answer to his own question is: "No, in all these things we are more than conquerors through him who loved us."

A conqueror is someone who fights a battle and wins; he overcomes his adversary. You are "more than a conqueror". That means you have the victory before the battle begins, for Jesus has already overcome your adversary. He wants you to proclaim *His* victory in every situation, not try to fight your own battles. If you try to fight in your own strength you will be overcome time and time again, and the victory of Jesus will seem only a pious hope. Paul goes on to say:

For I am convinced that neither death nor life, neither angels nor demons, neither the present nor the future, nor any powers, neither height nor depth, nor anything else in all creation, will be able to separate us from the love of God that is in Christ Jesus our Lord (Rom. 8:38–39).

Nothing and nobody can separate you from that love that is in Christ Jesus, for that is where you are, living in Him. You are more than a conqueror *through Him*, not in yourself. You can believe His victory, not yours. You can experience the faithfulness of His love for you over and over again. If your trust is in His love, you will not be overcome.

YOU ARE MORE THAN A CONQUEROR THROUGH JESUS WHO LOVES YOU.

NOTHING CAN SEPARATE YOU FROM HIS LOVE.

LED IN TRIUMPH

But thanks be to God, who always leads us in triumphal procession in Christ and through us spreads everywhere the fragrance of the knowledge of him (2 Cor. 2:14).

Jesus is leading you in His triumphal procession. By the victory of His cross, He leads you in triumph through one adverse situation after another, enabling you to bear witness to His love and goodness, His compassion and mercy, His life and power. There will come the time when all will have to bow the knee before Jesus and acknowledge that He is Lord. Those who are in His triumphal train are those who have already bowed the knee and submitted to His authority and Lordship.

He does not call you to spread fear, despair and doubt, but faith in His love and power and confidence in His word and promises. You are to spread "the fragrance of the knowledge of Him" for, Paul continues, "we are to God the aroma of Christ among those who are being saved and those who are perishing" (v. 15). Heed the warning that things will not always be easy. To those who are perishing "we are the smell of death"; to those who are being saved, "the fragrance of life" (v. 16). No wonder Paul asks: "And who is equal to such a task?" It can only be accomplished by Jesus working through us, leading us by His Spirit in His triumphal procession.

Stand firm in Victory

God does not spare His children from all adversity, but He carries them through it all, enabling them to have the victory over it. That is a far more meaningful witness to the world.

> I consider that our present sufferings are not worth comparing with the glory that will be revealed in us. The creation waits in eager expectation for the sons of God to be revealed (Rom. 8:18–19).

You are a son of God, and He is wanting the world to receive something of the sweetness of Jesus through you, even through the trials and difficulties of life.

YOU ARE IN CHRIST'S TRIUMPHAL PROCESSION.
THROUGH YOU THE FRAGRANCE OF THE KNOWLEDGE OF HIM IS TO BE SPREAD.

YOUR NAME IN HEAVEN

> However, do not rejoice that the spirits submit to you, but rejoice that your names are written in heaven (Luke 10:20).

Jesus sent the seventy-two disciples out with the command: "Heal the sick who are there and tell them, 'the kingdom of God is near you'" (Luke 10:9). When they returned they were overjoyed, wondering at the fact that even demons submitted to them in the name of Jesus. He replied:

> I saw Satan fall like lightning from heaven. I have given you authority to trample on snakes and scorpions, and to overcome all the power of the enemy; nothing will harm you. However, do not rejoice that the spirits submit to you, but rejoice that your names are written in heaven (Luke 10:18–20).

You are given that same power and authority. That is why you do not need to fear the power of the enemy. You live in Him who has overcome evil. Jesus reminds the disciples that they are not to rejoice in the power, the authority or the victory, but in why they have them. Satan and the spiritual beings who followed him in rebellion against God were all thrown out of heaven. But the disciples of Jesus belong to His Kingdom; their names are written in heaven.

You belong to His Kingdom. Your name is written in heaven. That is a cause for rejoicing. And it means that you can exercise the power, authority and victory that you have in Jesus. But He wants you to remember why you can do so; *because by His grace, in His love and mercy, He has chosen you to belong to His heavenly Kingdom*. You never need to feel defeated and overcome. Remember where you belong and rejoice in the Lord. He will renew your confidence in the victory that is already His.

That victory has to be established in each situation. It is there, an accomplished fact of the cross, waiting for you to take hold of and apply to the circumstances of your life. If you do not do so, then it will appear that the opposition is allowed to prevail. Stand firm in the victory that is yours in Christ.

YOUR NAME IS WRITTEN IN HEAVEN.

NOTHING WILL HARM YOU, AS YOU BELIEVE THE VICTORY YOU HAVE IN JESUS.

YOU ARE TO USE THE POWER AND AUTHORITY THAT GOD GIVES YOU OVER THE DEFEATED ENEMY.

REIGN IN LIFE

> It is true that through the sin of one man death began to rule because of that one man. But how much greater is the result of what was done by the one man, Jesus Christ! All who receive God's abundant grace and are freely put right with him will rule in life through Christ (Rom. 5:17 G.N.B.).

That is true for you: because you have received the gift of righteousness, you will reign in life through Jesus. *God wants you to see yourself as one who reigns in Him who is on top of his circumstances – not being ruled and governed by them*. Our God is the one who gives faith to see mountains moved – not falling on us to crush us!

Stand firm in Victory

You cannot reign in your own right; only as "the result of what was done by the one man, Jesus Christ!" It is in His reign that you live. He is never defeated. Don't bow down to the mountains, the seemingly immovable problems that loom large before you. You are to speak to those problems and command them to move. By His Spirit, Jesus wants to give you the faith and authority to do that. He wants to guide you in your prayer so that you see the fulfilment of His promise: "You may ask me for anything in my name and I will do it."

YOU HAVE RECEIVED GOD'S ABUNDANT GRACE AND ARE PUT RIGHT WITH HIM.

YOU WILL RULE IN LIFE THROUGH CHRIST.

VICTORY

> The sting of death is sin, and the power of sin is the law. But thanks be to God! He gives us the victory through our Lord Jesus Christ (1 Cor. 15:56–57).

Through Jesus, God has given you the victory over the power of sin. That power no longer needs to dominate your life. Sin itself exists, and the possibility will always be with you in this life. But so will the forgiveness of Jesus!

"The wages of sin is death" (Rom. 6:23). Through Jesus you have not only victory over sin, but even over death. That means you need not fear death, nor be uncertain of what will happen to you beyond death. *If you are living for the glory of God now, He will take you to His eternal glory then.*

> Listen, I tell you a mystery: we will not all sleep, but we will all be changed – in a flash, in the twinkling of an eye, at the last trumpet. For the trumpet will sound, the dead will be raised imperishable, and we will be changed (1 Cor. 15:51–52).

You will have a new resurrection body, not the flesh and blood of your earthly body. This is the great Christian hope, the promise that is held out to us in Jesus. And so Paul exhorts:

Therefore, my dear brothers, stand firm. Let nothing move you. Always give yourselves fully to the work of the Lord, because you know that your labour in the Lord is not in vain (1 Cor. 15:58).

Do not lose the rich inheritance that you have in Christ. That has been given you through His grace. Live in His victory now and look forward to the final victory that is to come.

GOD HAS GIVEN YOU THE VICTORY THROUGH JESUS.

YOU WILL BE CHANGED AND WILL BE LIKE HIM.

YOU ARE TO STAND FIRM IN YOUR INHERITANCE IN JESUS AND LET NOTHING MOVE YOU.

YOU ARE TO GIVE YOURSELF FULLY TO THE WORK OF THE LORD.

21

PROCLAIM THE VICTORY

OVERCOME THE WORLD

For everyone born of God has overcome the world. This is the victory that has overcome the world, even our faith. Who is it that overcomes the world? Only he who believes that Jesus is the Son of God (1 John 5:4–5).

You are born of God because you are a Christian who is born of the Spirit. You have overcome the world. It does not matter what happens to you in this world; you have the victory in Jesus and will ultimately see the full realisation of that victory in His glory.

It is by your faith in Jesus – He who has overcome the world – that it can truly be said that you have overcome the world. In your own strength such an assertion would be plainly ridiculous. However, this demonstrates the power

Proclaim the Victory

released through faith. "Who is it that overcomes the world?" John asks. "Only he who believes that Jesus is the Son of God." *You* believe that. So *you* overcome the world.

The power is not in your faith. Faith leads to the victory when it is centred upon God and His Son, Jesus. He is so great and so mighty that only a tiny mustard-seed of faith is enough to see mountains of need moved. Your faith is in Him who is victorious, and that gives you the victory.

Put your faith in fears and you will be paralysed with fear. Put your faith in doubts and you will be questioning and uncertain. Put your faith in yourself and you will fail time and time again. Put your faith in feelings and you will constantly be disappointed. But put your faith in Jesus and you will know His victory. *The one who puts his faith in the living Lord is the one who overcomes the world, who works that victory out in his daily life.*

You have to do that to experience His victory. Those who don't do it speak critically of a trite triumphalism. But the word of God is clear; "everyone born of God has overcome the world", and with it opposition, misunderstanding, selfishness and hatred. It is good to know you are on the winning side because you belong to Jesus.

BECAUSE YOU ARE BORN OF GOD, YOU HAVE OVERCOME THE WORLD.

BECAUSE YOU BELIEVE THAT JESUS IS THE SON OF GOD, YOU HAVE OVERCOME THE WORLD.

YOUR FAITH HAS GIVEN YOU THE VICTORY IN JESUS.

FAITH

Everything is possible for him who believes (Mark 9:23).

What is impossible without faith becomes possible with faith – so long as that faith is in God through Jesus.

Some believe in God and in His Son, Jesus, but they do not expect Him to intervene in their lives, to act in power and to answer their prayers. *The faith that God wants you to have is that expectant faith that not only acknowledges He is almighty, but also expects Him to act in almighty ways in the circumstances of your life*. That faith makes the impossible possible.

That is not to say that a believer can do anything and everything. God can do *for* him whatever is necessary. And God can enable him in supernatural ways to accomplish things that are His purpose, but beyond the natural powers of the Christian. So Paul says:

> I can do everything through him who gives me strength (Phil. 4:13).

God will allow you to fail when you try to achieve things in your own strength. He will enable you to do the impossible when you have faith in His strength. It is only *through Him* that you can do all things.

EVERYTHING IS POSSIBLE FOR YOU BECAUSE YOU BELIEVE IN JESUS.

YOU CAN DO EVERYTHING THROUGH HIM WHO GIVES YOU STRENGTH.

THE CHALLENGE TO FAITH

> I tell you the truth, anyone who has faith in me will do what I have been doing. He will do even greater things than these, because I am going to the Father (John 14:12).

Jesus uses the phrase "I tell you the truth" when He knows that what He is about to say will meet with doubt or unbelief. It is astonishing that He should promise that "anyone who has faith in me will do what I have been doing." He does not say that you need to have a great deal of faith; He does say that the faith needs to be in Him.

Faith in yourself is futile. Faith in your faith will prove fruitless. *Faith in Jesus will mean that you will do what He has been doing.* See this not only as a challenge to your faith, but also as a promise that God is giving you. He says even more about the believer: "he will do even greater things than these, because I am going to the Father."

It was when he returned to the Father that Jesus prayed for the Holy Spirit to be poured out on God's people. The

Proclaim the Victory

'greater things' began on the Day of Pentecost when the Spirit filled the 120 believers gathered together in Jerusalem. That had not happened during the earthly ministry of Jesus. The Acts of the Apostles is the record of how the ministry of Jesus continued through the early Christians. They were doing the same things as He had done. And they saw 'greater things' when 3,000 were converted and filled with the Spirit.

The works of power in Jesus's life cannot be separated from His fellowship with His Father and His submission to His authority. It is God's purpose to continue the ministry of Jesus in the world through you and all other believers. How far God can do that through you will depend upon your fellowship with Him and your obedience to Him. If that was true for Jesus, it is true for you, too.

YOU WILL DO THE WORKS OF JESUS IF YOUR FAITH IS IN HIM.
LIKE JESUS, YOU NEED TO BE IN CLOSE FELLOWSHIP WITH THE FATHER.
LIKE JESUS YOU NEED TO OBEY THE FATHER.

THE PRAYER OF FAITH

I tell you the truth, if anyone says to this mountain, "Go, throw yourself into the sea," and does not doubt in his heart but believes that what he says will happen, it will be done for him. Therefore I tell you, whatever you ask for in prayer, believe that you have received it, and it will be yours (Mark 11:23–24).

Jesus was a man of authority. He spoke to the need and commanded it to be met. He even controlled the winds and waves. He spoke to sickness and told it to depart; people were cleansed of sin by the words He spoke.

Jesus teaches His disciples to speak to the mountains of need that arise before them. He did not doubt the outcome when He spoke; He does not want you to doubt the outcome when *you* speak. *That authority will come from your own submission to God's authority in your life, and your willingness to follow obediently the leading of His Spirit*. He will inform and empower your speech and your prayer.

I tell you, whatever you ask for in prayer, believe that
you have received it, and it will be yours (v. 24).

Does that promise meet with faith or doubt in your
heart? Jesus means what He says. Of course, you can only
"believe that you have received it" if you pray with faith
given by God's Spirit. And He will not give you the witness
of faith for what is contrary to His purposes. If we do not
allow the Spirit to lead and guide our praying, then we shall
often pray in the wrong way and meet with a negative
response from the Lord.

YOU ARE TO SPEAK WITH FAITH TO THE MOUNTAINS OF
OPPOSITION AND NEED, AND COMMAND THEM TO DEPART.

YOU ARE TO PRAY WITH FAITH.

YOU ARE TO BELIEVE THAT YOU HAVE RECEIVED WHATEVER
YOU ASK FOR IN PRAYER.

ASK 'IN MY NAME'

And I will do whatever you ask in my name, so that the
Son may bring glory to the Father. You may ask me for
anything in my name, and I will do it (John 14:13–14).
I tell you the truth, my Father will give you whatever you
ask in my name . . . Ask and you will receive, and your
joy will be complete (John 16:23–4).

Jesus gives these prayer-promises to His disciples. *He
expects you to believe them and act upon them.* To ask "in
the name of Jesus" is to stand in His place before the throne
of God, knowing that your Father hears and answers you.
He has given you that privilege. You are to ask for what
Jesus would ask, with the expectant faith that He gives you.

It is not for your sake that God will answer you but for the
sake of Jesus "that the Son may bring glory to the Father".
As you receive, not only will He be glorified but also "your
joy will be complete." James warns: "You do not have
because you do not ask God. When you ask, you do not
receive because you ask with wrong motives, that you may
spend what you get on your pleasures" (James 4:2–3).

That shows the importance of praying from the right
motives: not out of selfishness, but "that the Son may bring

Proclaim the Victory

glory to the Father". Let the Father know that it is His interests that you have at heart; you delight to do His will and see His purposes fulfilled.

JESUS WILL DO WHATEVER YOU ASK IN HIS NAME.

HIS FATHER WILL GIVE YOU WHATEVER YOU ASK IN THE NAME OF JESUS.

NO ANXIETY

Do not be anxious about anything, but in everything, by prayer and petition, with thanksgiving, present your requests to God. And the peace of God, which transcends all understanding, will guard your hearts and your minds in Christ Jesus (Phil. 4:6–7).

Anxiety is present when faith is not operating. Jesus said: "I tell you, do not worry about your life" (Matt. 6:25). "Do not worry about tomorrow" (Matt. 6:34). If your trust is in Him you need not be anxious about anything. When you look at difficult situations, your initial reaction may be anxiety and doubt. In which case you need to ask the Lord for His forgiveness and then look at the situation through the eyes of Jesus. "In everything, by prayer and petition, with thanksgiving, present your requests to God." *If you are praying with faith, you will be praying with thanksgiving because you "believe that you have received it"*. That assurance of God's faithful answer is shown by the peace of God that "transcends all understanding". In the midst of circumstances when you would naturally be anxious and fearful, you experience the peace of God instead.

Jesus gives a good demonstration of this. When His friend, Lazarus, was critically ill, He did not hurry to Bethany. When He stood before the tomb where Lazarus's body had been for four days, He prayed: "Father, I thank you that you have heard me. I knew that you always hear me" (John 11:41–42). That is a fine demonstration of praying with faith, with thanksgiving. At that moment nothing had happened. Jesus only had the assurance that Lazarus was about to be raised.

YOU ARE NOT TO BE ANXIOUS ABOUT ANYTHING.

YOU ARE TO PRAY WITH THANKSGIVING.

THE PEACE OF GOD WILL GUARD YOUR HEART AND MIND IN CHRIST JESUS.

SIGNS

And these signs will accompany those who believe: in my name they will drive out demons; they will speak in new tongues; they will pick up snakes with their hands; and when they drink deadly poison, it will not hurt them at all; they will place their hands on sick people and they will get well (Mark 16:17–18).

The most reliable manuscripts do not contain the closing words of Mark's Gospel. However, we must be careful not to discredit the truths they contain. They demonstrate that the early believers expected to see miraculous signs of God's protection and power in their lives. They summarise other verses of direction and promise that Jesus gives to His followers. The signs will "accompany those who believe": again the emphasis on faith. They will be accomplished only in the name of Jesus.

SIGNS WILL ACCOMPANY YOUR FAITH.
IN THE NAME OF JESUS, GOD WILL WORK IN MIGHTY WAYS THROUGH YOU.

BOLDNESS

In him and through faith in him we may approach God with freedom and confidence (Eph. 3:12).

You no longer have to cringe before God, wondering whether He loves you and has accepted you. *You can be confident before Him because He has given you the freedom and privilege to approach Him in the name of the One who has always been acceptable to Him.* You do not come in your own name, but in His. You do not plead any righteousness of your own, but His. When God looks upon you He sees you in His Son. And when He hears your prayer, it comes to Him through Jesus in whom you live.

YOU MAY APPROACH GOD WITH FREEDOM AND CONFIDENCE BECAUSE YOU ARE IN HIM AND HAVE FAITH IN HIM.

GIVEN ALL THINGS WITH CHRIST

> He who did not spare his own Son, but gave him up for us all – how will he not also, along with him, graciously give us all things? (Rom. 8:32).

Because you live in Jesus, God wants to give you 'all things' that you need to live your life for Him, in loving obedience to Him. Paul makes this statement in the midst of reminding his readers that all things are working together for their good; that they have been predestined to be conformed to the likeness of Jesus; that they are more than conquerors, and nothing shall separate them from the love of God in Christ Jesus.

To live in Jesus means that you will know the fellowship of His sufferings; *but in every need your Father is wanting to meet with you and provide for you.* "Be faithful, even to the point of death, and I will give you the crown of life" (Rev. 2:10).

Know that God's purpose is graciously to give you all things. He never wants to withhold from you. He is a gracious giver. He has demonstrated that by not sparing His own Son, but by giving Him up for you and for all men. If He dealt with you as you deserve, He would give you nothing. Instead, He acts graciously towards you.

GOD GAVE HIS SON FOR YOU.

HE WILL GRACIOUSLY GIVE YOU ALL THINGS WITH HIM.

EVERY NEED MET

> And my God will meet all your needs according to his glorious riches in Christ Jesus (Phil. 4:19).

Every human need is met in Jesus, through His glorious riches. He is the Lord, the King, your Provider, your Healer, your Strength, your Saviour. He saves not only from sin and death, but also from sickness and need. How can you receive the answer to your needs from Jesus; how can you appropriate this glorious promise that all your needs will be met?

First, by realising afresh that the promises need to be believed. It is the prayer of faith that will release God's gracious gifts into your life.

Second, by understanding the context in which Paul gives this great promise. He has been congratulating the Philippians on their faithful giving to others. Jesus teaches us:

> Give, and it will be given to you. A good measure, pressed down, shaken together and running over, will be poured into your lap. For with the measure you use, it will be measured to you (Luke 6:38).

By expressing your love for God in faithful, generous giving to Him and others, you are able to receive those glorious riches which God gives in Jesus. Often needs are not apparently met in the way expected, not because He is slow to give, but because we are reticent in giving.

God has set you the example in this. He gave you His most treasured possession, His Son, so that you might belong to Him. All His glorious riches are in Christ Jesus – and so are you! Understand, then, that *God loves to provide for you because He is your Father who loves you perfectly.*

GOD WILL MEET ALL YOUR NEEDS ACCORDING TO HIS GLORIOUS RICHES IN CHRIST JESUS.

HE WANTS YOU TO BELIEVE HIS PROMISES.

HE WANTS YOU TO BE FAITHFUL IN YOUR GIVING TO HIM AND TO OTHERS.

JESUS – THE FULFILMENT OF ALL GOD'S PROMISES

> For no matter how many promises God has made, they are 'Yes' in Christ. And so through him the 'Amen' is spoken by us to the glory of God (2 Cor. 1:20).

God has chosen to work in the lives of His children through promise. In His word He makes many promises, in both the Old and New Testaments. Jesus is the 'Yes', the fulfilment of all these promises. In Christ you can see God's promises to you fulfilled.

Through your life in Him you can say 'Amen' to those promises. That means that you can expect to see the promises realised because you believe them. At the same time, you need to be sure that you fulfil any condition that is attached to the promise, and you need to know that the Spirit of God is speaking that particular promise to you at that particular time.

Be encouraged by the fact that you have already experienced the fulfilment of many great promises: you have received new life, the gift of the Holy Spirit, forgiveness. All those are received through faith in the promise of the Lord. Know that He is faithful to His word and wants you to go on believing His promises and seeing their fulfilment in your life.

YOU CAN SAY 'AMEN' TO THE PROMISES OF GOD.

YOU WILL SEE HIS PROMISES FULFILLED 'TO THE GLORY OF GOD'.

AGREEING TOGETHER

Again, I tell you that if two if you on earth agree about anything you ask for, it will be done for you by my Father in heaven (Matt. 18:19).

In praying and believing God's promises, the agreement of two people produces startling results: "it will be done for you by my Father in heaven." *When you put the words of Jesus to work you will discover their truth.* It is possible for you to determine what you will believe God to do or to provide without necessarily heeding the voice of the Holy Spirit. When two people are praying in the Spirit, seeking God's purpose, He will give them a common witness of what He will do, of what they are to ask and how they are to believe. That witness is a safeguard against someone trying to persuade God to do what he wants. Where the two are in harmony in their praying and believing in the Spirit, they shall see their heavenly Father answering them with His provision.

You need to take careful note of the importance of the Holy Spirit in this aspect of prayer – as, indeed, in all aspects of prayer.

LEARN TO AGREE WITH OTHERS IN PRAYER.

THE HOLY SPIRIT WILL LEAD YOUR AGREEING.

YOUR HEAVENLY FATHER WILL ANSWER YOU.

22

YOUR INHERITANCE

Praise be to the God and Father of our Lord Jesus Christ! In his great mercy he has given us new birth into a living hope through the resurrection of Jesus Christ from the dead, and into an inheritance that can never perish, spoil or fade – kept in heaven for you, who through faith are shielded by God's power until the coming of the salvation that is ready to be revealed in the last time (1 Pet. 1:3–5).

God has dealt with you in His mercy. He could have left you under judgment of death, which is what you deserved. But He had mercy on you, brought you to faith in Jesus and gave you the gift of eternal life. Your new birth has given you a living hope.

Faith is believing that you have what you cannot see. Hope is trusting that you will have what God promises. Faith is present. Hope is future.

By faith you appropriate the glorious riches that are made available to you in Jesus. Through hope you await the joys that are yet to come.

The living hope you have is that, because of the resurrection of Jesus, you will also be raised to "an inheritance that can never perish, spoil or fade". That inheritance is "kept in heaven for you" because you belong to Jesus. Through faith in Him, you are shielded, protected, kept by the power of God until He brings you to the fulfilment of the whole process of salvation. God will keep you until you reign with Him for ever.

YOU HAVE BEEN GIVEN A NEW BIRTH INTO A LIVING HOPE.

YOU HAVE BEEN GIVEN AN INHERITANCE THAT CAN NEVER PERISH, SPOIL OR FADE.

YOUR INHERITANCE IS KEPT FOR YOU IN HEAVEN.

Your Inheritance 169

THROUGH FAITH YOU ARE SHIELDED BY GOD'S POWER "UN-
TIL THE COMING OF THE SALVATION THAT IS READY TO BE
REVEALED IN THE LAST TIME".

FAITH TESTED

In this you greatly rejoice, though now for a little while you may have had to suffer grief in all kinds of trials. These have come so that your faith – of greater worth than gold, which perishes even though refined by fire – may be proved genuine and may result in praise, glory and honour when Jesus Christ is revealed (1 Pet. 1:6–7).

Faith delights the Lord. He loves to see His children believing Him, trusting Him and depending upon Him. Faith is tested and strengthened by the various difficulties that God allows you to encounter in this world. Instead of resenting these and feeling bitter about them, He wants you to look to Him with faith that He will carry you through. More important still, nothing is to cause you to doubt His love, His mercy and goodness that He shows you. *Faith that is genuine believes God regardless of the circumstances.* You do not have faith in Him, or love Him, because of what you can get out of Him, but because of who He is and the love He has shown you in Jesus. That love can never be disputed. He has declared it fully in the cross.

There may be situations that you cannot understand. Each one is a test of how genuine your faith is. Peter says that it is more precious than gold. Gold is refined by fire; it will often seem that you have to pass through the refining fires. Gold perishes; you shall not, because you have been born again "into a living hope". And through all the testing and refining God will keep you until you receive the reward of faith. "We rejoice in the hope of the glory of God" (Rom. 5:2).

And after you have suffered a little while, the God of all grace – who imparts all blessing and favour – who has called you to His (own) eternal glory in Christ Jesus, will Himself complete and make you what you ought to be, establish and ground you securely, and strengthen and settle you. To him be the dominion – power, authority, rule – for ever and ever. Amen – so be it (1 Pet. 5:10–11 Amplified).

You can echo the joy and gratitude that Peter expresses: "Praise be to the God and Father of our Lord Jesus Christ!"

YOU MAY HAVE TO SUFFER GRIEF IN ALL KINDS OF TRIALS.

YOUR FAITH IS REFINED BY FIRE.

YOUR FAITH WHEN PROVED GENUINE WILL RESULT "IN PRAISE, GLORY AND HONOUR WHEN JESUS CHRIST IS REVEALED".

THE GOD OF ALL GRACE HAS CALLED YOU TO ETERNAL GLORY IN CHRIST JESUS.

HE WILL COMPLETE AND MAKE YOU WHAT YOU OUGHT TO BE.

HE WILL "ESTABLISH AND GROUND YOU SECURELY, AND STRENGTHEN AND SETTLE YOU".

'WITH HIM'

Here is a trustworthy saying:
If we died with him,
    we will also live with him;
if we endure,
    we will also reign with him.
if we disown him
    he will also disown us;
if we are faithless,
    he will remain faithful,
    for he cannot disown himself (2 Tim. 2:11–13).

You have died with Christ; He took you to the cross. You live with Him now, and if you endure and remain faithful to Him, you will also reign with him. He will always remain faithful, for that is His nature, and even God cannot deny what He is. Even if you are unfaithful you cannot make Him unfaithful.

But there is this warning: if you disown Him, He will also disown you!

As you remain faithful to the Lord, so you will see Him fulfilling all that He promises you. You will receive the fulfilment of the 'living hope' that you will reign with Him for all eternity. *The Lord will never withdraw from you*, but

Your Inheritance

there is the awful possibility of you withdrawing from Him, deserting Him for your own way. That will always be a possibility in this life, because God will not interfere with your free will. It was a possibility even for Jesus: He could have been disobedient – but never was!

And the great promise of God is: "He who overcomes will . . . be dressed in white. I will never erase his name from the book of life, but will acknowledge his name before my Father and his angels" (Rom. 3:5).

IF YOU ENDURE, YOU WILL REIGN WITH JESUS.

IF YOU DISOWN HIM, HE WILL DISOWN YOU.

RESURRECTION

> For my Father's will is that everyone who looks to the Son and believes in him shall have eternal life, and I will raise him up at the last day (John 6:40).

God's purpose for you is that you should enjoy new life in Jesus now, and that He will raise you up 'at the last day'. Over and over again the scriptures promise us that Jesus will come again in triumph and will take to Himself all those who are His own.

> For the Lord himself will come down from heaven, with a loud command, with the voice of the archangel and with the trumpet call of God, and the dead in Christ will rise first. After that, we who are still alive and are left will be caught up with them in the clouds to meet the Lord in the air. And so we will be with the Lord for ever (1 Thess. 4:16–17).

When Jesus returns on that great Day of the Lord that the Bible repeatedly promises, "the dead in Christ will rise first". All that God has promised will be fulfilled. Then those who are still alive 'in Christ' will be gathered together with them. All those who have been perfected and made righteous through His sacrifice will be with Him for ever. That is the final outcome, that is the fulfilment of the promise that Jesus gives concerning those who remain faithful to Him. *Jesus will acknowledge all who are His and they shall know His glory eternally.*

GOD WILL RAISE YOU UP AT THE LAST DAY.
YOU WILL BE WITH THE LORD FOR EVER.

THE FRUIT OF BELONGING

For as in Adam all die, so in Christ all will be made alive. But each in his own turn: Christ, the firstfruits; then when he comes, those who belong to him (1 Cor. 15:22–23).

You inherited the sin of Adam and were worthy only of death. But Jesus is the second Adam and, through His obedience, He has redressed the disobedience of man. As God has raised Jesus from the dead in a new resurrection body which is incorruptible and cannot be destroyed, *so He will raise you also, together with all who belong to Christ Jesus*. God sees you as one whom He is leading to the fulfilment of that purpose. He who has begun that good work in you will bring it to completion.

YOU WILL HAVE A NEW RESURRECTION BODY.

WE SHALL BE LIKE HIM

Dear friends, now we are children of God, and what we will be has not yet been made known. But we know that when he appears, we shall be like him, for we shall see him as he is (1 John 3:2).

You cannot know what it will be like to be raised with Jesus and to have a new resurrection body. That body will not be like the present one. Jesus was not immediately identified by His disciples when He appeared to them in His risen body.

Speculating is a useless activity. Rather, rejoice in the truth that you shall be like Him. A Christian need have no other aspiration than to be like Jesus. And when He returns that desire will be fulfilled. *For when you see Him as He is, you will be like Him*. Hallelujah!

YOU SHALL SEE JESUS AS HE IS.
YOU SHALL BE LIKE HIM.

FUTURE GLORY

> When Christ, who is your life, appears, then you also will appear with him in glory (Col. 3:4).

In this life you will only receive snatches of insight as to the nature of His glory. Your great hope is that "you also will appear with him in glory". The brief glimpses one receives now are enough to convey the fact that the glory of God is beyond description. He will not give you glory of your own; He will allow you to enter fully into His glory.

Note the first part of this verse: "Christ, who is your life". Jesus is not a hobby or a part-time occupation for busy people. *He is your life*. Without Him you would be unacceptable to God, now and eternally, and your life would be without meaning or purpose. Your life is now to be lived 'in Christ Jesus' that He, who is your life, may lead you to the fulfilment of all of God's desires for you.

CHRIST IS YOUR LIFE.
YOU WILL APPEAR WITH HIM IN GLORY.

HE WILL COME AGAIN

> Christ was sacrificed once to take away the sins of many people; and he will appear a second time, not to bear sin, but to bring salvation to those who are waiting for him (Heb. 9:28).

Through all that Jesus accomplished when He came, you have entered the salvation of God. When He comes again, He will bring that process of salvation to completion. In the early Christian Church there was an obvious longing for the Lord's return. We are told to watch and pray for that great time. We are to be those who are waiting for him, prepared and ready like the wise virgins of whom Jesus spoke in the parable, which ends with the words: "Therefore keep watch, because you do not know the day or the hour" (Matt. 25:13).

When Jesus returns, He will not need to bear sin; He has already done that. *He will gather those who are His into His final victory and triumph.*

174   *In Christ Jesus*

YOU ARE TO WAIT FOR THE LORD'S RETURN.
YOU ARE TO BE READY BECAUSE YOU DO NOT KNOW WHEN HE
WILL COME.

YOUR KINGDOM COME

There is the sense in the New Testament of the Kingdom of God having already come because Jesus, the King, has already come. By faith in Him, you have entered into the life of His Kingdom.

However, there is also the sense in which the Kingdom is still to come. It will only be fully manifested when the King returns in triumph and glory at the end of the age. What does Jesus teach us about this?

> This is how it will be at the end of the age. The angels will come and separate the wicked from the righteous and throw them into the fiery furnace, where there will be weeping and gnashing of teeth (Matt. 13:49–50).
>
> Then the righteous will shine like the sun in the kingdom of their Father (Matt. 13:43).
>
> When the Son of Man comes in his glory, and all the angels with him, he will sit on his throne in heavenly glory. All the nations will be gathered before him, and he will separate the people one from another as a shepherd separates the sheep from the goats. He will put the sheep on his right and the goats on his left. Then the King will say to those on his right, "Come, you who are blessed by my Father; take your inheritance, the kingdom prepared for you since the creation of the world. For I was hungry and you gave me something to eat, I was thirsty and you gave me something to drink, I was a stranger and you invited me in, I needed clothes and you clothed me, I was sick and you looked after me, I was in prison and you came to visit me" (Matt. 25:31–36).

Jesus makes it clear that there will be a clear division between the wicked and the righteous, between the self-righteous and those who are made righteous by His blood. The wicked and self-righteous "will go away to eternal punishment, but the righteous to eternal life" (Matt. 25:46).

Nobody likes the idea of judgment, but it is an integral part of Jesus's teaching: it is a reality that faces those who do not belong to Jesus and who refuse to believe in Him.

> Whoever believes in him is not condemned, but whoever does not believe stands condemned already because he has not believed in the name of God's one and only Son (John 3:18).

Contrast this with what Jesus says about those who do believe in Him:

> I tell you the truth, whoever hears my word and believes him who sent me has eternal life and will not be condemned; he has crossed over from death to life (John 5:24). For my Father's will is that everyone who looks to the Son and believes in him shall have eternal life, and I will raise him up at the last day (John 6:40).
> I tell you the truth, he who believes has eternal life (John 6:47).
> I am the living bread that came down from heaven. If a man eats of this bread, he will live for ever (John 6:51).
> Whoever eats my flesh and drinks my blood has eternal life, and I will raise him up at the last day (John 6:54).
> He who feeds on this bread will live for ever (John 6:58).
> My sheep listen to my voice; I know them and they follow me. I give them eternal life, and they shall never perish, no one can snatch them out of my hand (John 10:27–28).
> I am the resurrection and the life. He who believes in me will live, even though he dies; and whoever lives and believes in me will never die. Do you believe this? (John 11:25–26).
> Did I not tell you that if you believed, you would see the glory of God? (John 11:40).

Such is the fruit of faith. Those who refuse to believe need to heed the warning that Jesus gives:

> There is a judge for the one who rejects me and does not accept my words; that very word which I spoke will condemn him at the last day (John 12:48).

That shows how important it is to believe the words of Jesus. Remember that He expects to see the fruit of righteousness in your life. Your faith in Jesus means that you will not be condemned. *But still you will have to give account of your new life and of the fruit that God expects to see produced in you by His grace and power*. That is clearly what Jesus is saying in those important verses from Matthew, chapter 25. To believe in Jesus is not an academic exercise, but faith that affects deeply the person you are and the things you do.

YOU WILL SHINE LIKE THE SUN IN THE KINGDOM OF YOUR FATHER.

THE REWARD JESUS WANTS FOR YOU IS TO "TAKE YOUR INHERITANCE, THE KINGDOM PREPARED FOR YOU SINCE THE CREATION OF THE WORLD".

HE WANTS TO SEE THE FRUIT OF RIGHTEOUSNESS IN YOUR LIFE.

YOU WILL NOT BE CONDEMNED.

YOU HAVE ETERNAL LIFE: YOU WILL LIVE FOR EVER.

YOU WILL BE RAISED ON THE LAST DAY.

NO ONE CAN SNATCH YOU FROM THE HAND OF JESUS.

YOU WILL SEE THE GLORY OF GOD.

23

AND SO . . .

ABIDING

Whoever eats my flesh and drinks my blood remains in me, and I in him (John 6:56).

Plainly, you need to abide, to remain, to live continually in Jesus, and so receive the heavenly reward that awaits you.

Jesus describes Himself as 'the bread of life'. Whether

you interpret 'eats my flesh' in a sacramental way or as feeding on His word, He is clearly saying that you need to go on feeding on Him. Whether you interpret 'drinks my blood' as a reference to Holy Communion or to the work of the cross, or both, Jesus is saying that to remain in Him will involve a continual need to live in His forgiveness.

The man who feeds on Jesus and lives in His righteousness, will continue to live in Him. And Jesus will continue to live in that man.

> Just as the living Father sent Me, and I live by (through, because of) the Father, even so whoever continues to feed on Me – who takes Me for his food and is nourished by Me – shall (in his turn) live through and because of me (John 6:57 Amplified).

YOU ARE TO CONTINUE TO FEED ON JESUS.
YOU WILL REMAIN IN HIM, AND HE IN YOU.

A GREAT PROMISE

> And surely I will be with you always, to the very end of the age (Matt. 28:20).

As you continue to feed on Jesus in word and sacrament, you will know the gift of His presence being continually renewed in you and with you. When delivering the Great Commission to the Church, Jesus gives His followers the promise of His presence until he returns to claim them for His own at the end of the age, when He comes in triumph and glory.

Jesus will never desert you. *He will take you through the refining that you need; He will uphold you in every difficulty; He will inspire faith to enable you to live in His victory.*

JESUS WILL BE WITH YOU ALWAYS.

GOD'S PRESENCE

God has said:

> "Never will I leave you;
> never will I forsake you."

So we say with confidence:

"The Lord is my helper; I will
not be afraid.
What can man do to me?" (Heb. 13:5–6).

Because of the great truth that Jesus will never withdraw His presence from you, you can make the response of faith. You can say with confidence: "The Lord is my helper; I will not be afraid." *There is nothing that man can do that can take from you your eternal inheritance in Jesus as you remain loyal and faithful to Him.* He has pledged Himself to love you with an everlasting love, and He will never go back on His word. You can leave Him if you so decide, but He will never leave you; He will never forsake you because you are His child. He has paid the price for you that you might belong to Him. It is His intention to keep you for Himself as one of His holy, set-apart people.

THE LORD WILL NEVER LEAVE YOU.

HE WILL NEVER FORSAKE YOU.

THE LORD IS YOUR HELPER IN EVERY SITUATION.

YOU WILL NOT BE AFRAID AS YOU TRUST IN HIM.

POWER OVER THE ENEMY

The one who is in you is greater than the one who is in the world (1 John 4:4).

Not only do you live in Jesus; He also lives in you by the power of His Spirit. That power within you is greater than the power of the enemy who inspires rebellion and disobedience in the world. You do not belong to the world, nor are you any longer under the rule of the evil one or any of the spiritual forces that acknowledge him. You do not need to fear human opposition, either. It does not matter what agency the enemy uses to try to put pressure upon you, *God has already equipped you in every way necessary to overcome the opposition and difficulties*.

You know well by now that to trust to yourself will only produce failure. Believe this great truth of God's word: "the one who is in you is greater than the one who is in the world."

And So . . .

THE ONE WHO IS IN YOU IS GREATER THAN THE ONE WHO IS IN THE WORLD.

FORGIVE

> And when you stand praying, if you hold anything against anyone, forgive him, so that your Father in heaven may forgive you your sins (Mark 11:25).

To live in the overcoming power of God means to live at one with Him – but also at one with others. Abiding in Jesus, living in Him, involves being at peace with others. Jesus tells you to pray for your enemies and those who treat you spitefully.

Just as you need to avail yourself of the Lord's forgiveness every time you sin, *so you need to learn to forgive immediately those who wrong you*. Do not harbour grudges, bitterness or resentment. You will not be able to live in the confidence of faith if you do. Let your forgiveness of others be as ready as your desire for God's forgiveness in your life.

Here Jesus says that there is this need to forgive whenever you pray. It is that important. To live in Jesus is to live in His forgiveness – and to live in ready forgiveness of others.

YOU ARE ALWAYS TO FORGIVE OTHERS.

COME TO ME

> Come to me, all you who are weary and burdened, and I will give you rest. Take my yoke upon you and learn from me, for I am gentle and humble in heart, and you will find rest for your souls. For my yoke is easy and my burden is light (Matt. 11:28–30).

There will be those times when the whole business will seem far too difficult. God will seem remote, and it will appear impossible for you to forgive others. It is at these times especially that you will need to turn to the word-portrait of who you are 'in Christ Jesus'. He will restore you in faith as you begin to see yourself as He sees you.

Turn to Jesus. Pray in the Spirit. Accept His invitation afresh. Do not think yourself some kind of spiritual martyr who is struggling on against all the odds, carrying your own burdens and possibly those of others around you.

Your life is now yoked to Jesus. That means that He is to take the strain, and you are to cast your burdens upon Him. Learn from Jesus; *depend upon your heavenly Father as He did*. Do not stray into that place of spiritual pride where you say: "I will do it." You will find rest for your soul when you learn to trust and depend upon Him.

JESUS WILL GIVE YOU REST.
HE WILL GIVE YOUR SOUL HIS PEACE.
YOU ARE YOKED WITH HIM.

GOD'S WILL FOR US

> Be joyful always; pray continually; give thanks in all circumstances, for this is God's will for you in Christ Jesus (1 Thess. 5:16–18).

How does God want you to live out your life in Christ Jesus? Paul gives the simple, direct answer.

First: "*Be joyful always*". That is a vital part of Christian witness, and will be a reality if you are living in the truth of what God has done for you in Jesus. How can you help rejoicing in what He has made you and His continual grace that is shown to you? This joy does not originate in the emotions, in the soul; it is the joy of the Spirit that flows into the soul. *It is joy that cannot be taken away from the Christian no matter how difficult the circumstances in which he finds himself.* It is the joy that enabled the apostles to rejoice in prison and that enables Christians today to bear great hardship and persecution willingly for the sake of Christ.

It is the joy that leads to the Christian's heart expressing praise to God for all His love and goodness, again regardless of circumstances. It is the joy that makes God's people a praising people.

Second: "*Pray continually*." God's will is that you never fall back on your own resources, but learn to look to Him in every situation as well as in every need. He has promised to do whatever you ask in His name for His glory. *Your God is the Lord who cares, the Lord who hears, the Lord who answers*. Like Jesus in His humanity, you are never to lose sight of your dependence upon your heavenly Father and the fact that He has ordained that He shall work in response to the faithful prayers of His children.

Third: "*Give thanks in all circumstances*", because "we know that in all things God works for the good of those who love him, who have been called according to his purpose" (Rom. 8:28). *Never does He lose control of your life*. He is the Lord, the Sovereign God who will keep His promises to care and protect and love His children, His holy 'set-apart' people. Nothing "will be able to separate us from the love of God that is in Christ Jesus our Lord" (Rom. 8:39). Even in the midst of "trouble or hardship or persecution or famine or nakedness or danger or sword" you belong to Christ; you live in Him and He in you. Nothing can separate you from that immense love of His.

And so the writer exhorts his readers:

> Through Jesus, therefore, let us continually offer to God a sacrifice of praise – the fruit of lips that confess his name. And do not forget to do good and to share with others, for with such sacrifices God is pleased (Heb. 13:15–16).

That is what we want – for God to be pleased with us. We cannot please Him ourselves, only through Jesus. In Him we can please God by what we allow Him to do through us by the power of His Spirit. By that Spirit we can offer the sacrifice of praise that pleases Him. And as we remain faithful to the Lord, we know that He will be pleased with the end product when we are presented "holy in his sight, without blemish and free from accusation".

YOU ARE TO BE JOYFUL ALWAYS.
YOU ARE TO PRAY CONTINUALLY.
YOU ARE TO GIVE THANKS IN ALL CIRCUMSTANCES.
THAT IS GOD'S WILL FOR YOU IN CHRIST JESUS.

24

YOUR PORTRAIT IN JESUS

From all these truths, you can build a picture of who you are 'in Christ Jesus'. The truths we have discovered in previous chapters are collated here to give you a comprehensive description of your new life. This is how God sees you, what He asks of you, and what He promises you.

CALLED AND CHOSEN BY GOD
God has chosen you.
He has chosen you in love.
He has chosen you through His glorious grace, which he has freely given you.
You have been called by God, by His own glory and goodness.
You were created by Him and for Him.
He has chosen you in accordance with His pleasure and will.
Your name is written in heaven.
He has chosen you to be holy and blameless in His sight.
The God of all grace has called you to eternal glory in Christ Jesus.
You are one of His own people, whom He is purifying.

CRUCIFIED WITH CHRIST
Jesus has paid the price for your sins.
You have been redeemed by Him.
You have been reconciled to God by Christ's physical body.
You have peace with God through His blood, shed on the cross.
You have forgiveness of sins through His blood.
You have received His mercy.

Your Portrait in Jesus

You have been freed from sin.
You are no longer a slave to sin.
Your total healing, salvation or wholeness was accomplished on the cross.

YOU HAVE DIED
You died.
You have died with Christ.
You have been crucified with Christ.
Your old self was crucified with Him.
You have taken off the old self with its practices.
You have been crucified to the world, and the world to you.
You died with Christ, to the basic principles of this world.
You died to sin.
You are to put to death whatever belongs to your earthly nature.
You died to the law through the body of Christ.
You were buried with Jesus through baptism.

YOU HAVE NEW LIFE
You have been raised with Christ.
You have passed from death to life.
God has raised you up with Christ.
You are a new creation.
You are born of God.
Your old life has gone; the new life has come.
God has made you alive with Christ.
Christ is your life.
You have been raised with Christ through your faith in the power of God.
You have been given a new birth into a living hope.
You have been given an inheritance that can never perish, spoil or fade.
Your inheritance is left for you in heaven.
You are free to live a new life.
You have put on the new self.
Your new self is being renewed in knowledge.
You do not have to continue to sin.
You live in His wonderful light.
Christ lives in you.

YOU ARE SET FREE
Through Jesus Christ you are set free.
You have freedom 'in Christ Jesus'.
You are to live in freedom.
You are set free from the fear of death.

YOU ARE MADE RIGHT WITH GOD
By the gift of God's grace you are put right with God.
You are made righteous in God's sight.
You are made righteous, not by good works, but by faith in Christ.
You are put right with God by Jesus.

YOU ARE MADE HOLY
You have been made holy through the sacrifice of Jesus.
You are sanctified in Christ.
You are one of God's holy people.
You have been set apart for God.
You are a holy temple in the Lord.
He suffered to make you holy.
You have been made pure and righteous through Jesus.
You have been made perfect for ever.
You have been washed – purified from sin.
You are called to be holy.
You are to purify yourself, as He is pure.
Your soul is being made holy.
You have been sanctified, made holy, set apart for God and dedicated to Him.
You will be presented perfect in Christ.

WHAT JESUS DOES FOR YOU
God has brought you into union with Christ Jesus.
He has cancelled the written code which stood opposed to you.
You have received the circumcision done by Christ.
Jesus has entered heaven and appears before God for you.
He lives to intercede for you.
Jesus, the Righteous One, speaks to the Father in your defence.
You have direct access to God the Father through Jesus.

Your Portrait in Jesus

God gave his Son for you.
You are yoked with Jesus – not sin.
Jesus is able to help you resist temptation.
He cares for you.
The Lord is your helper in every situation.
Jesus meets your need.
Jesus is your wisdom.
He has disarmed the powers of darkness that oppose you.
You live in the victory of Jesus.

YOU ARE 'IN CHRIST JESUS'

You live in God.
You have been included in Christ.
You are in Jesus.
You are a branch of the True Vine.
You are to live in Jesus.
You live in Christ Jesus, who is always the same, constant in His love for you and always faithful to His word.
You belong to another, to Him who was raised from the dead, to be fruitful.
If you remain in Him, you will bear much fruit.
Apart from Jesus you can do nothing.
You have been given fulness of life in Christ.
You have been enriched in every way in Him.
God has blessed you in Christ with every spiritual blessing in the heavenly places.
You have all the resources of heaven available to you.
You have been clothed with Christ.
He wants to work in you what is pleasing to Him.
You are light in the Lord.
You are light for the world.
You are growing in the image of your Creator.
You are raised up with Christ and seated with Him in the heavenly realms in Christ Jesus.

YOU LIVE BY FAITH

God has given you faith.
Your work is to live by faith in Jesus.
Through faith in Jesus, God has given you eternal life.
Through faith in Jesus you will not perish eternally.

You have believed the word of truth.
You are to continue to live in Jesus by faith.
You can live your life by faith in Him.
He will inspire faith in you; you are guaranteed what is to come.
You participate in the divine nature as you believe His promises.
You are to approach the throne of grace with confidence.
You are to believe God's willingness to give His riches to you, despite your own unworthiness and weakness.
Everything is possible for you because you believe in Jesus.
You are not to be anxious about anything.
You are to cast all your anxiety on God.
You will not be afraid as you trust in Him.
You are to hold firmly to your faith.
You will do the works of Jesus if your faith is in Him.
Signs will accompany your faith.
Your faith is refined by fire.
Your faith, when proved genuine, will result in praise, glory and honour when Jesus Christ is revealed.
Through faith you are shielded by God's power until the coming of the salvation that is ready to be revealed in the last time.
You are receiving the goal of your faith, the salvation of your soul.
You believe in Him and are filled with an inexpressible and glorious joy.

GOD LIVES IN YOU BY HIS SPIRIT
You are a dwelling in which God lives by His Spirit.
Through Jesus the law of the Spirit of life has set you free from the law of sin and death.
He has set His seal of ownership on you.
He has put His Spirit in your heart.
God's anointing remains in you.
The Spirit of God lives in you that you may live in freedom.
You are to remain in the Spirit, living 'in Christ Jesus'.
His Spirit will teach you.
He has given His Spirit to speak to you and lead you in obedience.

Your Portrait in Jesus

You have the Spirit of love to enable you to love your brothers.
The Father and Son come to you and make their home with you.
Jesus is in you.
God lives in you.

YOU LIVE IN GOD'S GRACE
You have received God's abundant grace and are put right with Him.
You have been saved by His grace.
God has lavished the riches of His grace on you.
God gives you His grace to resist temptation.
God gives you His Grace to live a self-controlled, upright and godly life.
You have been given God's grace 'in Christ Jesus'.
You are to be strong in the grace that is in Christ Jesus.
He has dealt kindly with you to show the extent of His grace.
Through faith in Jesus, you now stand in God's grace.

YOU ARE TO BE FRUITFUL IN CHRIST
Your life is now hidden with Christ in God.
You have everything you need for life and godliness by His divine power.
God wants to equip you with everything good for doing His will.
You can do everything through Him who gives you strength.
Like Jesus, you need to be in close fellowship with the Father.
He wants to see the fruit of righteousness in your life.
You are created 'in Christ Jesus' to do good works, which God has prepared for you.
He wants you to be faithful in your giving to Him and to others.
You are to bear much fruit.
You are to be eager to do good.
You are serving the Lord Christ.
You are His workmanship.

YOU ARE IN HIS LOVE
You are loved by God.
God has shown His great love for you.
God is rich in mercy towards you.
You are to remain in the love of Jesus.
You can overflow with thankfulness for His faithful love for you.
May your love abound more and more; then you will know what is best, you will be kept pure and blameless until the day of Christ; you will be filled with the fruit of righteousness through Jesus.
There is no condemnation for you because you are in Christ Jesus.
Nothing can separate you from the love of God in Christ Jesus.

YOU ARE A SON OF GOD
The Father has lavished His love upon you by making you His child.
You are no longer a slave, but are a son of God.
You are a son of God through faith in Jesus.
You live as a son of God to glorify your heavenly Father.
You are an heir of His.

AS A SON YOU ARE TO LIVE IN OBEDIENCE TO GOD
Like Jesus you need to obey the Father.
Because you live in Jesus, you are to obey Him.
You are to obey the commands of Jesus and then you will remain in His love.
As you obey the Lord, your joy will be full.
God's love is made complete in you through obedience to His word.
You are not to keep on sinning, persisting wilfully in disobedience.
You are not to persist in those sins, because you are born of God.
You are to give yourself fully to the work of the Lord.
You are to set your heart on heaven.
You are to set your mind on things above.

You are to have nothing to do with the fruitless deeds of darkness.
You are to let your light shine before men.
Through you the fragrance of the knowledge of Him is to be spread.
Your food is to do the will of God.
You are always to forgive others.
You are to do what Jesus would do – in His name.
You are to walk as Jesus did because you live in Him.
You are to speak as Jesus would speak – in His name.
Whatever you do you are to do with your heart as working for the Lord.
You are to submit yourself to God.
You are to be joyful always.
You are to give thanks in all circumstances, for this is God's will for you.
You are to wait for the Lord's return.
You are to be ready, because you do not know when He will come.

THE IMPORTANCE OF GOD'S WORD FOR YOU
You are to express your love for God by obeying His word.
You are to continue in the teaching of Christ.
You are to keep to the pattern of sound teaching with faith and love in Christ Jesus.
You will be rooted and built up in Him, by word and Spirit.
You are to allow His words to live in you.

YOU ARE WEAK
You are weak in Him.
Yet by God's power you will live with Him to serve Him.
You may have to suffer grief in all kinds of trials.

YOU ARE TO LIVE IN VICTORY IN JESUS
You are to be strong in the Lord.
You are to be strong in His mighty power.
In this world you will have trouble. You live in Jesus who has overcome the world.
Because you are born of God, you have overcome the world.

The one who is in you is greater than the one who is in the world.
You escape the corruption of the world and have victory over evil desires as you continue to put your faith in Jesus.
Nothing will harm you, as you believe the victory you have in Jesus.
God has given you the victory in Jesus.
You are in Christ's triumphal procession.
You are more than a conqueror through Jesus who loves you.
You are to use the power and authority that God gives you over the defeated enemy.
Your faith has given you the victory in Jesus.
You are to resist the devil – and he will flee from you.
You are to put on the whole armour of God.
You are to stand firm against sin.
God makes you stand firm in Christ.
He has redeemed you from all wickedness.
You can say 'No' to ungodliness and worldly passions.
You will rule in life through Christ.

YOU ARE PART OF THE BODY OF CHRIST
You are a member of the one body of Christ.
You belong to all the other members – and they to you.
You are joined together with them.
You are God's people, fellow-citizens of His Kingdom.
You are God's household.
You are a chosen people, a royal priesthood, a holy nation, a people belonging to God.
You have a specific function within the body of Christ.

GOD WILL ANSWER YOUR PRAYERS
You are to pray with faith.
You are to pray in the Spirit on all occasions.
You are to pray continually.
You are to pray with thanksgiving.
You are to believe that you have received whatever you ask for in prayer.
You are to speak with faith to the mountains of opposition and need, and command them to depart.

Your Portrait in Jesus

You may approach God with freedom and confidence because you are in Him and have faith in Him.
You are to come near to God – and He will come near to you.
Jesus will do whatever you ask in His name.
His Father will give you whatever you ask in the name of Jesus.
Learn to agree with others in prayer.
The Holy Spirit will lead your agreeing.
Your heavenly Father will answer you.
You will know the presence of Jesus when you come together with those in Christ.
You are to bind on earth what is bound in heaven.
You are to release on earth what is released in heaven.

THE PROMISES GOD GIVES YOU

God has given you His very great and precious promises.
God will forgive your sins and purify you from all unrighteousness when you confess your sins to Him.
You will possess the qualities of God's life in increasing measure.
You will receive mercy and grace to help you in your time of need.
You will not be ineffective and unproductive, but fruitful.
God will answer your prayers to enable that fruitfulness.
He wants you to believe His promises.
You will be strengthened in faith as you live in Him.
God will meet your needs according to His glorious riches in Christ Jesus.
The peace of God will guard your heart and mind in Christ Jesus.
Jesus will give you rest; He will give your soul His peace.
He will complete and make you what you ought to be.
He will establish and ground you securely, and strengthen and settle you.
He will graciously give you all things with Christ.
You will be changed and will be like Him.
You will remain in Him, and He in you.
Jesus will be with you always.
The Lord will never leave you.

He will never forsake you.
In the name of Jesus, God will work in mighty ways through you.
You will see His promises fulfilled to the glory of God.
You can say 'amen' to the promises of God.

YOUR FUTURE HOPE IN JESUS
If you disown Him, He will disown you.
If you endure, you will reign with Jesus.
You will not be condemned.
You have eternal life; you will live for ever.
You will be raised on the last day.
No one can snatch you from the hand of Jesus.
You will see the glory of Jesus.
You will be presented holy in His sight, without blemish and free from accusation.
You will receive an inheritance from the Lord as a reward.
The reward Jesus wants for you is to take your inheritance, the Kingdom prepared for you since the creation of the world.
You will shine like the sun in the Kingdom of your Father.
You will appear with Him in glory.
You will have a new resurrection body.
You will be confident and unashamed before Jesus at His coming.
When He appears you will be like Him, for you will see Him as He is.

25

CONFESSING THE WORD

We can rejoice in these wonderful truths of what it means to be 'in Christ Jesus'. But how can we apply them to our lives? Jesus said:

Confessing the Word 193

> Make a tree good and its fruit will be good, or make a tree bad and its fruit will be bad, for a tree is recognised by its fruit (Matt. 12:33).

Through His death on the cross Jesus has made us 'good', acceptable to God. He has given us His Spirit that good fruit may be seen in our lives. No matter what kind of 'tree' you used to be, or what kind you *feel* yourself to be, God has remade you so that you can produce good fruit.

The fruit will be good if the tree is good – not only in appearance, but also in heart.

> For out of the overflow of the heart the mouth speaks. The good man brings things out of the good stored up in him, and the evil man brings evil things out of the evil stored up in him (Matt. 12:34–35).

What a man says is a reflection of what he thinks, and his thinking is conditioned by what he believes. The 'good man' will speak the truth about God, about himself and about others, because the truth is in his heart, and his mind is set upon that truth. What he says is an expression of what he believes and of the kind of person he is.

The conversation of the man who is in Christ needs to reflect the fact that he is living in the power of his new nature. It is possible for a Christian repeatedly to deny the truth about himself, because the words he speaks are a denial of what God says about him.

Jesus attached great importance to the things we say. Among His most telling words are these:

> But I tell you that men will have to give account on the day of judgment for every careless word they have spoken. For by your words you will be acquitted, and by your words you will be condemned (Matt. 12:36–37).

RENEWED SPEAKING

Our speaking often gets us into trouble because we give expression to our negative fears and doubts and unbelief. Some time ago, God showed our community that He was not glorified by the negative things we thought and said about ourselves and others. Our conversation and thinking needed to be re-ordered to become consistent with the word of God. We did not walk around quoting Bible texts all day long, but began to encourage each other to see ourselves as God sees us. We can hardly be living in unity and harmony with Him if we are continually contradicting what He is saying about us as His children. And we have a responsibility to our friends in Christ to be positive in our speaking:

> Do not let any unwholesome talk come out of your mouths, but only what is helpful for building others up according to their needs, that it may benefit those who listen (Eph. 4:29).

Paul says that "each of you must put off falsehood and speak truthfully to his neighbour, for we are all members of one body" (Eph. 4:25). That is not to say that we were deliberately lying to one another within the community. If there is falsehood of that kind in our lives, God would surely want to deal with us. It is not a question of speaking to deceive others, but the false things we all tend to say when we are deceived, when we listen to fears and negative thoughts, when we believe doubts and suspicion, and react without immediate faith to difficult situations that arise.

Gently and lovingly, often with considerable humour, we would correct each other when anybody spoke negatively or denied the truths of their life in Christ by what they said.

"Is that the way the Lord sees you?" "That's not what the word says about you." Or just a reminder: "You are in Christ Jesus."

The initial human reaction to being corrected is often one of frustration and anger; we learned to be thankful. I was speaking to a group about this a few months later, telling them how we were learning to correct each other gently and to build each other up in the word. After the meeting, David, who was travelling with me, said, "Do you realise that we hardly ever have to correct each other now?" That was right. We had become far more accurate and positive in our speaking. What is more, some members of the community who had always been very negative in their attitudes towards themselves were becoming far more positive and confident in the Lord. They were beginning to see what it meant to be 'in Christ Jesus'.

Since then we have discovered how easy it is to slip back into the old habits and, every so often, we have to take another look at our speaking.

FIVE-FOLD CONFESSION OF FAITH

I want to share this five-fold Confession of Faith with you. As you discover from the scriptures more of the truth about yourself as a new creature in Christ, you will need to know how to use that truth, how to speak it and apply it to your life.

We often use the words 'to confess' to refer to our need for forgiveness. But the word means "to speak out in agreement". We need to speak out in agreement with the word of God – to declare our faith in God, in what He has done for us in Jesus, and in what He has made us because we live in Him.

1. CONFESS THE WORD TO YOURSELF

If you do not speak the word of God to yourself, then you will not think it or believe it with much conviction.

When I was a child a popular saying was: "Speaking to yourself is the first sign of madness." We can refute that utterly. All of us speak quietly to ourselves in our thinking, and there is good scriptural precedent for the practice. King David often knew what it was to face seemingly insuperable difficulties and to suffer from bouts of despair. Yet he knew the secret of turning to God in praise in the middle of all pressures:

> Praise the Lord, O my soul;
>   all my inmost being, praise his holy name.
> Praise the Lord, O my soul,
>   and forget not all his benefits (Ps. 103:1–2).

David is speaking to himself, to his own soul. He is saying: "David, take your eyes off your problems and away from yourself and centre them on the Lord with praise for all he has done for you." He continues:

> He forgives all my sins
> and heals all my diseases;
> he redeems my life from the pit
> and crowns me with love and compassion.
> He satisfies my desires with good things,
> so that my youth is renewed like the eagle's (vv. 3–5).

David could not speak or think of himself as being in Christ, but he could speak thankfully of the great love that the Lord has shown him. He knew God to be faithful in keeping His word; He would continue to show His love and mercy to him. David gives himself five good reasons for looking at himself and his situation with a positive faith:

> He forgives all my sins.
> He heals all my diseases.
> He redeems my life from the pit.
> He crowns me with love and compassion.
> He satisfies my desires with good things.

Notice that his concentration is on what God does. There are many situations where my natural human reaction is to fear. When younger, I was a very fearful person in many respects. My life in recent years has followed a course in which God had led me to do one thing after another that, humanly, I would have found impossible and would never have wanted to do.

When that initial reaction of fear occurs I could do one of two things. I could concentrate on the fear, consider the fear, listen to the fear, and before long I would be thinking of a dozen reasons why I needn't do what I knew I should do. I would have allowed the fear to take hold of me and make me useless in that situation.

Or I could meet the fear head on with faith – confessing the word of God. A suitable scripture for this particular need would be: "Fear not, Colin, I am with you always." I find it helpful to insert my name because I know God is addressing His word personally to me. In the use of this saying I am acknowledging my fear; I am not pretending that it is not there. But I am immediately hearing God's answer to that fearful reaction. There is no need to fear, because He is with me. My concentration is now on Him and not on my feelings.

A good acrostic for fear is: False Expectations Appearing Real. Jesus is the truth and His words set us free from false expectations.

Other appropriate words to use to counteract fear are the words of Paul addressed to Timothy.

> For God did not give us a spirit of timidity, but a spirit of power, of love and of self discipline (2 Tim. 1:7).

At my ordination I had that verse of scripture written on a piece of paper and tucked into my breast pocket. I considered it most appropriate.

When confessing the word to myself, I would direct it personally in this way. "Colin, God did not give you a spirit of fear, but a spirit of power, of love and of self-control." Then I could get on with the job. What further excuses could one make in the face of such a truth?

As you step out in faith, you will discover that God is as good as His word. His presence is with you and He supplies all the resources of His Spirit that you need to do whatever He asks of you.

Cultivate the habit of confessing the word to yourself, choosing scriptures that are relevant to your need.

2. CONFESS THE WORD TO GOD

Learn to speak the word to God in prayer; pray according to the word. Our God is a God of promise; that is the way He has chosen to work. The scriptures are full of the promises He makes, especially through the Old Testament prophets and through Jesus. He is God's 'Yes' to all those promises:

> For no matter how many promises God has made, they are all 'Yes' in Christ. And so through him the 'Amen' is spoken by us to the glory of God (2 Cor. 1:20).

Promises are to be believed. God wants you to pray according to those promises, believing that He is faithful in giving you what you ask. However, it is not only in asking that you need to confess the word in prayer.

In praising God, we praise Him whose nature is revealed to us in scripture. It is good to mark in your Bible those verses that tell you something of His nature, and when speaking to God you can address Him in that way. For example, in 1 Thess. 5:23 He is described as the 'God of peace'. You can speak to Him as your Father, who is the 'God of peace'. In the following verse He is described as 'faithful'; you can speak to Him as the one who is always faithful. Each phrase is part of an enormous picture that is the Bible's revelation of the nature of God.

It is good, if you are in particular need of peace, to know that you are praying to the God of peace, and if you are needing to believe some particular promise, that you are in fellowship with Him who is faithful.

Never lose sight of the place of the Holy Spirit in your praying. "Pray in the Holy Spirit" (Jude v. 20). That involves listening. It is good to listen before you speak, to allow the Holy Spirit to bring a word of scripture to your heart. He will do that frequently if you give Him the opportunity to do so. It will be a word that is relevant to you personally or to the situation that concerns you. The Holy Spirit will inform your prayer, teaching you what to pray when you are utterly perplexed. He may bring a promise of God to your mind, in which case you can then "confess the word" with conviction, because you will know that you are responding to the word that God has spoken to you.

3. CONFESS THE WORD TO SATAN

Be absolutely clear about this: to confess the word to Satan does not mean that you have a conversation with him or any of his minions. He is a nasty piece of work, the thief who "comes only to steal and kill and destroy". He is not worthy of a conversation with a child of God. He is also the 'deceiver' and "the father of all lies"; he has been a liar from the beginning. So you cannot trust anything that he says, anyway.

To confess the word to Satan is to *dismiss him* with the word. This is how Jesus dealt with him when he was tempted in the wilderness. "It is written . . ." He replied to each of the temptations:

Confessing the Word 199

> Jesus answered, "It is written: 'Man does not live on bread alone, but on every word that comes from the mouth of God'" (Matt. 4:4).

The word of God is our answer to the enemy. He is a liar; the word is the truth that reveals how the enemy is conquered on the cross and how we have been delivered out of his power, out of his kingdom of darkness, and have been brought into the light of the truth of Jesus Christ.

> Jesus said to him: "Away from me, Satan! For it is written, 'Worship the Lord your God, and serve him only.'" Then the devil left him, and angels came and attended him (Matt. 4:10–11).

That will often need to be your reply when he tempts you, or tries to bring you under condemnation. "Resist the devil, and he will flee from you" (James 4:7). Never try to argue with him. Dismiss him. "Away from me, Satan!"

> Put on the full armour of God so that you can take your stand against the devil's schemes (Eph. 6:11).
> Stand firm then, with the belt of truth buckled around your waist, with the breastplate of righteousness in place, and with your feet fitted with the readiness that comes from the gospel of peace. In addition to all this, take up the shield of faith, with which you can extinguish all the flaming arrows of the evil one. Take the helmet of salvation and the sword of the Spirit, which is the word of God (Eph. 6:14–17).

Here is the armour that is your defence against the enemy, and your weapon with which you can always defeat him. Around your waist you have the belt of truth with which to counteract all his lies and deceiving tactics.

You have the breastplate of righteousness. You have been made acceptable to God through the blood of Jesus, and need not heed the enemy's slanderous accusations and attempts to make you feel unacceptable and condemned.

You have the gospel of peace. Through that gospel you have been brought to a place of peace with God that the enemy has no right to destroy, although he will try his best to do so. It is the good news of what Jesus has done for us that gives you the certainty of victory over Satan.

You have the shield of faith. Believing what Jesus has done, and what He has made you, will enable you to "extinguish *all* the flaming arrows of the evil one". Yes, *all* of them, everything that Satan will throw against you. You are not confessing the truth if, as a Christian, you say: "The devil has really got a hold on me."

You have the sword of the Spirit. The armour is defensive; it prevents you from being wounded. The sword of the Spirit is your weapon with which to inflict defeat on the enemy. And what is this sword? It is the word of God.

> "It is written..."

Never argue with him; dismiss him: "Away from me, Satan." He now stands condemned (John 16:11).

4. CONFESS THE WORD TO ONE ANOTHER

I have already spoken of how we set about this in our community. We are to encourage one another and to build one another up in love and in the truth. We are made part of the body of Christ so that we can walk in faith together. When one is downcast, or tentative in his faith, he can be encouraged by the others. That is how the Church should be operating in any locality: a body of people who are walking together in faith, in the power of the Spirit.

> Let us not become conceited, provoking and envying each other (Gal. 5:26).

It is easy to be destructive in what we say to others and in what we say about them behind their backs.

> Therefore each of you must put off falsehood and speak truthfully to his neighbour, for we are all members of one body (Eph. 4:25).

Remember that Jesus said that "out of the overflow of the heart the mouth speaks". If your heart is full of pride you will be exalting yourself and trying to knock others down. If you are full of envy and jealousy, you will gossip

Confessing the Word

and find any opportunity to criticise. If you are angry and unforgiving, then you will be full of resentment and bitterness.

In contrast to all this, you have the continual opportunity to speak the truth with love. That does not entitle you to say whatever you want to someone so long as you add the words: "Of course, I tell you all this in love – brother!"

The truth that we are to confess to one another is the truth of what God has done for us in Christ, and what we are as those who are born and filled with the Holy Spirit. It is in that context that Paul is speaking in Ephesians, chapter 4:

> Surely you heard of him and were taught in him in accordance with the truth that is in Jesus. You were taught, with regard to your former way of life, to put off the old self, which is being corrupted by its deceitful desires; to be made new in the attitude of your minds; and to put on the new self, created to be like God in true righteousness and holiness (Eph. 4:21–24).

"Therefore," Paul continues, "each of you must put off falsehood and speak truthfully to his neighbour."

Learn to build one another up in the truth of the new life that we have together with Jesus. There are times when we have to "weep with those who weep", to be good listeners, to identify with someone in great need. But always direct them to the truth of what God has done, of what he has made them as a new creation. Do not simply wallow in the mire with them or you will both sink together. Do not indulge in a 'pity session'. Lovingly, gently, sensitively, yet firmly, direct them to the truth. Confess the word to them.

5. CONFESS THE WORD TO THE WORLD

These five ways of confessing the word are not given in any order of importance. They are all important and necessary. It is no use being content with three or four of the five. Every Christian needs constantly, daily, to be doing all five.

Confessing the word to non-Christians we meet does not start, therefore, when we are adept at the other four ways. It begins at the very start of our Christian lives.

> "The word is near you; it is in your mouth and in your hearts," that is, the word of faith we are proclaiming: That if you confess with your mouth, 'Jesus is Lord,' and believe in your heart that God raised him from the dead, you will be saved. For it is with your heart that you believe and are justified, and it is with your mouth that you confess and are saved (Rom. 10:8–10).

It is important to encourage those who have just come to faith in Jesus to share immediately that new-found faith with others. Every new convert is an evangelist, as he or she speaks with the obvious joy of the new life he has found in Jesus.

Once we have received a few rebuffs from others, there is a great temptation to stop witnessing verbally to the truth. Never mind the rebuffs! God does not tell us to force people to respond, but He does call us to proclaim the truth boldly:

> How, then, can they call on the one they have not believed in? And how can they believe in the one of whom they have not heard? (Rom. 10:14).

Again, we need to follow the leading of the Holy Spirit in what to say and when to say it. He will enable us to bring the right word at the right time, with love and sensitivity. It is not a question of having some Christian sales-patter. God uses most effectively those who desire to share the truth with others *in love*. They do not regard non-believers simply as further opportunities to gain more converts; they are seen as people whom God loves, people with a need for God and a need to know His love for them.

When your neighbour comes into your kitchen pouring out her heart and relating her latest tale of woe or frustration, point her to Him, the Answer. When you see the man at work sinking under the pressure, don't watch him drown; reach out to him with the lifeline of Jesus. They may not accept the help that is offered, but at least they have heard that help is possible and that life is not impossible. They may not respond until they have come to the end of themselves and every other possibility. But the word that is sown does not always produce an immediate harvest.

"How?" That is the burning question for many. *How* can I know Jesus? *How* do I pray? *How* do I know He has forgiven me?

There is only one answer and that is the cross. Point the one who needs God to the cross. Don't try to explain all you have come to understand of what God did in Jesus. Most of that understanding has been given you since you became a Christian, after you have turned to the cross yourself. Let the Holy Spirit give you the words to show that Jesus took that person, with all his need, to the cross, not just to help with the problem, but to make him a new man.

SPEAK IN LOVE

Put this five-fold Confession of Faith into operation and you will soon notice considerable changes, not only in your speaking, but also in your thinking and believing. As you constantly speak the truth, you will find that you are believing the truth with greater conviction. You will react to situations in a different way, too. Even if your immediate human response is to fear or doubt, as you counteract that with the truth, you will walk in the power of God instead of your own weakness.

Don't be discouraged at your failures when you start being negative and critical. You have been conditioned by wrong thinking for as many years as you are old. It takes some time to begin to think as God thinks, to see things as He sees them, to see yourself as the new creation who lives 'in Christ Jesus'.

Whenever you fail, ask the Lord to forgive you – and receive His forgiveness immediately:

> The mouth of the righteous is a fountain of life (Prov. 10.11).
> The tongue of the righteous is choice silver (Prov. 10:20).
> The lips of the righteous nourish many (Prov. 10:21).

PART 3

HOW YOU ARE TO LIVE IN JESUS

26

APPLYING THE TRUTHS

God has placed us in Christ that we may live in Him. Jesus said to His disciples:

Remain in me, and I will remain in you (John 15:4).

The word translated 'remain' means to abide, rest, go on continually living in Christ. It has the definite sense of Jesus telling them to continue to live where God has put them: 'in Christ Jesus'.

God has placed us in Christ by His own gracious act. He commands us to go on living in that privileged position. The implication is obvious: it is possible to be put in Christ but not to live as if you are in Him.

God has also given to every believer the gift of the Holy Spirit. His purpose is that all Christians should "walk in the Spirit", following the leading of God and allowing Him to empower them with love. Then they will be able to be obedient to His will. He wants to see the fruitfulness of the Holy Spirit in their lives.

It is possible to be in Christ, but to live as if not in Him. It is possible to be in Christ and not walk in the Spirit. That was obviously true for some of the Christians at Corinth in Paul's time, and indeed in every Church to which he wrote. It is true for Christians today.

Although God has placed me in Christ, I am living in the flesh if I am depending upon myself, seeking my own purpose of pleasing myself, rather than being faithful and obedient to the Lord's will. Although I have been crucified with Christ, I can still live as if my old nature had not passed away: I am able to live as if I am not born again, or filled with the Holy Spirit, or living in Christ.

Before becoming a Christian I could not live in the power

of God's Spirit. Now, as a child of God, a citizen of the Kingdom of Heaven, one baptised in the Holy Spirit, I am able to live in His power.

That does not mean that I will. I am not under compulsion. God gives me, and every Christian, the alternatives of living in the flesh or in the Spirit.

To live in the Spirit is to recognise that I can only please God by allowing Him to live out His life in me, to express Himself through me. For that to happen I shall need to learn what it is to trust in the Lord Jesus Christ, to abide or remain in Him, looking to Him to produce His fruit in me.

In the flesh we do not want to please God, for the sinful nature is unconcerned about Him or His purposes. The enemy will use every opportunity to encourage us to trust in the flesh rather than the Spirit. He will want us to act in our own strength, for while we are doing that, we cannot be acting in the power of God's Spirit.

By contrast, God's purpose is that all our activity should be in Christ:

> And whatever you do, whether in word or deed, do it all in the name of the Lord Jesus, giving thanks to God the Father through him (Col. 3:17).

We are not to hop about like spiritual kangaroos, living according to the new nature one minute, before going back to the sinful nature the next. We have to recognise that these two natures are diametrically opposed. Any attempt, therefore, to try to reconcile the two will meet with inevitable spiritual defeat.

> The sinful nature desires what is contrary to the Spirit, and the Spirit what is contrary to the sinful nature. They are in conflict with each other, so that you do not do what you want (Gal. 5:17).

The two cannot be reconciled; they are in conflict. Paul does not say: "Fight the old nature", for that has already been put to death in Christ. But the desire to please ourselves, to be independent and to act in our own strength is still there, and leads Christians into sin. That is why many doubt the reality of their death in Christ.

Applying the Truths

> So I say, live by the Spirit, and you will not gratify the desires of the sinful nature (Gal. 5:16).

It is not for the Christian to fight against himself; it is only by concentrating on the resources of the Holy Spirit that He will be victorious. Paul is saying that we are to turn away from the old and put our concentration on the new life that we have in Jesus, looking to the resources of the Holy Spirit. Do not look back to the past, or in upon yourself. For if you do, you will certainly see weakness and failure.

By concentrating on the desires of the flesh, you can easily become bound by those desires. By concentrating on your own weakness or failure, you can easily be obsessed by the failure. We have all come across the Christian who can do nothing but talk about his problems, and his whole relationship with God seems to revolve around those needs. There seems to be little giving to God, only a ceaseless wanting to receive from Him. There are times when even that is lacking, for he seems to enjoy his problems or being the centre of attention when he is receiving ministry. It may be that he is afraid to let go of them; if he does, he fears that part of his identity will be lost.

Of course, the truth is that, when he turns away from the old to the new, he will discover his true identity, the new man that He is in Christ.

THE MIND

> Those who live according to the sinful nature have their minds set on what that nature desires; but those who live in accordance with the Spirit have their minds set on what the Spirit desires (Rom. 8:5).

It is of crucial importance to direct our minds towards the new and not the old. To set the mind on the flesh, with its desires, weakness, failure, is sinful. We must not shirk that fact. Often we try to justify this preoccupation with self, and others around us do not help if they encourage self-pity.

Somebody only has to say: "Oh, you poor dear", for

most people to accept willingly the sympathy that statement conveys, to assent to it mentally and think: "At last here is someone who understands me and all my problems."

God understands us far better. He knows our needs, and how we can live above them instead of allowing them to be on top of us.

> The mind of sinful man is death, but the mind controlled by the Spirit is life and peace, because the sinful mind is hostile to God. It does not submit to God's law, nor can it do so. Those controlled by the sinful nature cannot please God (Rom. 8:6–8).

Preoccupation with self is spiritual death. The man who does not know God is imprisoned in his thinking, but not the man of the Spirit. If he concentrates on what the Spirit would teach him, he will have life and peace. It seems senseless for the new-born, Spirit-filled man to reject His inheritance by thinking of himself as an old creature. Now he needs to think as one who belongs to God.

"Those controlled by the sinful nature cannot please God." But we have seen that the Christian is not controlled by the sinful nature; he has been set free from it. So what is the point of putting himself back into prison? That is what happens to some. They protest that they cannot help it, they cannot believe that they are set free from the past. They do not radiate the love, joy, and peace of Jesus, even though they claim a living faith in Him.

"Live by the Spirit," Paul says, and the consequence will be that "you will not gratify the desires of the sinful nature." Let us contrast some of the desires of these two natures.

Desires of the flesh	*Desires of the Spirit*
Look in upon yourself;	Look to the Lord;
Be independent;	Be dependent upon Him;
Help yourself;	Let God enable you;
Use only your natural resources to do things;	Use the resources of the Holy Spirit;
Do what you want;	Do what Jesus wants;
You matter most.	God matters most.

We have only to look at the list in the left-hand column to see that Christians know the continuing presence of those desires, even after their new birth. It seems that the mind is often drawn to them, like metal to a magnet. They long to be able to enjoy the Lord without all these desires when they reign with Him in glory. Until then, He wants to teach them to live fulfilling the desires of the Spirit, not the flesh.

Victory over this preoccupation with self is not a matter of using our own fighting instincts. Often there is not the will to fight, because we desire to gratify the flesh and not reckon it dead.

> Those who belong to Christ Jesus have crucified the sinful nature with its passions and desires (Gal. 5:24).

Paul again uses the past tense to refer to what believers have already done. These works of the flesh will persist until we recognise that the flesh itself is crucified with Christ. Then, day by day, we can put to death all those desires to please ourselves in ways that are contrary to the purpose of God.

If our trust is in Jesus and the power of His Spirit, we shall experience the triumph of the Spirit over flesh and the temptation to concentrate on self; He will keep us from falling. If we undertake the fight ourselves, we shall be in constant need of God's forgiveness for our failure to resist temptations, even those subtle ones like trusting in ourselves, being independent, being too busy for God, or too busy doing for Him what we consider right. In that way we are often led back to the flesh and out of the will of the Spirit.

CHRIST IN YOU

Self-love naturally rises in rebellion against living our lives in obedience to the Spirit, and to trusting in the living Jesus within us. Before Jesus is allowed to establish His Lordship in different areas of our lives, we shall frequently experience conflict, as our initial and natural response is to resist what He wants. That conflict is only resolved when we submit to Him and gladly accept His will for us.

Even in that, Jesus is expressing His love for us. He wants to take us through the difficulties of faith that we experience, the problems that arise, and the needs that confront us. Because we live in Him and He in us, nothing can separate us from His loving purpose:

> Who shall separate us from the love of Christ? Shall trouble or hardship or persecution or famine or nakedness or danger or sword? . . . No, in all these things we are more than conquerors through him who loved us (Rom. 8:35-37).

To be more than a conqueror means that you have the victory without having to fight the battle. The battle is the Lord's; He fought it on the cross, and the resurrection is evidence that He has emerged triumphant.

The Lord does not want us to indulge in trite triumphal talk; He desires to see us living in the power of His victory. Every time we receive forgiveness the victory of the cross over sins is proclaimed.

We also experience the triumph of the cross when we reckon our old nature dead, and when we turn away from the desires to please self.

We see the victory of Jesus over the enemy when we apply the work of the cross where evil is gripping people's lives.

Several people came forward to receive the Lord's healing power at a meeting in Australia. They were standing along the communion rail as I prayed with them one by one.

I came to a certain woman, who told me that she had curvature of the spine and that a hard lump had developed on her spine. As I prayed with her she fell to the ground under the power of God and lay still. The next woman was suffering from rheumatoid arthritis and began to pour out an endless list of other complaints. For years she had suffered from one illness after another. She certainly looked the picture of misery.

When ministering to the sick, one must always seek to be open to the leading of the Holy Spirit. I felt that I could not pray immediately for this woman's healing. As I waited on the Lord, I realised that the problem was one of evil, that

Applying the Truths

this woman needed to be set free from spiritual bondage. In such instances, a simple prayer for healing is ineffective; Jesus gives us authority over the powers of darkness and tells us to use that authority in His name.

I exercised that authority, addressed the spirit of infirmity that had afflicted her with one sickness after another, and commanded it to release her in Jesus's name. It was apparent from the woman's appearance that there was an immediate release. She was set free not only from pain but from the spiritual forces of wickedness that had oppressed her and made her so unhappy. Paul reminds us:

> Our struggle is not against flesh and blood, but against the rulers, against the authorities, against the powers of this dark world and against the spiritual forces of evil in the heavenly realms (Eph. 6:12).

Jesus has won the victory over those "spiritual forces of evil in the heavenly realms", and He gives us the authority to proclaim that victory wherever we come up against those evil forces. I did not set that woman free; all I did was to proclaim the victory of Jesus which gives us power over these evil spirits.

The story does not end there, for while I was exercising that authority, the woman with the back problem began to feel the lump being pushed into the ground. She spoke to me after the meeting and explained what had happened. I believed that the Lord was saying that the woman had been under occult influence. When I questioned her about this, she told me that, when she was fifteen years old, her mother had taken her to a spine diviner. Divining, and all forms of spiritualism, are strictly forbidden in the scriptures and are described as an "abomination to the Lord". Ever since this episode with the diviner, over twenty years previously, the woman had suffered increasingly with her spinal condition, and this hard lump had developed.

Once again, we exercised the authority that Jesus gives, and proclaimed His victory over all the occult powers of darkness that had affected the life of that woman. Her back was immediately released and the lump disappeared. Praise the Lord for His victory!

It is possible for us to pray and not see the effective answer that we need, unless we are proclaiming the victory of Jesus on the cross.

He took every human need and met it there on Calvary as He poured out His blood for us. When we ask God for His healing, or to meet any other need, we come to Him in His love, grace and mercy. But we come also in the power of what He has already accomplished for us in Jesus. It is because of this that Paul proclaims:

> But thanks be to God, who always leads us in triumphal procession in Christ (2 Cor. 2:14).

He *always* leads us in triumph, but only because we are 'in Christ Jesus', in whom there can be no despair and defeat. How out of place it is, therefore, for Christians to mope around with negative attitudes!

The enemy wants us to feel defeated, that he has the upper hand. Defeat easily leads to a sense of condemnation. In Christ there can be no condemnation.

> Therefore, there is now no condemnation for those who are in Christ Jesus (Rom. 8:1).

Again and again the apostle reminds us of our place 'in Christ Jesus' so that we may "live a life worthy of the calling" we have received. When we are not looking to the resources of the Spirit we depend upon ourselves, think our own thoughts, desire our own desires, scheme our own schemes – and want to kick ourselves for grieving Him!

Apart from Christ we are weak and useless. In Him the whole situation is different. "I can do everything through him who gives me strength" (Phil. 4:13). Paul does not say that he can do everything; he can only do everything through Him. We come back to Jesus every time, to our need for complete dependence upon Him.

PROBLEMS OF UNBELIEF

It is impossible for us to live up to our full potential unless we believe what Jesus says about us.

Sometimes I ask people at meetings if they have faith in

Applying the Truths

Jesus. Usually a forest of arms is raised. I then ask them to turn to John 14:12 and read what Jesus says:

> I tell you the truth, anyone who has faith in me will do what I have been doing. He will do even greater things than these, because I am going to the Father.

I then ask those who are doing the same things as Jesus to raise their hands. There may be two or three brave ones; sometimes nobody moves. I explain why I have done this: to expose unbelief! One moment we have faith in Jesus; the next we are admitting that we do not believe what He says about us.

Whenever Jesus was about to tell the disciples something that He knew they would find it hard to accept, He prefixed His words with this phrase "I tell you the truth", or "Truly, truly". He is saying to them: "You may find this hard to believe but it is definitely the truth . . ."

He wants them to understand that *anyone* who has faith will do what He has been doing. This involves living a life that reflects something of the life of Jesus, but if you look at the context of this saying, it is apparent that He is thinking of the works of power that will be done in His name and in response to prayer. Jesus continues:

> And I will do whatever you ask in my name, so that the Son may bring glory to the Father. You may ask me for anything in my name, and I will do it (vv. 13–14).

Jesus tried to convince the disciples in different ways of this simple but profound truth: "Whatever I can do, you can do in my name, on my behalf." That is why He told them not to be discouraged about His imminent crucifixion. Something even more wonderful was about to happen. The Holy Spirit who had been with them would soon be in them. God Himself would be in them, enabling even greater things than Jesus had done. These greater things would be possible, says Jesus, "because I am going to the Father". It was then that He would ask His Father to pour His Spirit into the hearts and lives of His children.

'Those greater things' began on the day of Pentecost.

First God filled 120 disciples with His Spirit – that had never happened in the earthly ministry of Jesus. Then 3,000 were converted and the Spirit came upon them. The like of that had not happened before, either. This was the beginning of the fulfilment of what Jesus had promised: "I tell you the truth, anyone who has faith in me will do what I have been doing. He will do even greater things than these because I am going to the Father."

Don't regard these words as a threat; see them as a glorious promise. Jesus is talking about you, for He speaks of "anyone who has faith".

We are living in the days of the greater things of God. We do not have to look back into the past and wish that we could have lived with Jesus in the days of His manhood, able to witness the miracles we read about in the scriptures. He tells us that He will do greater things in these days, if our faith is in Him.

Don't imagine that you would have found it easier to believe if you had been one of those original disciples. Even after all they had seen and witnessed, including the resurrection appearances of Jesus, we are told that 'some doubted' (Matt. 28:17). But don't allow that to be an excuse for *your* doubt. The coming of the Holy Spirit upon them changed that doubt to a militant faith, and those same disciples witnessed God moving in mighty ways as a result.

It is a great privilege to see Jesus doing greater things in these days. This year I have witnessed things that I would never have thought possible – the Holy Spirit coming upon thousands at the same instant; hundreds of people being healed within a few minutes as the power of God moved through a congregation; hundreds coming into the Kingdom of God as the Spirit convicts them of sins and draws them to repentance.

We are living in the mighty days of the Spirit, the era of the Spirit, when God is ready to do great things. And in the coming years I believe we shall see even greater things happening, as our faith to believe God to move in such ways increases. There is already ample literature available testifying to the mighty working of God's Spirit in countries around the world.

Applying the Truths

And yet there are still those who want to close their eyes to what God is doing, pretending that it is all peripheral to the main mission of the Church: to proclaim the gospel. The simple fact is that the gospel is making greatest advances where the works of His power accompany the proclamation of the word. And that is the scriptural way. Paul would not have dared to proclaim the gospel without expecting to see God's mighty hand at work in the 'signs following'.

> Our gospel came to you not simply with words, but also with power, with the Holy Spirit and with deep conviction (1 Thess. 1:5).

We do not see more of the power of God, because of our unbelief in His word, in what He says about us and what we can do in His name. We may try to explain away that unbelief, or excuse ourselves for it, but God will only give us the increase of faith that we need when we are prepared to recognise that unbelief for what it is, come to Him in repentance for it, and let Him cleanse us from it. As we then seek that freshness of faith through the Holy Spirit, God will quicken His word in our hearts so that we dare to believe it: "*anyone* who has faith in me . . ."

> My message and my preaching were not with wise and persuasive words, but with a demonstration of the Spirit's power, so that your faith might not rest on men's wisdom, but on God's power (1 Cor. 2:4–5).

FEAR

There is still much fear among Christians concerning demonstration of the Spirit's power. As a result, the gifts of the Spirit are often stifled or even forbidden (which is contrary to scripture); healing is avoided by many, and not taught by others; exorcism is regarded as an outdated mode of fanaticism by many church leaders. The ministry of Jesus and the apostles would have been unacceptable in many churches today, when people want a nice, quiet, conventional, rationally acceptable, church life – with nothing much happening. In making sure that nothing wrong or bad or 'not of the Spirit' occurs, many pastors and leaders have made sure that nothing much of the Spirit happens, either. Listen to Paul again:

> I will not venture to speak of anything except what Christ has accomplished through me in leading the Gentiles to obey God by what I have said and done – by the power of signs and miracles, through the power of the Spirit. So from Jerusalem all the way around to Illyricum, I have fully proclaimed the gospel of Christ (Rom. 15:18–19).

In leading the Gentiles to obey God, the apostle points to what he had done, as well as what he had said, to the signs and miracles that were performed by the power of the Holy Spirit. Paul could only claim to "have fully proclaimed the gospel of Christ" because of what he had said *and done*. Our proclamation of the truth is incomplete if we ask men to believe words without substantiating those same words with the life and power of which they speak.

This is a great challenge for all who have the privilege and responsibility of preaching. I live with that verse from John 14:12. It is a continual encouragement and spur to faith, to believe God for greater and greater things – that He may be glorified.

Recently, I received a very gracious and loving letter from a man who said that he had greatly appreciated the preaching at a mission I had been leading. But he went on to question why it was necessary to ask people to commit their lives to Jesus, to ask to be filled with the Holy Spirit and to receive His healing. Could I not have left the Spirit to do His own work? I mention this because I believe that this dear man was expressing a widespread reaction. We do not mind hearing the gospel proclaimed, but, whether we are Christians or not, we are all challenged by any demonstration of the Spirit's power, of what He is actually doing in the lives of people. There can be plenty of good sowing, but little reaping.

One of the finest evangelistic sermons that I have ever heard was preached by a rector to a church full of people, most of whom worshipped only occasionally. It was fertile

Applying the Truths

soil for the gospel. The sermon had great impact. But the preacher finished by saying: "I want you to go away and think about what I said." The following week that congregation was back to its normal size.

The sowing was excellent, but there was no reaping. The preacher had spoken of repentance, but had not led anyone to repentance. He had spoken about committing one's life to Jesus, but had not led anyone actually to make that commitment.

I do not say this in criticism, but to explain how we can lose many opportunities when we present the gospel without providing the opportunity for God to do in people what He desires to do.

In my travels I meet many pastors who complain that they faithfully preach the gospel week in and week out, but see little or no response. "Why?" they ask. There could be many answers to this question. It may be that the preaching lacks the necessary anointing of the Spirit. The truth of the gospel can be communicated with the mind to the minds of the listeners. People may appreciate what they hear at that level, but their lives will not be changed or transformed by such preaching. The Spirit needs to take the truths of the word and speak them to the hearts of the congregation. When people's hearts are stirred, they need to be shown how they can respond to the Lord and receive the new life about which they have heard.

The Spirit of God needs to speak to the spirits of men, for it is only by their spirits that they can know God.

And the preacher needs to be bold in his faith that God will confirm His word with signs following. Paul writes to the Galatians:

> Does God give you his Spirit and work miracles among you because you observe the law, or because you believe what you heard? (Gal. 3:5).

To believe the word, to respond in faith to the proclamation of the gospel, leads to the outpouring of the Holy Spirit and to God working miracles. If we do not see the evidence of the Holy Spirit's power present, we can only conclude that this is the result of unbelief, that the word is not received with faith.

The initial response of faith is not enough, for God desires to continue working among His people, teaching them that "anyone who has faith in me will do what I have been doing." Paul has already said to the Galatians:

> Did you receive the Spirit by observing the law, or by believing what you heard? Are you so foolish? After beginning with the Spirit are you now trying to attain your goal by human effort? (Gal. 3:2–3).

That is the real temptation; to substitute our own effort for the genuine work of the Spirit, to imagine that God will conform to our ways, instead of allowing ourselves to be open to His immense possibilities.

RECOGNISING GOD'S MIGHTY POWER WITHIN US

The law of sin and death still exists; God has not removed that. But there is a different law at work within the Christians – "the law of the Spirit of life". It is to that Spirit of life that he is to look and entrust himself, so that he will no longer allow the old law of sin and death to have any place in him.

We often underestimate the power of God's Spirit at work within us. Paul speaks of "the immeasurable greatness of his (God's) power in us who believe" (Eph. 1:19 R.S.V.).

> I pray also that the eyes of your heart may be enlightened in order that you may know the hope to which he has called you, the riches of his glorious inheritance in the saints, and his incomparably great power for us who believe. That power is like the working of his mighty strength, which he exerted in Christ when he raised him from the dead and seated him at his right hand in the heavenly realms (Eph. 1:18–20).

"The power in us who believe" is that same power that raised Jesus from the dead. We rightly think of the power

Applying the Truths

belonging to God; yet we so easily forget that He has come to live in us with that power, and has blessed us in Christ with every blessing that heaven has.

When we trust in Him, we experience the new law of His Spirit at work in us, giving no room for the law of sin to be exercised. We cannot live by both laws at the same time. When the mind is set on the sinful nature, we contemplate our own sinfulness, weakness and failure. The old law from which Jesus has delivered us comes into operation again, and once more we suffer defeat.

Depression is like a spiral in which a person becomes more and more negative. It can start with a situation to which the person responds in some negative way, with fear, failure, guilt. One negative follows another, until the person is in the position where he finds it impossible to be positive.

The spiral would not come into effect in the life of a Christian if at the first sign of trouble the positive truth of who and what he is 'in Christ' was affirmed. If that does not happen in the early stages, the darkness seems to thicken, so that, for some, it seems utterly impenetrable.

To have new life does not mean that a man will trust to that new life. It is not that someone in such a situation needs to cry out to God to give him more power; he needs to learn to live in the power that He has already given.

A man in the depths of depression may need ministry to set him free from the oppressive bondage he is experiencing. But he needs to know how to live in that freedom without falling back into depression. The truth will not only set him free; it will also keep him in freedom.

The most difficult people to help are those who are full of these negative feelings and reactions that arise from a low opinion of themselves. No amount of talking helps, for every positive approach is met by a negative response.

It seems that their minds are set like concrete on the flesh, on themselves, on their weakness and failure. It doesn't matter what anybody says, even God, it could not possibly be true for them. That is a terrible place to be in, for it seems they are incapable of hearing or receiving the truth.

I have known many people to be set free from that depression by the prayer of faith. It is as if a great black cloud is lifted from them and they can see clearly again. It is then that these positive truths need to be ministered, for it is then that they can be received, and the person concerned be saved from falling back into bondage. His attention can be directed away from that destructive self-concern and placed on Jesus and his place in Him.

Instead of going endlessly back into the past and deeper into ourselves, God would teach us to look out and away from ourselves to Him.

The Lord once summed this up for me when He said:

Don't look back, look forward.
Don't look in, look out.
Don't look down, look up.

Your words of faith: "REMAIN IN ME, AND I WILL REMAIN IN YOU." "THOSE WHO LIVE IN ACCORDANCE WITH THE SPIRIT HAVE THEIR MINDS SET ON WHAT THE SPIRIT DESIRES." "I TELL YOU THE TRUTH, ANYONE WHO HAS FAITH IN ME WILL DO WHAT I HAVE BEEN DOING." ". . . HIS INCOMPARABLY GREAT POWER IN US WHO BELIEVE."

27

SONS AND BROTHERS

SONS OF GOD
Jesus referred to God as 'my Father'. When He appears to Mary Magdalene in His risen body, He tells her:

I am returning to my Father and your Father, to my God and your God (John 20:17).

Because Jesus has reconciled us to God we are able to call Him 'Abba, Father'. His Father becomes our Father. We become sons of God by virtue of our faith in Jesus and our new birth in the Spirit.

> Yet to all who received him, to those who believed in his name, he gave the right to become children of God – children born not of natural descent nor of human decision or a husband's will, but born of God (John 1:12–13). Everyone who believes that Jesus is the Christ is born of God (1 John 5:1).

In our modern western society a son is brought up by his parents to become independent of the family. He will have his own choice of career. He is expected to be financially independent and when he marries he will settle with his wife in their own house, which may be far removed geographically from the rest of the family. There they will have their own children, who will be brought up to be similarly independent.

All this is far removed from the father–son concept of the New Testament. In the Jewish society of the time, the son was brought up within a close-knit family, in which the father exercised considerable authority over the household. The son was not encouraged to grow away from the family, but to become like his father, so that he could eventually assume the leadership of the household. He was expected to hold the same beliefs as his father, to have the same job as his father; when he married, his wife was incorporated into the family. They did not move away to begin a separate, independent family.

While his father was alive, the son would be expected to respect the authority of his father, even when he had attained adult status. The son grew up to be like his father, rather than to grow away from him.

Jesus did not come to work or speak independently of His Father.

> I tell you the truth, the Son can do nothing by himself; he can do only what he sees his Father doing, because whatever the Father does the Son also does (John 5:19).

Those listening to Jesus would have respected the principle of what He was saying, but they were offended that He should speak of His relationship with God in such a way.

Jesus clearly says that "the Son can do nothing by himself." He would not act independently of His Father. In His humanity He was totally submitted to the Father and was dependent upon Him. "Whatever the Father does the Son also does."

Jesus lived with the tension of two truths: "The Father and I are one", and "the Father is greater than I." The first of these sayings speaks of the relationship, the unity, the fellowship between Jesus and His Father – a fellowship He maintained by drawing aside to be alone with Him. The second speaks of the right filial submission and dependence upon the Father. He would not act independently of His will and direction.

Adam and Eve were thrown out of the Garden of Eden and lost their natural fellowship with God, because they fell into the trap of acting independently of Him. They were tempted to do that by Satan, who was himself thrown out of heaven for acting independently of God and rebelling against Him.

The devil tempted Jesus in the wilderness with this same temptation – to act independently of the will and direction of His Father. That Jesus would never do. If He had done so He would have denied His Sonship, and the whole process of salvation could not have been fulfilled.

> By myself I can do nothing; I judge only as I hear, and my judgment is just, for I seek not to please myself but him who sent me (John 5:30).

That is the perfect Son speaking. He does not please Himself; He lives to please His Father. He faced the physical pain of the crucifixion and temporary separation from Him, because that was His Father's will.

You would think that the Son of God would have the right to act on His own initiative, but He never did. You would think, as the Word of God, He would have spoken for Himself and would have said what He wanted to say. But He makes it clear that He didn't do that either.

> I did not speak of my own accord, but the Father who sent me commanded me what to say and how to say it

... So whatever I say is just what the Father has told me to say (John 12:49–50).

Again, that is the perfect Son speaking. He came to do the works of the Father and speak the words of His Father. He did not come to seek His own glory but to draw men to Himself so that He could lead them into the Kingdom of His Father.

WE ARE SONS

It is a mighty privilege to be made sons of God; words cannot adequately express our gratitutde to God that He should have forgiven us, accepted us and drawn us into His family.

But we can see that to be sons involves considerable responsibilities. We are not to be like modern sons brought up to grow away from our Father and be independent of Him. God does not say to us: "Now that you are my children, I will bless you and you can go off and do whatever you please." Neither does He say: "I want you to be independent and to stand on your own two feet."

Like Jesus He wants us to be:

1. Sons who live in close fellowship with Him and are prepared to draw aside to foster that relationship that He has given us.
2. Sons who are submitted to His authority, who do not want any purpose of their own that is contrary to His will.
3. Sons who seek to reflect the life of the Father in their lives.
4. Sons who are living not for their own glory, but for the glory of the one who has made them His sons.

BROTHERS OF JESUS

> Those whom God had already chosen he also set apart to become like his Son, so that the Son would be the first among many brothers. And so those whom God set apart, he called, and those he called, he put right with himself; and he shared his glory with them (Rom. 8:29–30 G.N.B.).

Jesus is the "first-born among many brothers". Those who are sons of God are brothers of the Lord Jesus. Like Him they are to reflect the Father in their lives and will inherit the glory of God.

In the parable of the prodigal son, the younger brother laments: "I am no longer worthy to be called your son." The father, however, wants to shower him with honour when he returns home repentant. For this is his son, born to share the inheritance of his father: "This son of mine was dead and is alive again; he was lost and is found" (Luke 15:24). The father had been waiting to welcome him back to the 'glory' for which he had been born. His sinful waste of his inheritance in the past was forgiven, and he was restored to his former place in the family of his father.

That boy had to go through the process of dying to himself, of living his life in his own way for his own sake. The waste was obvious to all except the boy himself. God often has to wait until we come to the end of our own purposes, before we take seriously His will for our lives.

> I tell you the truth, unless an ear of wheat falls to the ground and dies, it remains only a single seed. But if it dies, it produces many seeds (John 12:24).

Jesus was the grain of wheat that had to fall into the ground and die. The death of that one seed produced many seeds; one Son died, many sons of God could now be born. We, and all Christians of all ages, are the fruit that has come from that single 'grain of wheat' dying.

This same principle, however, has to be worked out in each of us if we are to be fruitful in our Christian lives in the way that God intends. The principle of death and resurrection runs throughout the gospel. We can only be raised to new life once we have known the death of the cross. Throughout our Christian lives we have to die to our own desires in order to be obedient to what the Lord asks of us. Jesus spells out clearly the implications of this:

> The man who loves his life will lose it, while the man who hates his life in this world will keep it for eternal life. Whoever serves me must follow me; and where I am, my

servant also will be. My Father will honour the one who serves me (John 12:25–26).

We need to recognise the weakness and uselessness of the flesh, and welcome the fact that we have been crucified with Christ. We do not have to live in bondage to that sinful self any longer. We do not have to live to please ourselves.

Not only do you need to count the old nature dead; you need also to offer yourself continually to God. Then you will begin to understand what Jesus means when He speaks of a man hating his life in this world. Sin will still try to drag you back to that life of self-pleasing. You will need to count yourself dead to sin daily; to know that you are willing for your desires to be submitted to His will at all times.

When God first began to teach me the importance of this, He allowed me to go through a series of incidents where everything seemed to conflict with what I wanted. I learned to welcome this rather than resent it, and to accept that God was not allowing that self any room to manoeuvre. I was being taught what John the Baptist knew well: "He must become greater; I must become less" (John 3:30).

God wants us to know His glory. Sin's destructiveness is seen in the fact that it prevents men from knowing that glory for which they were created: "For all have sinned and fall short of the glory of God" (Rom. 3:23). The work of the cross undoes that consequence of our sin and restores us to our inheritance of glory.

> Now if we are children, then we are heirs – heirs of God and co-heirs with Christ, if indeed we share in his sufferings in order that we may also share in his glory (Rom. 8:17).

The apostle continues:

> I consider that our present sufferings are not worth comparing with the glory that will be revealed in us (v. 18).

It does not matter what God asks of us; He will always give back more to us in this life, and assures us that we will share in his glory; His glory will be revealed in us.

The word 'sufferings' does not refer to physical or mental sickness, but to Christ's sufferings. We are to share in the cost of spreading the good news of His cross and resurrection in a world that is opposed to Him and His ways. We are not to concentrate on the sufferings, but on the glorious truth that we are His sons and co-heirs with Christ, who are given the privilege of sharing in His ministry of reconciling all things to Himself in Christ.

CLOTHED WITH CHRIST

> You are all sons of God through faith in Christ Jesus, for all of you who were baptised into Christ have been clothed with Christ (Gal. 3:26–27).

God does not expect us to reflect His love, His life, His power or His glory, of ourselves or in our own strength. Only because we live in Christ can we reflect anything of God Himself. He has clothed us with Christ. We appear before God, clothed in His righteousness and holiness.

> It is because of him that you are in Christ Jesus, who has become for us wisdom from God – that is, our righteousness, holiness and redemption (1 Cor. 1:30).

Because of Jesus we can appear before God made right and acceptable to Him, set apart and cleansed by the blood of Jesus, belonging to Him. We are His children, made worthy through the only one who is of Himself worthy.

Sons of God! Brothers of Jesus Christ! Clothed with Jesus! The wonder of it!

As we die to that life of self, more of what we are in Him can actually be manifested through our souls and bodies. That will give blessing and honour to our heavenly Father.

It is only *new* men who can be raised to the glory of God, through whom He can work now in the way that He desires, and to whom He will give the heavenly reward that He promises.

> In bringing many sons to glory, it was fitting that God, for whom and through whom everything exists, should make the Pioneer of their salvation perfect through

suffering. Both the one who makes men holy and those who are made holy are of the same family. So Jesus is not ashamed to call them brothers (Heb. 2:10–11).

You are of the same family as Jesus; He is your brother. God is bringing you to glory, as one of His sons. He has a plan and purpose for you. With Paul you can say that your "present sufferings are not worth comparing with the glory that will be revealed" in you. But God does not want you to imagine that obedience to Him will necessarily be a painful process. *He asks nothing of you without making available to you all the supernatural resources that you need to accomplish His will.*

Christians are new men who live in Christ, who are His brothers, filled with the same life and power that filled him. *Your words of faith:* "THOSE WHOM GOD HAS ALREADY CHOSEN HE HAS ALSO SET APART TO BECOME LIKE HIS SON, SO THAT THE SON WOULD BE FIRST AMONG MANY BROTHERS." "WHATEVER THE FATHER DOES THE SON ALSO DOES."

28

CALLED TO BE HOLY

God calls His people to be a holy people.

I am the Lord your God; consecrate yourselves and be holy, because I am holy (Lev. 11:44).

There is much misunderstanding of this word 'holy', which means "being separated for God". When Paul writes to the Ephesians, he addresses them as "the saints in Ephesus, the faithful in Christ Jesus" (Eph. 1:1). All Christians are saints, in the proper sense of that word. In fact, you are not a Christian unless you are a saint.

It is unfortunate that the term 'saint' has become so misused in the life of the Church. It is commonly used as a title for great men and women of God, such as the original disciples of Jesus and those who have led outstandingly pious or courageous lives, often facing martyrdom for the sake of the gospel. All those notable Christians are indeed saints, but so is every other Christian, all who are "the faithful in Christ Jesus".

Christians are people who are set apart for God, to be His own special possession, those who have received His life and are called to live the life of His heavenly Kingdom here on earth. They are those whom God has chosen and placed 'in Christ Jesus'. They are not ordinary people in the sense of living in the same way as everyone else; God has done an extraordinary thing to them and for them. Something unique has happened to them because they have put their faith in the Lord Jesus Christ. They have become sons of God.

A Christian is a Christian, a saint, not by virtue of what he has done or achieved, but because of what God has done to him. It is God who calls him, sets him apart to be His child, forgives him and places him 'in Christ Jesus'. It is God who has called him and chosen him to be separate from the world. Every saint belongs to Him, not to the world, and is to reflect His life, not that of the world. He can only belong to God because he has been forgiven, accepted, made righteous in His sight through the blood of Jesus.

To be a saint, therefore, is to recognise that God has separated you from the world even though you live in it. You live in the physical world but dissociate yourself from the ways and standards of the world, from worldliness. You are not concerned about being accepted by the world. You have been accepted by God and that is what matters most to you. You recognise that the life God calls you to live will be a challenge, a threat even, to those of the world around you. And you appreciate that you cannot compromise your position as a Christian, or your witness as one who belongs to Christ Jesus.

Whoever acknowledges me before men, I will also acknowledge him before my Father in heaven. But whoever disowns me before men, I will disown him before my Father in heaven (Matt. 10:32–33).

The Christian knows that he will be misunderstood, ridiculed, abused and even persecuted. But nothing can destroy the fact that God has chosen him to be one of His 'set-apart' people. No matter what he has to suffer for the sake of the gospel in this life, that suffering will be far outweighed by the glory that shall be his in Christ. Jesus said:

> Blessed are you when people insult you, persecute you and falsely say all kinds of evil against you because of me. Rejoice and be glad, because great is your reward in heaven (Matt. 5:11–12).

The Christian is not basing his life on the standards of this world; Christ is his life. He is not longing for the things that the world counts dear, but only for what the Lord values. He already has greater riches than the world can offer him – "every spiritual blessing in the heavenly places".

When a man dies to the flesh, to that sinful nature with which he was born, he dies to the world, too, and to all that the flesh counts dear. He is no longer a child of Satan; he is a child of God. He no longer belongs to the kingdom of this world, but to the Kingdom of heaven.

> I am not ashamed of the gospel, because it is the power of God for the salvation of everyone who believes (Rom. 1:16).

The gospel is the power of God that turns sinners into saints. A man cannot make himself a saint, he cannot gradually attain that status, nor does he have to be canonised by some church body. God makes him a saint when he believes the gospel. God says to him in effect: "You are mine. I have chosen you for myself to belong to me. I give you the rich inheritance of my heavenly Kingdom. You do not belong to the world any longer. You are a saint, made holy in my sight, set apart for me and my purposes, to live a holy and faithful life for my glory."

FAITHFUL

Paul describes the saints at Ephesus as "the faithful in Christ Jesus". To be faithful is to be 'full of faith'. The initial act of faith should lead to a life that is lived by faith, a constant trusting in what God has done for us in Jesus.

As saints we are to be full of faith in the love of God the Father that caused Him to send His Son to make it possible for us to be reconciled to Him. It is through that same love that God called and chose us to be adopted as His sons, to know Him and love Him.

> For he chose us in him before the creation of the world to be holy and blameless in his sight (Eph. 1:4).

We are to be full of faith that He has begun His good work in us and will bring it to completion – that we shall be presented pure and spotless before Him.

We are to be full of faith in the Lord Jesus Christ, that He is the Word of God that "became flesh and lived for a while among us" (John 1:14). That He who had no sin became "sin for us, so that in him we might become the righteousness of God" (2 Cor. 5:21). That He died, was raised on the third day, and lives and reigns in glory with the Father.

We are to be full of faith in the Holy Spirit, God living in us with the fulness of His life and power. That Spirit is the Comforter sent from God to be the strength of our new life, to guide us into all truth and to be our teacher, the one who will lead us in the ways of God, the One who desires the holiness of His nature to be expressed in our lives.

God knows that if we are "those who, hearing the word, hold it fast in an honest and good heart", we shall "bring forth fruit with patience" (Luke 8:15). That faithful abiding in His word will produce the fruit that God wants to create in us, by the power and activity of His Holy Spirit.

That involves holding on to our faith in the love of God despite all the pressure of adverse circumstances, all the contrary feelings we may have from time to time, through human and satanic opposition.

The faithful in Christ do not only believe in Him; they also live in Him. God has placed them in His Son so that they "will in all things grow up into him" (Eph. 4:15). They are identified completely with the whole work of salvation that God has accomplished in Jesus. They were crucified with Him, died with Him, were buried with Him, have been raised with Him, and are seated with him in the heavenly realms in Christ Jesus (Eph. 2:6).

> We will in all things grow up into him who is the Head, that is, Christ. From him the whole body, joined and held together by every supporting ligament, grows and builds itself up in love, as each part does its work (Eph. 4:15–16).

The Christian is part of the Body of which Christ is the head. He is joined to Him; he is a branch of the true Vine, who is Jesus.

How this contrasts with the negative talk that so often comes from Christians. They speak as if they are cut off from God, unacceptable to Him, spiritual failures who do nothing except grieve Him. God wants to impress upon us again and again that we live in Him and He in us.

> If anyone acknowledges that Jesus is the Son of God, God lives in him and he in God (1 John 4:15).
> For in him we live and move and have our being (Acts 17:28).

A Christian is not only a saint; he is also one who lives in Christ, in God. God has come to live in him with His Holy Spirit that he might be empowered to live a holy, faithful, set-apart life, not belonging to this world, but to Him!

THE OLD AND THE NEW

It does not matter how good and pleasant a person may be in the old life, in his or her natural being, that person still belongs to the old until the act of new birth. No amount of personal goodness can make him part of the new creation. Only Jesus can do that through what He has achieved by His crucifixion and resurrection. The old life is under sentence of death. That sentence must be executed before the new life can begin.

Some imagine that they can gradually transfer from one

to the other. But that is to deny what both Jesus and the teaching of the New Testament writers say. Others make the mistake of thinking that they can carry over some of their old life into the new.

> Neither do men pour new wine into old wineskins. If they do, the skins will burst, the wine will run out and the wineskins will be ruined. No, they pour new wine into new wineskins, and both are preserved (Matt. 9:17).

They may think that some of the old is of great value, and imagine that God has a similar evaluation of its worth. Others carry their old problems into their new life because they do not believe that they can be set free from them.

God's evaluation of the old is that it had to be put to death, even what we imagine to be good and worthy. The new creation is different and far better. Neither does God want us to believe that we need to be bound by the problems of the past. So why aren't all these problems dealt with at the moment of new birth?

In one sense they are – all of them! For every need has been met in the cross. It is common for people to experience deliverance from alcohol, drug or tobacco addiction at the time of their conversion, when they turn their lives over to God. Similarly many receive healing of their physical and emotional needs. When leading people to the Lord, I tell them to lay their needs as well as their sins before God, because I have found that He is so gracious to the repentant sinner.

Much depends on what people are taught to expect. If they are told to look to Him as Saviour, they will know His forgiveness. If they look to Him as Saviour and Healer, they will know forgiveness and healing.

I was asked to see a man who had become an alcoholic. His life had fallen apart and he was desperate for help. When we met, I showed him his need to repent, to turn his life over to Jesus, so that he could be made new. He needed time to consider all that he should bring to the cross. When I prayed with him a few days later, he was obviously intoxicated. He knew what he had to lay before Jesus, but he had felt the need for some solid drinking before coming to the point of actually giving himself to the Lord in prayer.

It was hardly the ideal atmosphere for prayer. But this man was coming to the Lord in his need. He prayed in a slurred voice, but it seemed that he was genuine in his search for God. I prayed with him for forgiveness and then laid hands on him asking God to fill him with the Holy Spirit and set him free from his drinking problem.

I heard nothing of him for two years. It was then that I discovered that from that day he was set free from his alcoholism and was now working in a centre for alcoholics, ministering to the needs of others.

But we should not be surprised if we are aware of old problems and needs after our new birth. These problems relate to our souls and bodies. It is the human spirit that is brought to life at the time of conversion. The Holy Spirit working through the human spirit can now begin His work on the soul, changing, transforming, purifying and healing. That is a gradual process of growth. Remember, your soul has been conditioned by the old patterns of thought and action for many years.

The new birth marks a new beginning in another sense:

> May I never boast except in the cross of our Lord Jesus Christ, through which the world has been crucified to me, and I to the world (Gal. 6:14).

The initial act of repentance marks the turning away from the desires and values of the world in which we live. It is in this area that perhaps Christians living in affluent societies show little success. It is too easy to try to justify our wanting to maintain the standard of living to which we have become accustomed, to see the new life as something to place alongside the old, rather than as a new way of life that supercedes the old.

That new birth can and should mark an entirely new beginning. We are set free not only from the sins of the past, but also from problems, needs and the desire to live as the world lives. For many Christians there is a marked change, a radical transformation in their lives, as a result of coming to the cross.

I could tell of many instances. I told earlier of a visit to a prison when several prisoners were converted. About a year later I visited that same city again. On the Saturday evening there was a big rally in the main concert hall, and many people came to new life, faith and healing. God moved powerfully in our midst and I asked those with specific testimonies of healing to come forward at the end of the meeting to give me a brief account of what God had done in their lives that evening.

Soon a long queue developed, comprising about 300 people. It took over an hour to hear those people testify to the wonderful graciousness of our God. During that hour, my colleague David and others were praying with other sick folk, and the power of God was being mightily manifested. People from that group started to drift over to me to share how they too had been healed.

I discovered afterwards that one of those who had been laying hands on people in the name of Jesus, and seeing Him heal them, was one of the prisoners who had been converted during my previous visit. He had since been released from prison and had become a mighty witness to the truth of the gospel, and one who was not afraid to pray with others with a bold faith in Jesus.

I rejoiced to hear that, but I could not help reflecting sadly upon the fact that in churches throughout this land there are many dear folk who have never dared to witness or pray for the sick. What a mighty transformation God can make in the life of a man when he is born again!

Do not doubt your new birth. If you love the Lord Jesus Christ, rejoice that He has forgiven you, accepts you, that He loves you, that you have been crucified with Him and raised to a new life in Him.

> I have been crucified with Christ and I no longer live, but Christ lives in me. The life I live in the body, I live by faith in the Son of God, who loved me and gave himself for me (Gal. 2:20).

God has made you a saint, you are a holy, 'set-apart' person. And yet that holiness has to be worked out in your character, behaviour, attitudes and conversation. You still have a natural life, but you also have a supernatural life in

Christ. And God desires that you live in the power of that supernatural life.

Holiness is not reflecting human goodness alone, it is reflecting Jesus. That is only possible because He has given His *Holy* Spirit to live within us. As we learn to live in the power of the Spirit, so we can demonstrate in practical ways what it means to live for God and for God to live in us.

God has made you a saint so that you can live as a saint. He does not ask you to become one, but to reflect more and more of the saintliness that you have 'in Christ Jesus'.

And what He asks of you personally, He asks of His whole Church corporately. He wants the Church to demonstrate that it is the body of God's holy, set-apart people, who live uncompromisingly for Him: the people who have forsaken worldliness and have made the Kingdom of God their priority.

> Your kingdom come, your will be done on earth as it is in heaven . . . (Matt. 6:10).

Your words of faith: "I AM THE LORD YOUR GOD; CONSECRATE YOURSELVES AND BE HOLY, FOR I AM HOLY." "MAY I NEVER BOAST EXCEPT IN THE CROSS OF OUR LORD JESUS CHRIST, THROUGH WHICH THE WORLD WAS CRUCIFIED TO ME, AND I TO THE WORLD."

29

CALLED TO OBEY

The saint is called to live a holy life, one that is set apart for God. If there is not a continual and conscious giving to Him, the Christian will live independently and selfishly. And every expression of independence and selfishness is an expression of unholiness.

God wants to change and transform your soul by the

influence of His Spirit, so that you do not express yourself in selfishness but express Him who now lives in you. Selfishness means that God is not a part of that action, nor the decision to perform it.

God is not impressed by our acts of commitment. There do need to be those times when we make conscious decisions concerning obedience and discipline. We need, also, to renew that deliberate handing over of ourselves to Him, asking Him to exercise His reign and authority over every area of our lives. There will also be those occasions when we have to submit to that authority and agree to do what God wants, rather than to fulfil our own desires.

But we need to beware of grandiose statements of commitment. They sound good and are no doubt well-intentioned. God is concerned, not in our saying that we will be obedient, but in the actual obedience. Jesus told a simple parable to illustrate this:

> There was a man who had two sons. He went to the first and said, "Son, go and work today in the vineyard." "I will not," he answered, but later he changed his mind and went. Then the father went to the other son and said the same thing. He answered, "I will, sir," but he did not go. "Which of the two did what his father wanted?" "The first," they answered (Matt. 21:28–31).

We are called by God, not to do what we consider to be good works, but to do His will as He reveals it. The constant offering of ourselves is a continual yielding to that will.

That does not mean that we sit around waiting for a voice from heaven to be clearly heard directing us, for God can be heard in the needs that He places before us and the people that He places around us. However, it is possible for us to rush into feverish activity, depending on our human resources, taking it upon ourselves to meet those needs and love all those people.

We need the right balance between those two extremes. We do need to know the Lord directing us, so that whatever we undertake is in His purpose and can be done in the power of His resources.

The human will is part of that soul life that is naturally

self-assertive, and therefore opposed to the purposes of God. To follow the desires of the old nature will naturally lead to disobedience to God. The self-will needs to know that it has been crucified.

GIVING TO GOD

God uses only what is willingly given to Him to use. Many Christians look with envy at the way in which God uses others; there is an obvious anointing upon them and a greater fruitfulness in their lives. They wonder why this should be when they, too, desire to work for God and to be used effectively by Him.

The way in which the man under the anointing is giving himself to the Lord cannot be seen by others. In that giving to God he is single-minded; he does not count the cost for himself. It matters to him only that he is being obedient to all that God is asking of Him.

> Give, and it will be given to you. A good measure, pressed down, shaken together and running over, will be poured into your lap. For with the measure you use, it will be measured to you (Luke 6:38).

Some covet the anointing and the fruitfulness, but do not want to face the cost of giving. Those who look wistfully at the way God uses others are usually not willing to submit themselves to His authority in the same way. They listen to their fears and the fears of loved ones around them. They are not prepared for that boldness of faith that God asks of those whom He would send out in His name, the boldness that is necessary to lead others in the ways of God and in obedience to His Spirit.

To give yourself, and go on giving yourself, will affect every area of your life, not only the doing of good works. It will affect relationships in marriage, family, church, business; it will affect personal attitudes towards the use of time and money.

God deals lovingly and gently with us. His desire is that everything be offered to Him, but He will not take everything away from us. All needs to be at His disposal, remembering always that it is His purpose to give. He only takes in order that He may measure back to us immeasurably more than we have given.

When my extended family and I moved from the parish in Luton, where God had done a particularly gracious work by His Spirit it seemed that we were giving up everything. I knew God was calling me to a full-time itinerant ministry, and the only way that I could effectively fulfil that was to resign from the responsibilities of the pastorate. That meant giving up the house in which we lived, the security of a regular income, the close fellowship of those we loved, and going out with little money and no security into an unknown future.

The Lord was going to teach us what it meant for Him to be our security, the Lord our Provider.

> "I tell you the truth," Jesus replied, "no one who has left home or brothers or sisters or mother or father or children or fields for me and for the gospel will fail to receive a hundred times as much in this present age (homes, brothers, sisters, mothers, children and fields – and with them persecutions) and in the age to come, eternal life" (Mark 10:29–30).

It would be a long story to show you how God has honoured His word in our lives. He has built around us a community of people who have devoted their lives to the Lord and His Kingdom. He has provided a most beautiful home in Sussex, set in lovely surroundings, to be the base for our travelling ministry. Here we can live out the gospel, reaching out to the locality, the nation and other countries around the world.

> Seek first his kingdom and his righteousness, and all these things will be given to you as well (Matt. 6:33).

The Lord promises us the right kind of prosperity in this life as well as the reward of life with Him eternally. His condition is that we put His Kingdom first in our lives; that we are giving ourselves to Him in whatever ways He is asking of us, for that is what it means to be submitted to His reign and sovereignty.

> You cannot give to God without receiving infinitely more back from Him. That is not the motive for giving to Him; He simply will not allow you to outdo Him in giving.

> Anyone who does not take his cross and follow me is not worthy of me. Whoever finds his life will lose it, and whoever loses his life for my sake will find it (Matt. 10:38–39).

This does not mean that we are to seek crucifixion, for we have already been crucified with Christ. There is to be a daily willing carrying of the cross to enable us to follow Him. A daily dying.

This does not mean that our souls cease to exist, that we lose our personality, or that God takes away all our natural abilities.

It does mean that there needs to be that daily dying to independent, self-motivated action. Our emotions are part of our soul-life and wield a very powerful influence in our lives. It is not that they are of themselves sinful, but they can so easily lead us into sin when they are not under the authority of God's Spirit.

> Anyone who loves his father or mother more than me is not worthy of me; anyone who loves his son or daughter more than me is not worthy of me (Matt. 10:37).

Loving father or mother, son or daughter is not wrong; such love is a fulfilment of the law of God. When that human affection over-rides our love for God it becomes sinful. Jesus says that the man who puts human affection above his love for God 'is not worthy of me'.

GOD FIRST
Putting God first is the only right course for a Christian: "Whoever loses his life (soul) for my sake will find it." I shall continually need to die to the desires of the soul in order that the will of the Spirit of God may be fulfilled in me.

To give in to the desires of the soul is to experience the loss of the Spirit's activity in that area of our being. To gratify the soul is to grieve the Spirit. The Christian can discover a new joy and a greater satisfaction when he knows that he has obeyed the Lord.

The stronger the self-dependence of the soul, the harder it is for God to have His way.

The great temptation is to try to please God and ourselves at the same time. That is rarely possible. There has to be that daily dying to self in order that the life of the Spirit may keep us in God's way.

Whenever the soul acts independently of the Spirit, that is tantamount to telling God to mind His own business. We can hate ourselves for the things we do, and yet still persist in doing them, because somehow or other they gratify our self-love.

And so the work of the cross and the Spirit is to bring purity to each particular area of the soul-life; then our feelings and emotions can be ruled by the Holy Spirit for the glory of the Father.

> Then he called the crowd to him along with his disciples and said: "If anyone would come after me, he must deny himself and take up his cross and follow me" (Mark 8:34).

These words are spoken to anyone who would be a follower of Jesus.

Some seem to imagine that the life of self-denial is only for advanced disciples. Jesus says otherwise. The Christian life begins at the cross, the place where Jesus took that naturally sinful self and crucified it. From that moment the believer is to count himself dead to sin, but alive in Christ. The soul, acting independently of the Spirit, will lead him into sin unless deliberately denied. That is a daily necessity, for the soul-life would rise up at any opportunity it is given to assume control.

These words were spoken during the momentous time at Caeserea Philippi when Peter was the first to proclaim openly: "You are the Christ." That was a revelation given him by the Father.

Jesus chooses this as the appropriate time to prophesy His forthcoming rejection and crucifixion: "He then began to teach them that the Son of Man must suffer many things and be rejected by the elders, chief priests and teachers of the law, and that he must be killed and after three days rise again" (Mark 8:31).

This was to be the destiny of the Christ, the Messiah, the Son of God: not what Peter, nor the other disciples, would want for the man they had come to admire and love deeply. The implication of Peter's confession of faith is that Jesus should be worshipped. Surely it could not be true that He would suffer, be rejected and killed.

> He spoke plainly about this, and Peter took him aside and began to rebuke him (v. 32).

One moment Peter, inspired by God, utters the profound revelation "You are the Christ." In almost the next breath, he dares to rebuke the one he has just acknowledged as the Son of God. That is the soul of Peter at work, overcome by his human reason, his human affection for Jesus, and his human will for His future. Jesus does not spare Peter in His reply:

> But when Jesus turned and looked at his disciples, he rebuked Peter: "Out of my sight, Satan!" he said. "You do not have in mind the things of God, but the things of men" (v. 33).

Because the soul can function apart from the spirit, and will do so whenever allowed, it can easily be used by Satan to oppose the work of God's Spirit. The natural reason does not understand the things of God. The soul needs to be informed by the mind of the Spirit, the mind of Christ. The will needs to conform with His will, even when that means facing suffering and death. The emotions of human love need to be subject to God's love – and that will inevitably involve a denial of selfish, unconsecrated affections.

Jesus is showing the disciples that to love Him is to love God's purpose for Him – not to argue against it. He calls the crowd to Him and teaches them that anyone who loves God will need to accept His purpose lovingly, too. That, in turn, will mean that "he must deny himself and take up his cross and follow me."

> For whoever wants to save his life (soul) will lose it, but whoever loses his life (soul) for me and for the gospel will save it. What good is it for a man to gain the whole world, yet forfeit his soul? Or what can a man exchange for his soul? (vv. 35–37).

The soul wants to hold on to its own life. The mind wants to press its own opinions, the will its own decisions, and the affections their own desires. Over against that is the life of the Holy Spirit. Working through the regenerated human spirit, God wants to inform the mind of His thoughts, inform the will of His will, inform the affections of what He loves.

Yet never will God force His mind, His will or His love upon us. His Spirit lives in us to inform us of His purpose and to provide all His resources to enable us to face and accomplish whatever His will is revealed to be.

LISTENING TO GOD

Every Christian knows a confusion of voices within himself, a confusion that seems often to be intensified when he is trying to seek the purpose of God for some particular situation. "Is that my own voice, the voice of God, or Satan trying to mislead me?" he will often ask himself.

God speaks with a 'still, small voice' that can so easily be drowned by the clamour of our own desires, understanding and will. And it is true that the enemy prompts us to consider the problem and our own feelings – anything to distract us from that quiet witness of the Spirit within us.

The more the soul is given free expression, the more difficult it is to hear the voice of God. The Christian who leads a disciplined, obedient life will be able to hear God more readily than the Christian who is casual about his waiting upon God, or who is being undisciplined and disobedient in his way of life.

Many are led to fast during a time of waiting upon the Lord for His answer to a specific need. That act of self-denial can intensify one's sensitivity to the voice of God. The soul is subject to the Spirit and can more easily hear, receive and respond to what God is saying.

When told that Jesus would suffer and die, Peter was confronted with the fact that he did not want the will of God. All of us hope God will change His mind when He confronts us with something we don't want to do. When they do not like what He is saying, Christians sometimes continue to wait upon Him in the hope that they will hear Him say something else. They reject what they hear at first, saying that it is not of the Lord, because they do not want it to be of the Lord. And so they wait and wait for Him to say something different, and wonder why He is so silent.

God is not going to change His will for anyone. He often has to wait until we are prepared to have a change of mind and will be obedient to Him. It is the Lord who has to wait and wait for us to respond to what He has already said.

OUR WILLINGNESS TO CHANGE

Often the soul will reject what God is saying because the man is fearful of the cost of obedience, of his own inability to measure up to the Lord's will, of what others think. The soul has to learn to trust to the Spirit, that He will empower and enable God's children to do anything that He is asking of them.

At other times the soul plainly does not want to face the sacrifice of yielding to God what that man finds precious and enjoyable. He has to decide whether his treasures are on earth or in heaven.

> Whoever tries to keep his life (soul) will lose it, and whoever loses his life will preserve it (Luke 17:33).

This is not only denying ourselves things that are obviously expressions of self-indulgence. There will be times when we have to let go of good things, that have been truly appointed and anointed of God, because now His will is for something different.

There are many different organisations and structures within the institutional churches which began years (sometimes centuries) ago, as genuine fruit of the Holy Spirit working through particular men and groups. God's appointing and anointing of that particular work have long since passed, but the work is carried on by the appointment and determination of men. In the process God can only be grieved, for that work will seem uninspired and lifeless, even if to the human mind it seems a good and worthy thing to do.

One of the most important aspects of obedience is not only to start when God says "Start!", but also to stop when He says "Stop!"

The real work of the Spirit of God can never be institutionalised:

> The wind blows wherever it pleases. You hear its sound, but you cannot tell where it comes from or where it is going. So it is with everyone born of the Spirit (John 3:8).

The Spirit can work within institutions, but never because of them. The Spirit will move within denominations, but never because of them.

To resist the Lord only produces conflict and agony for the Christian. Who can resist God and be at peace? Certainly nobody filled with the Spirit can easily do so, because he will have the witness of God within him that he is being disobedient. And if he drowns the voice of the Spirit by his stubborn refusal to listen to what He is saying, he will soon experience a spiritual dryness. It will seem that everything is falling apart in his life.

There will be many occasions when God's will comes into conflict with our human wills. Even Jesus experienced that conflict in the Garden of Gethsemene when He prayed: "Abba, Father, everything is possible for you. Take this cup from me. Yet not what I will, but what you will" (Mark 14:36).

In His humanity Jesus wanted to avoid the crucifixion; in His divinity He embraced the will of His Father. No one would question that Jesus had already given His life to be lived in obedience to His Father, and yet here we see the need for Him to offer Himself in a renewed act of obedience to His Father's authority.

It is not enough for any of us to say: "Lord, I *desire* to do your will." His answer to that is: "Do it, then!"

NOT GRUDGINGLY

Doing the will of God is not a matter of being made to do what we do not want to do. His will comes into conflict with our own natural desires. But the desire of the new nature, of the new heart that God gives us, is to please the Lord. The more we are built up in the power of that new nature, the greater our desire will be to please the Lord. We shall be able to say with the psalmist:

> To do your will, O my God, is my desire; your law is within my heart (Ps. 40:8).

Paul says we are to offer the parts of the body 'in slavery to righteousness'. A slave is one who is owned and possessed by the master. It is not bondage, but freedom, to know that we are possessed by Jesus, that we are precious to Him, that He desires obedience in us because that is best for us.

And yet, although He is the Master, He does not compel the slave to obey. We are to offer obedience to Him; He does not enforce it upon us. He awaits that offering of the servant in willing, loving, joyful service.

Your words of faith: "WHOEVER FINDS HIS LIFE WILL LOSE IT, AND WHOEVER LOSES HIS LIFE FOR MY SAKE WILL FIND IT." "IF ANYONE WOULD COME AFTER ME, HE MUST TAKE UP HIS CROSS AND FOLLOW ME."

30

OFFER YOURSELF

God has given you new life and placed you in His Son, Jesus. The spiritual worship that He asks of you is to offer yourself to Him: body, soul and spirit. Paul says to the Romans:

> I urge you, brothers, in view of God's mercy, to offer your bodies as living sacrifices, holy and pleasing to God – which is your spiritual worship (Rom. 12:1).

It is not your old life that is to be offered to God, for that has been put to death and is buried with Christ. It is the new life, you as a new creature, that needs to be offered back to God. Even the parts of your body are to be given to Him so that they can serve Him, being directed now, not by the old self, but by the new self – Christ in you. Offer yourselves to God "as those who have been brought from death to life".

> Therefore do not let sin reign in your mortal body so that you obey its evil desires. Do not offer the parts of your body to sin, as instruments of wickedness, but rather offer yourselves to God, as those who have been brought from death to life; and offer the parts of your body to him as instruments of righteousness (Rom. 6:12–13).

What belongs to the old cannot be consecrated to the Lord's service; it is dead. Only that which has passed through the process of death into resurrection can be offered acceptably to God. It is only as new creatures, living 'in Christ Jesus' that we can give our lives to Him in the way He desires. It is possible to be filled with zeal for God without knowing the new life. That was the tragedy of Saul of Tarsus before he became Paul.

Paul does not speak of some token offering of our new lives to God. He is more specific: "offer the parts of your body to him as instruments of righteousness." That means that we are prepared to do what is right in God's sight, to allow ourselves to be led and directed by Him. Paul emphasises this further:

> Just as you used to offer the parts of your body in slavery to impurity and to ever-increasing wickedness, so now offer them in slavery to righteousness leading to holiness (Rom. 6:19).

Here again is the total contrast between the old and the new. In the old, the body was used to gratify the desires of the self. In the new, the body is to fulfil the purpose of God.

Offer Yourself

Everything about the Christian belongs to the Lord; he has been "bought with a price".

The new man is to be "in slavery to righteousness". His concern is to do what God regards as right, not to satisfy his own desires and longings. It is peace and freedom to know that all you are and possess rightfully belongs to the Lord, and you give everything freely to Him. It is the recognition of this truth that will determine the use of your physical body, your time, abilities, money and other material resources.

What about your natural abilities? Are they of no use to God? Has He not given those to you? Yes, He has given them and He will use them once they are brought under the direction and sovereignty of the Spirit.

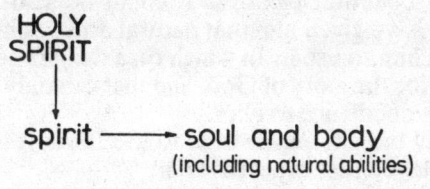

```
HOLY
SPIRIT
   │
   ▼
spirit ───▶ soul and body
            (including natural abilities)
```

God does not limit what He can do with you to making use of your natural abilities. Many discover that He chooses to use them in ways where they have no natural ability. That is certainly true in my own life. The reason for this is not difficult to see. When we are using natural resources it is easy to trust to those abilities to accomplish what we are doing, and that can involve missing God's best. Our abilities cannot compare with His. On the other hand, He knows that we shall have to depend utterly upon Him to enable us to do things we feel totally inadequate to attempt. That is what the new life in Christ is about: trust, not in ourselves, but in Him.

NATURAL GIFTS

Does that mean that God does not value the natural gifts and does not want us to use them? Not at all. All good gifts come from God. His concern is *how* they are used. They are to be consecrated to Him, which means that they come under His authority to be used at the direction of His Spirit.

A Christian may be a gifted artist. His desire may be to sit and give expression to that gift as often as possible, producing many canvases. That is fine if this is what God is wanting of him. But if the Lord has made him an evangelist, his painting could be an expression of self-indulgence that prevents him from devoting himself to his true vocation.

It could be said that he produces beautiful pictures that give pleasure to many people; yet he would be indulging his soul-life to please the soul-life of others. There would not be the 'abiding' fruit that would result from employing his supernatural gift of evangelism. Many could enter the eternal life of God's Kingdom and know His loving forgiveness and acceptance, which is far more important than looking at beautiful pictures. It could be said that God would not have given him that natural artistic gift if he did not intend him to use it. In which case the gift needs to be employed for the glory of God, and that can only happen if it is used in obedience to Him.

Certainly the gift means little to the Lord; it is how the gift is employed that concerns Him.

That is not to say that God will not use at least some of our natural abilities. But it is to say that He will not depend on them and He will teach us, likewise, not to depend on them.

Whatever we give to God will have to be 'broken' and brought under the direction and authority of His Spirit. That can be a painful process, for attempts to use our gifts in the way we think best are met with repeated frustration and failure. But to resist this process of breaking, of allowing God to deal with us, with our strong self-wills, only results in hindering fruitfulness. For we may be prepared to offer the gift, but it is unruly and needs to be trained by Him.

In offering the gift of ourselves to God we need to recognise that in many ways our lives are spiritually unruly and undisciplined. The Lord sets about the process of making us disciples, 'disciplined people' in our following of Him. Because He is the Lord of our lives we have to recognise that He is in charge. He is in control, and He does not make mistakes. That often-quoted verse of scripture is true which says:

> And we know that in all things God works for the good of those who love him, who have been called according to his purpose (Rom. 8:28).

That is the death-blow to murmuring against the Lord, complaining that He doesn't know what He is doing with you, or that He has made a whole series of dreadful mistakes in allowing so many difficulties in your life. It is the end of grumbling about your lot in life or the state of the world around you, the economic situation or the latest political crisis. God is in control and He knows what He is doing.

The Christian realises that even the destiny of the nations is in God's hands. As far as his own seemingly insignificant life is concerned, he learns that in everything God is dealing with him, teaching him, and all the time wanting to encourage his faith and build him in love.

> The reason my Father loves me is that I lay down my life – only to take it up again. No one takes it from me, but I lay it down of my own accord. I have authority to lay it down and authority to take it up again. This command I received from my Father (John 10:17–18).

Jesus did not desire to act independently, for that would be to deny the relationship He had with His Father: "the Father is in me, and I in the Father" (John 10:38).

Likewise, for us to act independently of Jesus is for us to deny the relationship that we have with Him: "Abide in me, and I in you" (John 15:4 R.S.V.). "Apart from me you can do nothing" (v. 5).

Jesus "has been tempted in every way, just as we are – yet was without sin" (Heb. 4:15). That means that He was tempted to act independently, to trust to Himself instead of to His Father. You would think that if anybody had the right to do his own thing it would be the Son of God. But He makes it perfectly clear that He was sent to do His Father's will, not His own.

Satan's method of attack, during the temptations in the wilderness at the outset of His ministry, was aimed at trying to persuade Jesus to do something out of His own initiative, that would fulfil His own desires and draw attention to Himself. He stood firm against all these attempts, quoting the scriptures as His answers to the taunts of the devil.

> My food is to do the will of him who sent me, and to finish his work (John 4:34).

Even God the Father held to His principle of working: "The measure you give will be the measure you get" (Matt. 7:2 R.S.V.). He had to give the life of His beloved Son in order to receive the harvest of sons He wanted in His heavenly Kingdom.

God's way of working is through death and resurrection. It was the way with Jesus; it is His way with us.

OBEDIENCE TO THE SPIRIT

The heart of the individual believer is readily exposed when God commands him to obey. He commanded Abram: "Leave your country, your people and your father's household and go to the land I will show you" (Gen. 12:1). "So Abram went . . ." (Gen. 13:1). It is for that faithful, obedient response that Abraham is the father of faith in the scriptures.

And in the New Testament, the Lord spoke to one of His children named Ananias.

> The Lord called to him in a vision "Ananias".
> "Yes Lord," he answered.

That is always the faithful response of the loving servant to his Master. Little did Ananias suspect God's purpose:

> "Go to the house of Judas on Straight Street and ask for a man from Tarsus named Saul, for he is praying. In a vision he has seen a man named Ananias come and place his hands on him to restore his sight."

This is more than the dear disciple can understand. His soul begins to argue:

"Lord," Ananias answered, "I have heard many reports about this man and all the harm he has done to your saints in Jerusalem. And he has come here with authority from the chief priests to arrest all who call on your name."

'But Lord' is the common answer for God to receive from His children when they cannot understand what He is commanding. Far from changing His mind, the Lord is emphatic in His command to Ananias, and shows that His purpose is even more extraordinary than His first statement had indicated. In fact, He was breaking him in gently:

"Go! This man is my chosen instrument to carry my name before the Gentiles and their kings and before the people of Israel. I will show him how much he must suffer for my name."
Then Ananias went . . . (Acts 9:10–17).

As he went, no doubt he was still utterly perplexed that the arch-persecutor of the Church should be chosen by God to become a great apostle. No doubt the enemy was sowing as much fear in him as possible, telling him that he was a fool to go near such a man; he must be misheraing God; he would be in chains for his faith as soon as Saul realised he was a Christian.

But Ananias went. He had heard the voice of the Spirit of God and he obeyed. He obeyed the Spirit rather than the reactions of his own soul to the situation. Like Ananias we need to be in constant readiness to hear the Lord's voice and respond to His commands: "I delight to do thy will, O my God" (Ps. 40:8 R.S.V.).

OUR TRUE MOTIVE
It is easy to be so preoccupied with the things of the soul that we miss the leading of the Spirit. That raises questions of the true motivation within our hearts.

Is your desire to please yourself or to please Him? It is easy to say that you want to please Him, for you know that is the answer you ought to give. What if pleasing Him meant that He was to take from you the possessions that you treasure most, or the interests that give you pleasure, or even someone you love dearly? What if God shows you that His purpose for your life will involve suffering, persecution, rejection? Would your response be: "If that is your will, Lord, then it is good and I continue to rejoice in you?"

Only this week a woman came to me in great distress. She lived in fear that something terrible would happen to her two children, that God would find a way of taking them from her because she loved them so dearly.

Christian friends had tried to assure her that He would not want to do that. But still the fears persisted. I asked her if she had ever given her children to the Lord. She hadn't, because she had been afraid to do so. I told her that was the very thing she needed to do. She needed to acknowledge that they were His children and He had the right to do with them whatever He pleased.

There and then amid tears she prayed and surrendered her children to the Lord. Immediately she was filled with peace and went on her way rejoicing. The panic she had experienced for so long had disappeared. She will discover that God's purpose is to bless her children and use them for His glory.

Nothing is more important to Him than the fulfilling of His purpose in our lives for His glory. If we allow anything to stand between us and that purpose, God will have to deal with those unruly soul-lives of ours. He has our own welfare at stake in doing that.

The soul can hinder the work of the Spirit in our human relationships. We cannot manipulate God or His love. And if we love with His love, we shall not attempt to manipulate people into doing what we want. Even God does not manipulate. He speaks quietly, revealing His purpose, and awaits our response to His will. Manipulation is only a device to encourage self-love, or to make others conform to our wishes. It encourages the soul to act independently of the Spirit and is therefore to be resisted.

I tell you the truth, unless an ear of wheat falls to the ground and dies, it remains only a single seed. But if it dies, it produces many seeds. The man who loves his life (soul) will lose it, while the man who hates his life in this world will keep it for eternal life (John 12:24–25).

That soul-life must die in order that it may become fruitful. It is a solitary seed until the process of death is accomplished.

We have seen this principle in Jesus Himself; He died that many sons might know the glory of God. That was a willing response to His Father's will. He had the power to lay His life down, or to refuse to do so.

So with us. If the new life that we have been given is to be expressed fully and freely, then we shall need to die to the wrong kind of self-expression. The soul in the Christian is to express the new self (Jesus), not the old self.

The Holy Spirit is alive in every true Christian, but often it is difficult for Him to find real expression in his life because of the strong self-life of the soul. Often the soul tries to contain that life, rather than give it free expression. In that case the believer is still ready to trust in his own human resources rather than in the supernatural resources that God has made available to him.

The soul is not able to express the life of the Spirit freely, unless it is constantly drawing upon the resources of the Spirit. This is a continuous process. Once the soul stops drawing on the resources of Jesus, it will begin to project its own life instead. A person can switch from one to the other in a moment of time, as with Peter at Caeserea Philippi.

It is for anyone who would follow Jesus to deny himself and take up his cross. That is a joyful thing. It is wonderful to be able to please the Lord by our ready obedience. That is to praise Him in more than words; it is to honour Him in our lives, to show that we truly love Him and are sincere in calling Him 'Lord'.

> Not everyone who says to me, 'Lord Lord', will enter the kingdom of heaven, but only he who does the will of my Father who is in heaven (Matt. 7:21).

The denial of the soul is not something that is done momentarily; it is not an event you can look back on as being already accomplished. It is a way of life, that the soul may be kept in a right and proper relationship to the Spirit at all times. Then the Spirit will be able to produce in the believer the fruit of love, joy, peace, patience, kindness, goodness, faithfulness, gentleness and self-control in the way that He desires.

God is not content with occasional flashes of His Spirit being seen in our lives; He wants our souls to be consistent in showing forth the life of Jesus.

You may ask yourself how you will ever come to the end of yourself, to that place where you will no longer trust to your own resources and no longer desire your own will. God will have a way for you. Inevitably it will involve Him confronting you with things about yourself that you would much rather not see. Perhaps He will have to take you through some traumatic times to deal with you. But He will do that. Somehow or other He will do it because He is committed to presenting you perfect before Him.

When God does this work, you will wonder how He managed to bless you in the past when there was so much of self remaining and being expressed in your life. You will see that there has been a great deal of compromise in your life, compromise of God's word, of His will, of the leading of His Spirit.

Such times will increase your sense of your total inadequacy, but, more important, they will increase your awareness of the grace of God and of the wonder of His love for you. The end result will be encouraging.

God will speak to you about your motives. He will show you that many things you do are done in the expectation of receiving praise from men. He will reveal the things about you that do not give Him glory. He will make clear when you are obedient out of a sense of duty, or with a grudging attitude, and when you truly delight to do His will.

He will want to remove the filter through which you put His word, allowing the things you are ready to face to pass through, but deliberately turning away from those things you do not want to face.

Offer Yourself 257

> Whoever serves me must follow me; and where I am, my servant also will be (John 12:26).

God wants us with Him, hearing Him, obeying Him. In whatever way He needs to deal with us to bring us to that place of willingly following Him, He will always act in love. "Endure hardship as discipline; God is treating you as sons" (Heb. 12:7).

All the time God has in view that final purpose that He has for us: that we should know His glory.

> The Spirit himself testifies with our spirit that we are God's children. Now if we are children, then we are heirs – heirs of God and co-heirs with Christ, if indeed we share in his sufferings in order that we may also share in his glory (Rom. 8:16–17).

Sensitivity to that Spirit has nothing to do with the level of our intelligence, but it is essential if we are to be obedient to the Lord. We can be so eager to work for God that we will not allow Him to deal with us.

It is easy to go rushing forward armed with some fresh revelation from God, imagining that we carry everything before us. We can be full of great ideas for the extending of the Kingdom, without being prepared to wait upon God for His orders. Jesus led Paul into obscurity for three years to teach him the gospel.

GOD DEALING WITH US

We so easily believe our feelings when God is dealing with us that we imagine He has deserted us, that He has forgotten us in our time of need, that He doesn't appreciate what is going on inside us, or even that He doesn't *care*! And all the time He is teaching us to abandon that self-concern, to believe that everything is working together for good, that we can "rejoice in the Lord always" because He is sovereign Lord and has not lost control of our lives, of the world, of His purpose in all creation.

> For it is we who are the circumcision, we who worship by the Spirit of God, who glory in Christ Jesus, and who put no confidence in the flesh (Phil. 3:3).

Before his conversion, his very strong and able soul-life was spent in what he considered a holy and righteous zeal for God. What does he now realise?

> But whatever was to my profit I now consider loss for the sake of Christ. What is more, I consider everything a loss compared to the surpassing greatness of knowing Christ Jesus my Lord, for whose sake I have lost all things. I consider them rubbish, that I may gain Christ and be found in him, not having a righteousness of my own that comes from the law, but that which is through faith in Christ – the righteousness that comes from God and is by faith. I want to know Christ and the power of his resurrection and the fellowship of sharing in his sufferings, becoming like him in his death, and so, somehow, to attain to the resurrection from the dead (Phil. 3:7–11).

Thus speaks a man who has spent his soul in serving God and has now discovered the power of His Spirit. He continues:

> Not that I have already obtained all this, or have already been made perfect, but I press on to take hold of that for which Christ Jesus took hold of me. Brothers, I do not consider myself yet to have taken hold of it. But one thing I do: Forgetting what is behind and straining towards what is ahead, I press on towards the goal to win the prize for which God has called me heavenwards in Christ Jesus. All of us who are mature should take such a view of things (Phil. 3:12–15).

That is the secret: not looking back upon past failure, but "straining towards what is ahead", allowing the Spirit of God to lead us on in His purposes, making us what He desires us to be, completing that good work in us that He has begun, and causing us to be fruitful for the glory of the Father. "All of us who are mature should take such a view of things.

Your words of faith: "OFFER YOURSELVES TO GOD, AS THOSE WHO HAVE BEEN BROUGHT FROM DEATH TO LIFE; AND OFFER THE PARTS OF YOUR BODY TO LIVE AS INSTRUMENTS OF RIGHT-

EOUSNESS." "I DELIGHT TO DO THY WILL, O MY GOD." "BUT ONE THING I DO: FORGETTING WHAT IS BEHIND AND STRAINING TOWARDS WHAT IS AHEAD, I PRESS ON TOWARDS THE GOAL TO WIN THE PRIZE FOR WHICH GOD HAS CALLED ME HEAVENWARDS IN CHRIST JESUS."

31

GOD'S DIVIDING WORD

Often the work of the Spirit in the Christian is hindered by his soul, his mind, will and emotions. His own thinking, his intellectual, rational understanding and assessment of a situation are very different from the revelation given by God's Spirit. There is often a conflict between the will of the believer and the will of God, as revealed in His word. The emotions, affections and feelings will draw our attention away from the Lord whenever given free rein.

It is essential to know when we are truly being led and motivated by God's Spirit, and when our own souls are in charge of the decisions we make. It is His word that will enable us to distinguish between the two:

> The word of God is living and active. Sharper than any double-edged sword, it penetrates even to dividing soul and spirit, joints and marrow; it judges the thoughts and attitudes of the heart (Heb. 4:12).

God's word 'cleaves asunder' the soul and spirit like a sharp sword, or cleaver, cutting through a carcass. Many mistake the urging of the soul for the voice of the Spirit, and so claim that they are acting in obedience to God when, truly, they are following their own inclinations.

The life of God's Spirit is to be expressed through every part of our beings and personalities: through our minds, our wills and our affections. The soul is, therefore, to be subject to the human spirit, operating in harmony with the Holy Spirit:

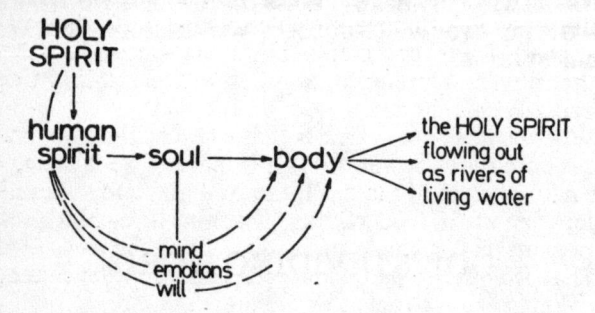

```
HOLY
SPIRIT
  \ /
human
spirit → soul → body ⟨ the HOLY SPIRIT
                       flowing out
                       as rivers of
                       living water
           mind
           emotions
           will
```

The soul is to manifest the love of the Spirit through the will exercising obedience to the Lord; the wisdom of God through the mind, and so on. The Holy Spirit needs to be expressed through the human personalities of Christians. God expressed Himself perfectly in Jesus and expresses Himself today through the Holy Spirit living in His children.

If, however, we allow our souls to be influenced by self, then we shall be expressing our own opinions rather than the mind of Christ, our own feelings and our own wilfulness. At all times the soul needs to be the vehicle through which God can express His life. And then, not only his soul, but his body as well, will reflect something of the life and vitality of the indwelling presence of God. In the early days of our life in the Spirit, the soul seemed to react sympathetically to this new presence. It was not long before the soul-life wanted to reassert its claim to be the central controlling factor of our lives instead of the servant of the spirit. That is another way of expressing the temptation to depend upon self and not the Spirit of God at work within us.

There has to be a daily dying to self-motivated, self-inspired, self-initiated action if one is to follow the leading of the Spirit as God's children. The soul is very powerful, and the new birth does not reduce that power. We can summon up all the resources of the soul intellectually, wilfully

God's Dividing Word

and emotionally, and let that be the motivating force that will determine our actions.

We can pay lip-service to the will and purpose of God, while imagining that we are able to cope perfectly well on our own. There are many things the Christian will do without even stopping to consider whether this is God's purpose for him or not.

What he does not realise is that when he does not act in the supernatural power of his new nature, he is acting on the natural level of the flesh, the soul and body operating independently of God's Spirit. That may bring him a sense of personal satisfaction, but it will not bring glory to God.

That offends the soul, which cries out for independence, for often it *wants* to act independently of God.

Even when we see an objective which we know to be the will of God, it is easy to employ the natural endowments of the soul to try to achieve that end, rather than to use the supernatural power of God's Spirit. It is a grave temptation, once having received the revelation of His purpose, to rush into human activity to achieve it. That leads to frustration and perplexity. For on such occasions it is difficult to fathom why God should give such clear direction, and yet not enable us to do what He wants. The answer to this perplexity is not difficult to see. When God reveals His purpose He does not send us away to try to accomplish that in our own strength, with the resources of the soul. He wants it done His way, in the power of His Spirit.

LIVING IN THE SPIRIT

The ability of any Christian to live in the power of God will depend upon his awareness of the life and activity of the Holy Spirit at work within him:

> You, however, are controlled not by the sinful nature but by the Spirit, if the Spirit of God lives in you (Rom. 8:9).

The life and power of the Holy Spirit enables the Christian to live according to his new nature. The Spirit of God Himself living within him, giving life to his mortal body:

If the Spirit of him who raised Jesus from the dead is living in you, he who raised Christ from the dead will also give life to your mortal bodies through his Spirit who lives in you (Rom. 8:11).

The Christian who is filled with the Holy Spirit does not need to be lured back into behaviour that belongs to the flesh. It seems extraordinary that the Christians at Corinth could manifest gifts of the Spirit so profusely and see God performing miracles among them, while at the same time harbouring sexual immorality and drunkenness at some of their meetings. Paul reminds them that they are the living temple of God because the Holy Spirit dwells in them. God has given His power, not only to enable the miraculous, but also to enable His children to live holy lives.

Don't you know that you yourselves are God's temple and that God's Spirit lives in you? . . . God's temple is sacred, and you are that temple (1 Cor. 3:16–17).

GRIEVING THE SPIRIT

They were to remember who and what they were as new creatures living 'in Christ Jesus'. That is true for Christians today. From time to time we hear of the scandal of someone whom God has used to be a blessing to many people, suddenly "going off the rails". It may be a pastor who suddenly leaves his congregation and disappears with another woman, or the tragedy of a Christian unaccountably becoming involved in a homosexual offence.

It is easy to frown and criticise, for it is certainly true that these things should not happen and are an offence to God when they do. It is perplexing to many to know why such things happen. Of course, we cannot analyse the details of particular cases here. But it is important to see why these moral lapses are possible for men who have been greatly blessed and used by God. Those concerned have been given new natures, but they cease to live in the power of that new nature – at least in that particular area of their lives which gives rise to the problem. They cease to follow the Holy Spirit and follow their own desires and inclinations instead.

God's Dividing Word

This may begin in a subtle way. For example, a counselling relationship can develop into an emotional bondage. People can be easily deceived by their emotions (which are part of the soul, not the spirit), even to the extent of claiming that an adulterous relationship is a beautiful thing of the Spirit.

That is a complete contradiction and denial of the teaching of scripture; so clearly it could not be the will of God. We could dismiss the claim as saying that the people involved simply want to justify their sinful actions. But that is only part of the answer.

We need to be concerned at the element of deception that is always present in such circumstances. When Paul was writing to the Galatians he said:

> So I say, live by the Spirit, and you will not gratify the desires of the sinful nature. For the sinful nature desires what is contrary to the Spirit, and the Spirit what is contrary to be sinful nature. They are in conflict with each other, so that you do not do what you want (Gal. 5:16–17).

The sinful nature has been crucified, and that means that we are no longer bound by the power of sin; we do not have to obey its promptings. But sin itself and the temptation to sin still exist, and that temptation often attacks through the emotions. Feelings are stirred and desires roused that conflict with the will of God. If we do not turn away from the temptation and look to the resources of the Holy Spirit to enable us to stand firm against these desires, other parts of the soul soon become affected. The will is weakened to resist and the mind begins to justify the actions. Step by step the people concerned slip into the sinful relationship. Their reason is distorted by the intensity of the emotional involvement.

In no way are we to excuse what is sin. But we are to understand it, and know compassion for those who become involved in such relationships. A little later Paul says to the Galatians:

> Brothers, if someone is caught in a sin, you who are spiritual should restore him gently. But watch yourself, or you also may be tempted (Gal. 6:1).

We all need to heed that advice and warning. That is the reason we have looked at this matter at some length. It is obvious that those who give in to sexual sin have offended the holiness of God. But for every person of the Spirit, sin is always "lurking at the door". The power of sin no longer controls him, but exists and will try to reclaim his life. Look at the other things Paul puts alongside sexual immorality when he is writing to Christians:

> The acts of the sinful nature are obvious, sexual immorality, impurity and debauchery; idolatry and witchcraft; hatred, discord, jealousy, fits of rage, selfish ambition, dissensions, factions and envy; drunkenness, orgies and the like (Gal. 5:19–21).

All these are acts of the sinful nature. Discord, jealousy, envy, rage, selfish ambition are not the outworking of the new nature; they are not evidence of the Holy Spirit at work; they are not the fruit of those living 'in Christ Jesus'. Paul continues:

> I warn you, as I did before, that those who live like this will not inherit the kingdom of God (v. 21).

This is a warning that he has needed to repeat. God desires His children to be living lives that are a demonstration of the life of His Kingdom. In the midst of the self-willed disobedience of the world, God's children are to be seen living holy lives, set apart for Him, reflecting His life. Any of those things that Paul lists here is a denial of that life.

It is easy for Christians to be led into jealousy, rage, selfish ambition, etc., because these are the natural emotional response of their souls to situations in which they are placed. God intends the soul to be under the influence and direction of the Holy Spirit. When the soul is fulfilling selfish desires it is utterly opposing the working of His Spirit. Before pointing the finger at the misdemeanour of others, grievous though their sins may be to the witness of the Church, let us heed what Paul says: "But watch yourself, or you also may be tempted."

FRUIT OF THE SPIRIT
Contrast all this with what the Spirit of God produces as His fruit in our lives:

> But the fruit of the Spirit is love, joy, peace, patience, kindness, goodness, faithfulness, gentleness and self-control. Against such things there is no law (Gal. 5:22 –23).

The sinful nature is "a slave to the law of sin". Through the cross we are delivered from that sinful nature and thereby set free from the law of sin. That law still exists, but is no longer the guiding principle in the life of the faithful Christian. In him, the Holy Spirit wants to produce His fruit, and Paul says that no law can withstand the power of that fruit. "Love, joy, peace, patience, kindness, goodness, faithfulness, gentleness and self-control": those are the qualities that we most want to see in our own lives and that others desire to see in us. They only grow through the power of the Holy Spirit within us.

The most effective way to withstand the pressures of sin around us is to be built up in the life of the Spirit. For the Spirit of God guides us into all truth, directs us to the will and purpose of God, and creates in us the qualities of life against which sin will not prevail.

The Holy Spirit, it needs to be repeated, is not given simply to enable gifts and to lead us into the right demonstration of God's miraculous power in our lives. He is also given to create that holiness of life that God intends for us, to produce the fruit of the Spirit within us, to enable us to stand firm against the pressures of sin around us. It is only in the power of the Holy Spirit that we can live in the power of the new nature that God has given us, confessing His words of truth that we are 'in Christ Jesus'.

FREEDOM

> It is for freedom that Christ has set us free. Stand firm, then, and do not let yourselves be burdened again by a yoke of slavery (Gal. 5:1).

God does not want our lives to come under any bondage again; instead, He wants to be leading us into a greater experience of liberty – freedom to do God's will in the power of the Holy Spirit, and to resist the temptations of the world, the flesh and the devil.

That yoke of slavery is law. We can interpret that as the law of sin from which we have been freed, as well as trying to please God by any legalistic form of religious practice.

> You, my brothers, were called to be free. But do not use your freedom to indulge the sinful nature; rather, serve one another in love (Gal. 5:13).

Learn this lesson well. You may be born of the Spirit and be filled with the Holy Spirit, but do not imagine that every thought and desire you have is the work of the Spirit. Your soul is not yet perfected; it is not fully trained. You can still have thoughts, desires and feelings that are contrary to the Spirit. God is wanting that soul of yours to come exclusively under the direction of the Holy Spirit. You are deceiving yourself if you imagine you have already attained that.

> Not that I have already obtained all this, or have already been made perfect, but I press on to take hold of that for which Christ Jesus took hold of me. I do not consider myself yet to have taken hold of it. But one thing I do; forgetting what is behind and straining towards what is ahead, I press on towards the goal to win the prize for which God has called me heavenwards in Christ Jesus. All of us who are mature should take such a view of things. . . . Only let us live up to what we have already attained (Phil. 3:12–16).

NOT BOUND BY THE PAST

Christians do not need to live by the past, as if they are still under compulsion to sin or to grieve God by wilful disobedience.

Since we live by the Spirit, let us keep in step with the Spirit (Gal. 5:25).

His own Presence lives within us to enable faithful obedience to Him, if we will only look to the resources of the Holy Spirit. To live in victory over temptation and sin and to know the victory of faith over adverse circumstances is to trust in the Person of God the Holy Spirit living within us. For it is the Spirit who directs us to the truth of God's word, the truth that sets us free and enables us to live in freedom.

The only alternative is to believe the circumstances around us and the fears and negative feelings within us, that are our natural reactions to problems. The Spirit declares Jesus and His promises to our hearts and minds. So we need to be sensitive to His indwelling Presence.

That sensitivity is crucial. It is one thing to know that God has filled you with the Holy Spirit; it is another to learn sensitivity in His presence and leading. It was that sensitivity that was obviously lacking among some of the Christians at Corinth. No one could question the validity or power of the Holy Spirit's presence among them. But they lacked the sensitivity that comes with love for God and others.

Chapter 13 of 1 Corinthians is not, as some wrongly claim, an appeal by Paul to show that he prefers the way of love to the way of spiritual gifts. He tells the Corinthians to desire those gifts. The most excellent way is not the way of love without gifts, but the way of gifts used and expressed in love.

The life, work, fruit and gifts of the Spirit are to be expressed in human lives, through human personalities. Any manifestation of the Holy Spirit's Presence can be marred by the attitude of the one through whom that manifestation occurs. If it is manifested without love, it is of no value. In fact, it will be counter-productive.

And if I have a faith that can move mountains, but have not love, I am nothing (1 Cor. 13:2).

The Holy Spirit is God. God is love. The Holy Spirit is the Spirit of love. The man of the Spirit will increasingly manifest a life of love that will demonstrate obedience to the Lord's threefold command of love – to love Him, to love our neighbour, and to love our fellow Christians as He has loved us.

> Love is patient, love is kind. It does not envy, it does not boast, it is not proud. It is not rude, it is not self-seeking, it is not easily angered, it keeps no record of wrongs. Love does not delight in evil but rejoices with the truth. It always protects, always trusts, always hopes, always perseveres. Love never fails (1 Cor. 13:4–8).

Such love is the fulfilment of one living in the power of his new nature 'in Christ Jesus'. Notice again how these qualities of love are the direct opposite of the natural inclinations of the sinful self.

THE ACTIONS OF THE SOUL UNDER THE POWER OF THE NEW NATURE

OLD NATURE SELF	NEW NATURE SPIRIT
Envies	Loves
Boasting	Joyful
Proud	Patient
Rude	Kind
Self-seeking	Good
Angry	Faithful
Resentful	Gentle
Impure	Self-controlled
Unfaithful	Humble
Helpless	Forgiving
Fickle	Truthful
Untruthful	Protecting
Enjoys evil –	Full of hope
sexual immorality	Persevering
witchcraft	Dependable
occult practices	
drunkenness	

God's Dividing Word

These lists are not exhaustive, but they give some impression of the way in which the old and new natures are contrasted in the New Testament. We cannot expect people to demonstrate the right-hand column unless they are 'born of the Spirit', and are allowing the Holy Spirit to direct their lives and reproduce His life in them. Neither should we be surprised that there is so much of the left-hand column evident in the world around us, in the society in which we live.

Your soul was conditioned by much of the 'old' before your conversion. The transformation that the Holy Spirit is bringing about in you will enable more of the 'new' to be seen in you. Your new birth is the event that initiates that process. The process itself is a gradual one, for fruit is produced as the result of growth. How rapid that growth is will depend upon whether your concentration is on the things of the Spirit, or whether you still want to run your own life in your own way, trying to make God fit into the framework of the life you have constructed for yourself.

There can be no doubt which God intends. Any half-hearted response to Him only results in conflict between the old and the new. You are not truly reckoning yourself dead to that old life of self.

> You are not your own; you were bought at a price. Therefore honour God with your body (1 Cor. 6:19–20).

He lives in us that we may recognise His complete claim upon our lives as His holy people. That can only be effected as we constantly affirm the offering of ourselves to Him, to live for His will and glory. That is the worship that He desires. Is all worship acceptable to God? Is it acceptable if it comes from self-seeking hearts, disobedient lives, from those concerned to live by their own selfish intent rather than by His Spirit? Is that what He wants? Does that glorify Him? Or is it a reflection of this scripture?

> These people honour me with their lips, but their hearts are far from me.
> They worship me in vain; their teachings are but rules taught by men (Mark 7:6–7).

That does not imply that we shall need to reach perfection of soul before our worship is acceptable to God, but that we are to co-operate with the working of His Spirit within us, yielding ourselves to His will and purpose, that more of His life may be expressed in us.

> Therefore, I urge you, brothers, in view of God's mercy, to offer your bodies as living sacrifices, holy and pleasing to God – which is your spiritual worship (Rom. 12:1).

The imperfections of our offering, of the worship of our lives, are covered by the cross. We offer ourselves as those who know that the self-principle has been put to death in us. We do not need to indulge that self or seek fulfilment of that self any longer. Now we are free to seek the glory of God in our lives.

THE HOLY SPIRIT LEADS

Although the Holy Spirit lives within us, how much He will be allowed to order our lives will depend upon how readily we submit to the Lordship of Jesus. The Holy Spirit does not 'take us over', He does not interfere with the response of our wills to the love of God. He will lead us, not compel us.

The Holy Spirit will only lead those Christians who are willing to be led by Him, those who want to be guided by Jesus and to be obedient to Him. This is true both personally and corporately.

The individual Christian remains a Christian, even if He is disobedient to the Lord and closed in His attitude to the work of the Holy Spirit in His life. The Holy Spirit can lead the Christian congregation that is willing to submit to God's authority, recognising that it is *His* church. But there are many congregations that do not even seek His will, let alone want it or fulfil it; there is little or no concept of the Holy Spirit having a particular purpose for them that can only be fulfilled in His power and love and under His anointing. One thing is certain, any congregation that sees its purpose as something that does not require that constant, fresh, spontaneous anointing of the Holy Spirit has substituted something of the soul for the genuine work of the Spirit.

The Holy Spirit can be present without being powerful. He is present in every child of God, but is only powerful when the life of that child is truly submitted to the purposes of the Lord.

The flow of the Spirit in every part of our lives is hindered by disobedience. The flow of the Spirit in the life of any congregation will be hindered by disobedience in that congregation.

Your words of faith: "THE WORD OF GOD IS LIVING AND ACTIVE, SHARPER THAN ANY DOUBLE-EDGED SWORD; IT PENETRATES EVEN TO DIVIDING SOUL AND SPIRIT, JOINTS AND MARROW; IT JUDGES THE THOUGHTS AND ATTITUDES OF THE HEART." "YOU, HOWEVER, ARE CONTROLLED NOT BY THE SINFUL NATURE BUT BY THE SPIRIT, IF THE SPIRIT OF GOD LIVES IN YOU." "LIVE BY THE SPIRIT AND YOU WILL NOT GRATIFY THE DESIRES OF THE SINFUL NATURE."

32

FOR THE GLORY OF GOD

Is all this really possible or practical? Does God expect us to be so spiritual? Surely He knows the limitations of our humanity and has given us our souls and bodies, with all their desires? Does He, therefore, expect such a life of self-denial?

And what about the world we live in? Isn't it true that we can be so heavenly-minded that we are no earthly good? What about all the practical needs of men: the starving, the refugees, the social outcasts? Isn't this preoccupation with spiritual life a retreat from reality and from facing the needs of such people? How can you talk about waiting on the Lord and His refining in our lives, when there is so much to *do*?

The questions continue to pour out of our souls, and if not from our own souls, there are plenty of others around us who will voice them for us.

TRUE WORSHIP

Jesus addressed Himself to the root cause of men's needs, to the heart of their problem. He shows us, above all, that the purpose of life is for the glory of God.

> Yet a time is coming and has now come when the true worshipers will worship the Father in spirit and truth; for they are the kind of worshippers the Father seeks. God is spirit, and his worshippers must worship in spirit and in truth (John 4:23–24).

We are called to a life of worship. That does not mean a life of services. It is a life of losing ourselves for God, of pouring ourselves out for Him.

He is more aware of the needs of the world and cares more about the welfare of individual people than any of us does. He knows that the only way to save people is the way of Jesus. He calls us, therefore, to share His life, His love and His power with all men. It is for Him to give to each Christian his own particular ministry or service. Every Christian is a gift from God to the Church and to the world:

> We have different gifts, according to the grace given us. If a man's gift is prophesying, let him use it in proportion to his faith. If it is serving, let him serve; if it is teaching, let him teach; if it is encouraging, let him encourage; if it is contributing to the needs of others, let him give generously; if it is leadership, let him govern diligently; if it is showing mercy, let him do it cheerfully (Rom. 12:6–8).

The Christian's ability to minister the life of Jesus to others is dependent upon his ministry in love and worship to the Lord. His ability to meet the needs of others is dependent upon his faith in the Lord.

There is a huge difference between supporting people in their needs and actually meeting those needs. Jesus came to do the latter, although often we will only allow Him to do the former. The soul reaches out in sympathy and compassion to human affliction; the Spirit of God wants to meet the total need of those who are afflicted.

The natural man, if moved to do good, says: "Get on with the job." The spiritual man is no less active, but is not compelled by the urge for activity. In his actions, he is led and guided by the Spirit; when he does act there will be much "fruit that will last" (John 15:16).

This principle applies to such 'practical' needs as feeding the hungry. Paul says that if it is a man's ministry to give, he should give generously. But he needs to know where to give, when to give, to whom to give, that the gift may be used in the best possible way.

And no amount of activity, of serving, of ministering must ever get in the way of the giving of ourselves in worship to the Lord. It is He who is worthy of our total self-giving. It is He who has paid the price for us that we might be His. It is He who has given His all to us, that we might give our all to Him.

He will not waste what is offered and given to Him. The humanist would say that such worship is a waste of good time that could be spent in meeting the needs of others; that giving financially for the sake of the gospel is denying food to empty stomachs.

The Christian understands human needs better. What is the purpose of filling a stomach if the spirit of the man remains alienated from Jesus, the living Lord? What, on the other hand, is the purpose of preaching the gospel if one is not prepared to meet the physical needs of those to whom one is ministering? It is not an 'either-or' situation, but 'both-and'. Because God is concerned about the whole man, so should the Christian be. He has food to give, spiritual as well as physical food, that will meet the need of body, soul and spirit.

GIVING WHOLENESS
The man who is sensitive to the Spirit of God will be more acutely aware of the needs of others, and more sacrificial in his giving to meet those needs. And yet he will know that the secret of his life is his giving to God, his worship of the

Lord, his dependence upon Him in prayer. Praise needs to flow freely from his heart. If there was no one else to serve, it would be worth living to minister only to the Lord.

When that is our attitude, then we see that every act of giving is in expression of our giving to Him. Giving to others must never become a substitute for our giving to Him; it is not something we do to try to impress Him with our goodness. Neither is it a spectacle to impress others; nor do we give to satisfy a personal need to give. We give as God directs us, remembering that He will waste nothing; and to those who give, He gives back "good measure, pressed down, shaken together and running over".

> When you give to the needy, do not let your left hand know what your right hand is doing, so that your giving may be in secret. Then your Father, who sees what is done in secret, will reward you (Matt. 6:3–4).

Gaining reward is not the motive for giving, but it is the result of giving and serving quietly and without fuss, in obedience to the Lord.

One of the problems of the soul is the desire to see immediate fruit. The Christian craves to be used, and often to be used in great and impressive ways. And yet serving the Lord does not always produce tangible results immediately.

One of the ways in which the Lord deals with that strong soul-life is to take us through a period when we feel utterly useless, as if there is no fruit being produced in our lives. We feel that we are of no use to the Lord or to anyone else. He shows us the futility of so much of our scheming and planning, and of our activity, even though it is done with the best of intentions – in His name even!

If we minister to the Lord, He will minister through us to others. If we serve the Lord, putting Him before all else, He will serve others through us. If we give ourselves wholeheartedly to the Lord in worship, He will minister His presence and His life through us. If we acknowledge that all our money is rightfully His, then He will be able to use far more of it to meet the needs of others than if we only apportioned a certain amount for specific charities. If our

For the Glory of God

lives are given wholly to Him, then our attitude will be that the Lord has the right to take whatever He wants whenever He wants. We are not concerned to pursue our own careers, paying a bit of 'conscience money' to the Lord's work.

The Spirit needs to be the governing force in the soul, that the body may respond to His purpose and be doing His will. It is easy to become preoccupied in doing and serving, and miss what God is saying to us. The way in which we fill our lives with over-activity is the demonstration of the fact that we still place value in that activity, whether it is led or inspired by God or not. This is true even of the proclaiming of the Gospel. The truth is often preached without the preacher seeking the anointing of God. The sick go away unhealed, because the minister has not sought the faith of God.

Unless the Spirit is the guiding influence in our lives, much of our thinking, speaking and activity is useless. "Apart from me, you can do nothing." Never mind the taunts of those who claim it is a waste of time to worship, to pray, to study the word of God! They speak only in ignorance.

> "For my thoughts are not your thoughts, neither are your ways my ways," declares the Lord. "As the heavens are higher than the earth, so are my ways higher than your ways and my thoughts than your thoughts" (Isa. 55:8–9).

God promises fruitfulness to those who act in obedience to His word.

> As the rain and the snow come down from heaven, and do not return to it without watering the earth and making it bud and flourish, so that it yields seed for the sower and bread for the eater, so is my word that goes out from my mouth. It will not return to me empty, but will accomplish what I desire and achieve the purpose for which I sent it (Isa. 55:10–11).

It is the word that will accomplish the purposes of God in us and through us. It is by putting His word into practice that we shall be fruitful and increase in fruitfulness. It is by speaking His word to our hearts that God will prune out of our lives those things that cause His work in us to be hindered.

FOR THE LORD

We live for the Lord Himself – not for some work that He gives us. We are, therefore, to seek the Lord for Himself, not only for the answers to the problems that arise in the ministry that He gives us.

Never do you need to look to the ways in which God uses others, and try to copy them. That will have disastrous results. As you seek the Lord for Himself, so He will give you that unique ministry that is right for you. The way the Lord can use you is dependent upon how much you love and praise Him.

He knows you better than you know yourself. He knows best what to do with the lives of His children. He never makes mistakes.

Sometimes Christians complain about the premature death of a believer whose love for the Lord is great, "What a waste! Why didn't God heal him? He could have done so much good in the world."

Is it really a waste to see a life poured out for God, even to the point of death? Have you not seen much fruit coming from those who meet their deaths with joy and an unshaken faith in the love and goodness of God?

His economy is often very different from ours. It is only a waste from *our* point of view. That is usually the response of the soul, of our affection for that person. Many have come into the Kingdom of God through the witness of dying Christians. He redeems every situation through the cross of Jesus. Even when His purpose of healing is not effected He will turn the situation for His own glory and the good of His Kingdom.

God will not waste even the death of His children. And death reminds us of the absolute sovereignty of our God, of our total dependence upon Him.

Through His Spirit and His word, God wants to reveal not only His ways to us; He wants also to reveal Himself.

For the Glory of God

He wants us to know Him. "I want to know *him* and the power of his resurrection," says Paul (Phil. 3:10).

And we only know *Him* as we spend time with Him in worship, adoration and praise. We can know much about Him through studying the word. Study is no substitute for union with Him in the bond of the Spirit. It is as we give to Him that we grow to appreciate Him and know more of the wonder of His glory, His grace, His love and power.

This is not the seeking of God in intercession and petition, asking for needs to be met, important though that is, but a giving of ourselves to Him, enjoying His presence, abiding in Him. It is not a question of seeking great emotional experiences of God, although the emotions cannot remain untouched by a revelation of God's love, for the Spirit floods the life of the soul at such times. Rather it is learning the truth: "Be still, and know that I am God" (Ps. 46:10 R.S.V.).

How can a husband and wife grow in love for one another unless they spend time together, not only in doing things, but also in enjoying each other's company? God wants us to enjoy His Presence, to spend time being with Him – asking nothing, wanting nothing more than to know Him.

> But thanks be to God, who always leads us in triumphal procession in Christ and through us spreads everywhere the fragrance of the knowledge of him. For we are to God the aroma of Christ among those who are being saved and those who are perishing. To the one we are the smell of death; to the other, the fragrance of life. And who is equal to such a task? (2 Cor. 2:14–16).

To many in the world there is no fragrance coming from Christians. They can ignore them as an irrelevance, a quaint overhang from the past. The sweetness of Jesus can only be seen in the lives of those who not only talk about Him, *but also know Him*. And that knowledge of Him will come out of their union with Him in adoration, worship and praise. We can be full of zeal for His work, for His Kingdom, for the spreading of His word, but God wants to see us giving the world the fragrance of *Him*. That can only happen in as much as we are prepared to give ourselves to Him for Himself.

Otherwise, our evangelism will seem hard and unloving, for all its good intention and zeal. It is what we are that we give to others, not only what we say or do. And what we are is dependent solely upon what God has made us, and how much of His Presence is communicated through us.

And so the Lord will deal with and remove from our lives those things that are unworthy of His presence, and obscure the fact that we live in Him.

Others need to see Jesus in us so that they desire Him, that where there is no hunger for Him hunger is created.

And so the work of the cross will cut more and more deeply into our lives; there will be that dying to self that more of the risen Saviour may be communicated through us.

> Now I commit you to God and to the word of his grace, which can build you up and give you an inheritance among all those who are sanctified (Acts. 20:32).

Your words of faith: "GOD IS SPIRIT, AND HIS WORSHIPPERS MUST WORSHIP IN SPIRIT AND TRUTH." "THANKS BE TO GOD, WHO ALWAYS LEADS US IN TRIUMPHAL PROCESSION IN CHRIST, AND THROUGH US SPREADS EVERYWHERE THE FRAGRANCE OF THE KNOWLEDGE OF HIM."

33

IN CHRIST TOGETHER

As we discover the rich inheritance that we have in Christ, we see that this is shared with every other believer in Christ. Each of us needs the personal revelation of the Holy Spirit to enable us to understand what it is to be dead and raised to new life with Jesus and to live as a child of God. Similarly the Church needs revelation to understand how the corporate

In Christ Together

body of believers appears to the Lord, and what His intentions and purposes are for His Body.

Our concepts of the Church are marred by the imperfect expressions of the Church seen in denominational structures. The Church is to demonstrate the new life of Jesus Christ. The Son gave His life that many sons might be born of the Spirit. Those sons are to live in fellowship with God the Father and Jesus, and also in fellowship with one another.

> Our fellowship is with the Father and with his Son, Jesus Christ (1 John 1:3).
> But if we walk in the light, as he is in the light, we have fellowship with one another, and the blood of Jesus, his Son, purifies us from every sin (1 John 1:7).

The word 'fellowship' means literally 'the sharing of life'. We share in the life of the Father and the Son. We live in God and He in us. Christians are also to share their lives with one another. This was clearly seen in the early days of the Church, not simply in terms of spiritual theory, but in the practical details of their lives:

> All the believers were one in heart and mind. No one claimed that any of his possessions was his own, but they shared everything they had. With great power the apostles continued to testify to the resurrection of the Lord Jesus, and much grace was with them all. There were no needy persons among them (Acts. 4:32–34).

The Holy Spirit led those Christians into a corporate sharing of their lives, and therefore of their assets. Any church fellowship today should be a similar expression of the unity that the Holy Spirit wants to express among God's children.

It was this unity for which Jesus prayed in the great prayer recorded in John, chapter 17, a unity that was to be a reflection of the fellowship, the unity, that exists between the Father and the Son.

> Holy Father, protect them by the power of your name – the name you gave me – so that they may be one as we

are one (v. 11). I pray also for those who will believe in me through their message, that all of them may be one, Father, just as you are in me and I am in you. May they also be in us so that the world may believe that you have sent me (vv. 20–21).

We think of the unity of the Church in terms of the need to break down the barriers of denominationalism. God surely does not want to see His Church divided, even structurally. But Jesus is not praying that here. He is concerned about the unity which Christians are to express in their relationships with one another. He is praying about relationships, not structures. It does not matter how men reorganise the structures of the denominations, there will never be the unity for which Jesus prayed until there is unity in the relationships between believers. And that starts in every locality where the Church exists. Jesus continued:

I have given them the glory that you gave me, that they may be one as we are one; I in them and you in me. May they be brought to complete unity to let the world know that you sent me and have loved them even as you have loved me (vv. 22–23).

The unity for which Jesus prayed has been made possible because He has restored us to the glory of the Father. Without the cross there could never be fellowship with God or with others. Twice Jesus states that this unity among Christians is essential, because it will affect the witness of the Church in the world: "so that the world may believe that you have sent me". The scandal of disunity among Christians is an obvious and easy target of criticism for those who oppose the gospel.

More than that, the quality of love that should exist between believers should be such that it is a witness to non-believers of the power of God's love for His children. There should be an obvious unity of relationship within any congregation or fellowship, so that the people living in that locality know there is a love among them that is powerful and is to be found nowhere else.

Jesus gave a new command to His disciples:

In Christ Together

> My command is this: love each other as I have loved you (John 15:12).

The love between Christians is to be a reflection of the sacrificial love that Jesus has for them. And He spells out clearly what this means:

> Greater love has no one than this, that one lay down his life for his friends. You are my friends if you do what I command (vv. 13–14).

Jesus showed that to love meant to serve, to live for others and not yourself. That is what it means to be a member of the true Church. God draws us into His Body, that we may learn what it is to live for one another, to love and serve others.

We have to recognise that we do not want to do that – that is why there are so few congregations and fellowships that manifest that quality of love. Living for others, serving, loving, giving, is certainly what the Spirit wants, but it is diametrically opposed to the desires of the flesh, of the sinful, selfish nature.

We have to learn the personal victory of the new nature not only within our individual lives, but also in our relationships with others. Of ourselves, we do not want to be too deeply involved with others. A common attitude is: "I will keep myself to myself", or "I don't want to get involved." And so church-going has become a routine for many people, who perhaps never have any real contact or fellowship with other members of the congregation.

Such attitudes are the evidence of a lack of new life, or of unwillingness to live in the power of that new life by recognising that the old independent attitudes have been crucified with Christ. The cross is the death-blow to independence, not only from God but also from other believers. It cannot be God's will for any congregation to manifest the isolated, independent attitudes of the old nature.

This problem is so grave and deep-seated that it is always the 'crunch-point' for any body of believers seeking to be renewed in the power of the Holy Spirit. Many people are willing to receive personal blessing from God, but when He says to that group that the time has come for them to face realistically what it means to love one another, there is always a violent reaction from some who feel threatened by such a suggestion.

That can be a demonstration of fear. It may be that they have never had any real and meaningful relationships with others, and will need to be led lovingly and gently into such relationships. For others, the word of the Spirit has come up against the desires of self.

Some will long for such relationships of love; others want the Lord to be real to them, but still want to order their own lives around their own independent attitudes.

No Christian can be a one-man church. He is part of a body of believers.

> In Christ we who are many form one body, and each member belongs to all the others (Rom. 12:5).

We need each other. We are not to be battling alone in our Christian lives and witness. By His Spirit God gives to each believer a ministry and gifts that are not self-sufficient, but that will enable him to contribute towards the life of the whole body of loving people:

> Now the body is not made up of one part but of many. If the foot should say, "Because I am not a hand, I do not belong to the body", it would not for that reason cease to be part of the body. And if the ear should say, "Because I am not an eye, I do not belong to the body", it would not for that reason cease to be part of the body. If the whole body were an eye, where would the sense of hearing be? If the whole body were an ear, where would the sense of smell be? But in fact God has arranged the parts in the body, every one of them, just as he wanted them to be (1 Cor. 12:14–18).

EXPRESSING THE UNITY WE HAVE
Jesus is not asking us to create a unity or a fellowship of our own; He wants us to express the unity we already have 'in Him' because together we live in Him. He desires that we

In Christ Together

take off the old attitudes of fear, independence and selfishness, and put on the new nature corporately of love, unity and fellowship; that we express corporately our life 'in Christ Jesus'.

That means giving up to Him all our ideas and wishes for a particular congregation, and yielding to the leading of the Holy Spirit. Very few congregations are in fact submitted to His leadership. The church is plagued by 'what-I-want' sickness, everybody wanting the worship and life of that local congregation to reflect his own views and wishes. And if anybody upsets those wishes, then there are plenty of other churches to attend.

That is the heart of the problem. You cannot attend the real Church; you have to be part of it, the living body of Christ, ready to devote your life to God in loving obedience to the leading of the Holy Spirit.

We are one in Christ; that unity is to be expressed between us. All Christians bear the same surname: 'in Christ'. We meet together in His name and that means in His Presence:

> For where two or three come together in my name, there am I with them (Matt. 18:20).

God has promised that His presence will be with us always; so Jesus is obviously referring to a very particular awareness of the power of His Presence when we meet together in His name.

He has promised to answer our prayers as individual believers, but He also gives this stunning promise:

> Again, I tell you that if two of you agree on earth about anything you ask for, it will be done for you by my Father in heaven (Matt. 18:19).

I see constant evidence of this in my ministry. At any meeting, one of the most important factors as to how powerfully the Holy Spirit will be able to move to change lives and bring healing to God's people is the corporate faith of the congregation. If the level of faith in the Body is high (and it is easy to sense when it is) then you know that many powerful demonstrations of God's Presence are going to take place.

By the same token, when the 'faithometer' reads zero (or even sub-zero!) you know that you are going to have to proceed on your own faith in the sheer grace of God to work despite the unbelief of the people. When faith in the Body is high, the one who is ministering is carried along by the response of the congregation. Where the opposite is the case, one feels empty and 'wrung-out' by the end of the service.

There are many 'wrung-out' Christians longing for unity and meaningful fellowship in their congregations. For God wants us all to bear each other up in faith, that the Spirit may carry us along together in His purposes.

> Carry each other's burdens, and in this way you will fulfil the law of Christ (Gal. 6:2).

WHERE WE BELONG

We belong *together* to God; we live *together* in Christ. The great truths about being in Christ are truths that relate to *all* who are born of the Spirit.

We cannot belong to Jesus and live in Him, and belong to the world at the same time. Jesus did not pray that His Father would take His disciples out of the world, because it is in the world that their witness was needed.

We do not belong to the kingdom of this world, but to the Kingdom of heaven. God's calling upon our lives is to continue the ministry of Jesus in the world, to be part of the answer to the prayer that He told us to pray:

> Your kingdom come, your will be done on earth as it is in heaven (Matt. 6:10).

It is for that reason that God has put us in His Son *now*, while we are in this world.

Clearly, no individual can continue the ministry of Jesus. But each has a contribution to make to the life of the Body, and *together*, by the power of the Holy Spirit, we are to be the 'new incarnation', the Body of Christ in the world.

Our life together, then, is to demonstrate the life and

power of God's heavenly Kingdom within His creation, bringing His light into darkness, His life where there is living death, His healing where there is pain and sickness, His provision where there is need.

Jesus ended His prayer in John 17 with these words about all believers:

> I have made you known to them, and will continue to make you known in order that the love you have for me may be in them and that I myself may be in them (v. 26).

To enable us to continue His ministry, Jesus prays that the Father's own love for the Son may be in us. That love has been given to us in the gift of the Holy Spirit. It is only by the power of that love overflowing our lives that we will be able to have the relationships of love that will be the witness of God's Presence among us and that the world needs to see.

No individual Christian can be the Body of Christ. To live 'in Christ Jesus' is to be one with all others who are in Him, regardless of their denomination, colour or tradition:

> You are all one in Christ Jesus (Gal. 3:28).

God knows where His true Church is: those who live in Him. That true Church cannot be identified with any denominational structure, nor any non-denominational group, either! It comprises all those who are accepted, redeemed, and who live in Jesus. This mystical union is deeper than any apparent disunity. It is a unity that is recognised whenever believers come together in the power of the Holy Spirit.

All the gifts that God gives by His Holy Spirit are to build up the life of the Body; they are not for the glorification of the one through whom they are expressed.

> Now to each one the manifestation of the Spirit is given for the common good (1 Cor. 12:7).
>
> It was he who gave some to be apostles, some to be prophets, some to be evangelists, and some to be pastors and teachers, to prepare God's people for works of service, so that the body of Christ may be built up until

we all reach unity in the faith and in the knowledge of the Son of God and become mature, attaining to the whole measure of the fulness of Christ (Eph. 4:11–13).

Clearly, as Paul says, that 'unity in the faith' does not yet exist, although our essential unity in Christ does. It is together that we are to grow to maturity in the knowledge and fulness of Christ.

That same Spirit will guide us into all truth, because He is the Spirit of truth. None of us has our doctrine perfect; certainly none of us has our living-out of that doctrine perfect. As together our lives become open to the Spirit, so He will draw us together in our understanding of the truth and our ability to live it by His grace.

Those who will not commit themselves to the life of the body will not truly commit themselves to the authority of God Himself:

> For anyone who does not love his brother, whom he has seen, cannot love God, whom he has not seen. And he has given us this command: whoever loves God must also love his brother (1 John 4:20–21).

The cross has to deal with that streak of independence that is so strong in so many. When a man becomes a Christian, that should be the end of his independence, for that has been crucified with Christ along with all that belongs to the sinful nature. Paul includes 'hatred, discord, jealousy, fits of rage, selfish ambition, dissensions, factions and envy' in the list of things that lead to this warning: "those who live like this will not inherit the kingdom of God" (Gal. 5:21). For all these are manifestations of the pride of independence and self-sufficiency.

> Christ loved the church and gave himself up for her to make her holy, cleansing her by the washing with water through the word, and to present her to himself as a radiant church, without stain or wrinkle or any other blemish, but holy and blameless (Eph. 5:25–27).

It is God's enemy that seeks to sow rebellion, disharmony and disunity among God's children, for he recognises the power that is manifested whenever a group of Christians do express their unity in Christ. He likes nothing more than to encourage Christians to act independently of God and of one another, just as he tempted Eve first and then Adam through her. He knows our individual weakness; but he also knows the potential effectiveness of our corporate strength.

It is because of this that Jesus needed to pray to the Father: "May they be one." We Christians need to see ourselves as part of the answer to that prayer, 'so that the world might know that you have sent me and have loved them even as you have loved me'.

Your words of faith: "OUR FELLOWSHIP IS WITH THE FATHER AND WITH HIS SON, JESUS CHRIST." "MAY THEY ALSO BE ONE IN US SO THAT THE WORLD MAY BELIEVE THAT YOU HAVE SENT ME." "MAY THEY BE BROUGHT TO COMPLETE UNITY TO LET THE WORLD KNOW THAT YOU SENT ME AND HAVE LOVED THEM EVEN AS YOU HAVE LOVED ME."

34

THE NEW AND THE LIVING WAY

Through the cross, men are freed not only from sin but also from law, from trying to please God through religious observance and practices, even if they are in a Christian format.

LAW OF THE OLD TESTAMENT
The law of the Old Testament was not wrong or bad; it was given by God Himself and reveals what He wants of His people. But it had no power to change men or to give them the spiritual birth of which Jesus speaks.

> We know that the law is spiritual; but I am unspiritual, sold as a slave to sin (Rom. 7:14).

Even though the law is spiritual, it cannot meet the needs of unspiritual men. They need to be born of the Spirit to become spiritual. Only when crucified with Christ and cleansed with His blood could they be made acceptable in God's sight, and only through the activity of His own Holy Spirit within them could they possibly please Him.

Again, we are face to face with the utter weakness and uselessness of our old nature. Our flesh immediately wants to deny that, and claim some value for itself. But God has shown His estimate of it in the cross; the old life had to be crucified with Jesus:

> I know that nothing good lives in me, that is in my sinful nature. For I have the desire to do what is good, but I cannot carry it out (Rom. 7:18).

And so Paul comes to the conclusion: "Those controlled by the sinful nature cannot please God" (Rom. 8:8).

The old nature will want to insist that it is not all that bad, that it is capable of good works and lofty ideals. It is a great temptation to say that natural man is good in himself.

But that is not how God thinks. It does not matter what that unredeemed man produces; it cannot be acceptable to God because that man is unacceptable until he has come through the cross into the new life of Jesus. He can strive to produce the most beautiful and exquisite offerings, but unless he acknowledges that he is a sinner who needs to be reborn and made a new creature, he remains separated from the Lord by his sin and cannot please Him. He still needs to humble himself before God and accept the salvation that is made available to him through the death and resurrection of Jesus Christ.

Our failure to be able to keep the commandments of God demonstrates that, no matter how determined we are, we cannot please God of ourselves. Jesus reminded the disciples: "apart from me you can do nothing" (John 15:5). Such truth strikes at our pride.

Under the terms of the old covenant God made it clear what He expected of His people. The promise that He gave concerning the new covenant demonstrated that He was aware that men could not fulfil His expectations. Therefore

The New and Living Way

God Himself would come and do in them what He wanted. *He* would do it.

The Spirit-filled man wants to believe that he can do great things for God. God has done so much for him; now surely there is something that he can do for God!

The Lord confronts us with the fact that, even if we are born of the Spirit and are filled with the Spirit, there is still nothing we can do for Him – nothing that He will value, that is. Still, we are to live in His grace, allowing Him to do through us much greater things than we could ever achieve ourselves.

> So, my brothers, you also died to the law through the body of Christ, that you might belong to another, to him who was raised from the dead, in order that we might bear fruit to God (Rom. 7:4).

The law cannot produce the fruit in your life that God desires; that comes only through the Holy Spirit at work within you. The reason for this is clear. The law could not deal with man's sinful nature, the flesh. It could control that nature to a limited degree through effort and discipline. But that is all. It could not deal with the essential issue of sin and the power of sin that grips the man living under the influence of the sinful nature with which he was born.

Religious observance can control that sinful self, but cannot deal with those essential problems. Dependence upon church tradition and practice, rather than on the direct working of the cross in men's lives, produces only a travesty of the Christian faith, for such dependence cannot create new life nor produce the power of the Holy Spirit.

To be a Christian is to belong to a Person, not a religious institution: "that you might belong to another, to him who was raised from the dead".

Each year I witness great numbers of church-goers coming into the Kingdom of God. At a single service there can be hundreds who come to the cross and receive new life.

A few days ago I was leading a mission in the south-west of England. At the end of the service on the first evening a middle-aged man came forward to speak to me. He said that he had been a strong churchman all his life. Never had he heard the gospel presented before in such a way that clearly demanded a response from him. For the first time he had come to repentance, and knew that he had entered into a personal relationship with God.

For the rest of that mission I noticed this man sitting near the front every night. His face was aglow with the love of Jesus, his eyes wide open with interest as he soaked in the word of God.

That man is typical of thousands that I meet or who write to me. Why should this be? How can people attend church services for years and be inoculated against the heart of the gospel?

There are probably a number of answers: the essence of the gospel of salvation is not proclaimed to every congregation; people are not necessarily led to personal repentance; there can be good, faithful sowing of the word of God, but little effective reaping; often the gospel is presented without the anointing of the Spirit that quickens the hearts of those who hear; it is assumed wrongly by some pastors that their people have already come to repentance and new life.

Some church-going people do not want anything more than a Sunday religious acknowledgment of God. They do not think of Him as the Lord who will intervene in the circumstances of their lives with His love and mighty power. God is to be respected but not embraced too closely.

On the other hand, there are those who are crying out for reality in their spiritual lives. They want to know God, to be drawn closer to Him, and to experience His love in their lives. Without such reality the church will appear to be little more than a social club or friendly society with slight worship overtones. Services can appear lifeless and joyless – and they are. Young people can be deterred from seeking the living Christ, because those who claim to be His followers seem to them dowdy, solemn, lifeless people.

May God forgive us for such a witness. When we understand the work of the cross and live in the power of that revelation, our lives will be filled with wonder, joy and praise. All that will be experienced in our worship, too.

The New and Living Way

When the lives of God's children are filled with the vibrant love and power of the Holy Spirit, His Presence will be manifested among them in ways that are obvious to all observers.

I count it a great privilege to see God meeting with so many, some of whom have been longing for years to know the Lord in a personal way. I count it a privilege to see God empowering them with His Spirit, healing them and encouraging their faith.

What is it that sets them free? It is the word of truth. Perhaps they have never heard the truth; perhaps they have never received it; perhaps they have never responded to it; but when they do they are set free.

> So if the Son sets you free, you will be free indeed (John 8:36). Do you not know, brothers, – for I am speaking to men who know the law – that the law has authority over a man only as long as he lives? (Rom. 7:1).

If that is the case, death is called for – death to trying to please God by obeying commandments. Our human weakness only results in our continual failure to obey the Lord. His purpose was not to replace the law of the Old Testament by some kind of Christian law or church tradition.

> So, my brothers, you also died to the law through the body of Christ (Rom. 7:4).

Notice the tense "*you also died.*" That death has already taken place on the cross with Jesus.

Paul uses the illustration of marriage to point out that if a woman marries another man while her first husband is still alive, "she is called an adulteress." (Rom. 7:3).

It is 'spiritual adultery' to be united with Christ while still being wedded to the law! That is why Paul is so emphatic about the need to be dead to the impossibility of trying to please God by the observance of law, before being raised to new life with Jesus. That new life includes God's new way of working. He is working in us to achieve His purpose rather than by making legal demands that we cannot fulfil. It is only through the new way that we can be fruitful.

Under the new covenant it is Jesus Himself, living in us by the power of His Spirit, who will carry out God's purpose in us. That cannot happen as long as we still employ our weakness to try to please Him. Every time we do that, He allows us to fail. He wants us to trust His strength, not our own weakness. Then we shall look to Him for the power, anointing and strengthening of His Spirit. We shall be prepared to spend time waiting upon Him, to know His will and purpose, for to pursue any course of our own will not only be to employ our weakness, but will also be obvious disobedience that will grieve the Lord.

To be set free from the law does not invite disobedience to the will of God. It simply points out to us that there is only one way of obedience and that is through the activity of Jesus Christ in us. Because we are filled with God's own Spirit, His expectations of us are greater, not less – not that we should strive to please Him ourselves, but to allow Him to work in us and through us as He desires.

> May God himself, the God of peace, sanctify you through and through. May your whole spirit, soul and body be kept blameless at the coming of our Lord Jesus Christ. The one who calls you is faithful and he will do it (1 Thess. 5:23–24).

Yes, God is faithful and He will do it.

COMPLETE RELIANCE ON GOD

It is difficult for us to stop trying to achieve things ourselves. We live in a world where it is deemed successful to achieve, to accomplish, to prove your physical strength or ability, or your intellectual prowess. We are taught to be independent, to "stand on our own two feet" and not to rely upon others.

All this is totally different from God's way. He shows us that all human achievement is nothing. What really matters is what He has accomplished in His Son and what we allow Him to accomplish in us by His Spirit.

The more self-effort, the less scope is given for the activity of God's Spirit. Many would testify to God's sustaining grace through times of great difficulty, when human

The New and Living Way

resources were totally inadequate to meet the need. It is easier to turn a situation over to God when you recognise your inability to cope. God desires to teach us to turn every situation over to Him, even when we *can* humanly cope. God is not a last resort when all other devices have failed. Neither is it valid to say that we do not want to trouble Him unless it is absolutely necessary.

The extent to which He desires to be concerned and involved in every aspect of our lives is demonstrated by the fact that He comes to live in us in the Person of His Holy Spirit, that He may be pre-eminent in everything. Not to 'trouble' Him is to neglect that Presence and waste the resources that He has made available to us. It is to act as if still operating in the old life, instead of living in the power of our new nature.

It is a great day when a Christian realises that he is not expected to do anything *for* the Lord, but to allow Him to do everything through him. That is the gateway to a truly fruitful life. How else could the words of Jesus ever be fulfilled?

> I tell you the truth, anyone who has faith in me will do what I have been doing. He will do even greater things than these, because I am going to the Father (John 14:12).

And what happened when He returned to be with the Father? The Holy Spirit could then be poured out upon God's children. How could we ever do the same works as Jesus, except through the working of the same Spirit in us?

One thing is certain: we cannot depend on our own resources and on God's Spirit at the same time. If we are to trust Him, we shall have to learn not to trust in ourselves.

In the verses in which Paul expresses his dilemma notice how often the word 'I' occurs:

> *I* do not understand what *I* do. For what *I* want to do, *I* do not do, but what *I* hate *I* do. And if *I* do what *I* do not want to do, *I* agree that the law is good. As it is, it is no longer *I myself* who do it, but it is sin living in *me*. I know that nothing good lives in *me*, that is in *my* sinful nature.

> For *I* have the desire to do what is good, but *I* cannot carry it out. For what *I* do is not the good *I* want to do; no, the evil *I* do not want to do – this *I* keep on doing. Now if *I* do what *I* do not want to do, it is no longer *I* who do it, but it is sin living in *me* that does it.
> So *I* find this law at work. When *I* want to do good, evil is right there with *me*. For in my inner being *I* delight in God's law; but *I* see another law at work in the members of *my* body, waging war against the law of *my* mind and making *me* a prisoner of the law of sin at work within *my* members. What a wretched man *I* am! Who will rescue *me* from this body of death? (Rom. 7:15–24).

It is that 'I', the self, that is taken to the cross and put to death so that it may no longer dominate the lives of those who trust in Him.

Christian writers have argued endlessly as to whether this conflict refers to pre-conversion or post-conversion experience. Is Paul putting himself in the dilemma of a man before he comes to new life? He is seeking God and may be under conviction of sin, but is still not born again. Or is he speaking of his own conflict as a Christian, one who has been born again, but who needs to reckon that his old nature has been crucified with Christ?

Good arguments, each supported by abundant scriptural quotations, can be given for either case. Part of the genius of the scriptures is that they can speak in different ways to different people in different situations. We can rob them of that richness when we try to confine their meaning to one interpretation. Often several different interpretations each contain elements of the truth.

This passage certainly relates to the conflict of the man who is trying to serve God by law, by religious observance, and is not alive in the Spirit. Of him it is true when Paul says:

> I know that nothing good lives in me, that is in my sinful nature. For what I do is not the good I want to do; no, the evil I do not want to do – this I keep on doing.

The New and Living Way

But then the following verses can also describe the dilemma of the man who is born of the Spirit, but who does not reckon his old nature dead:

> When I want to do good, evil is right there with me. For in my inner being I delight in God's law; but I see another law at work in the members of my body, waging war against the law of my mind and making me a prisoner of the law of sin at work within my members.

We need spend no further time on the argument, for what Paul goes on to say gives the answer to either predicament: that of the man needing a new life, and that of the one who needs to reckon his old life dead.

For Paul's answer to this preoccupation with self, this striving and wanting to do what is right, while at the same time failing to accomplish it, is simple:

> Thanks be to God – through Jesus Christ our Lord! (Rom. 7:25).

He is the answer. It is He who cancels out the 'I'. Because of what He has done, we no longer need to depend upon law, upon self, upon our weakness:

> I have been crucified with Christ and I no longer live, but Christ lives in me. The life I live in the body, I live by faith in the Son of God, who loved me and gave himself for me (Gal. 2:20).

The life Paul previously lived 'in the body' was doomed to spiritual failure, because "I see another law at work in the members of my body, waging war against the law of my mind and making me a prisoner of the law of sin at work within my members." But *now* he stresses that "the life I live *in the body*, I live by faith in the Son of God." It is the same body, but a different principle is now at work within him. The Lord Jesus Himself lives there by the life and power of His Spirit. Paul can, therefore, live by faith in Him – that active continual trusting in His indwelling Presence.

Instead of the body being ruled by the law of sin and

death, it is now under the influence of the law of the Spirit of life. The weakness of the physical body, with all its desires and longings, persists. And Paul was conscious of the times when that body needed to be kept in its right place – not ruling his life with its appetites, but being in submission to the reign of God in His life.

So even doing good in the old way falls short of God's best purpose, for what He does in us and through us will be better still! Because He "has blessed us in the heavenly realms with every spiritual blessing in Christ", it would seem the height of folly to resort to our own weakness to try to please Him. Yet, sadly, this is why so much Christian endeavour ends in fruitless futility.

Unless God initiates it, the work will be fruitless for Him. That means that it has to be His idea. And unless He does it in us, it will likewise be unfruitful. As Paul points out to the Philippians: 'For it is God who works in you to will and to act according to his good purpose' (2:13).

> No, I beat my body and make it my slave so that after I have preached to others, I myself will not be disqualified for the prize (1 Cor. 9:27).

The soul and the body need to be kept under the direction of the Holy Spirit. We shall easily drift back to a life of spiritual indiscipline and self-pleasing if we do not maintain that conscious daily offering of ourselves to God, body, soul and spirit.

> I do not set aside the grace of God, for if righteousness could be gained through the law, Christ died for nothing! (Gal. 2:21).

Do not set the grace of God aside by self-dependence, or by thinking that God can be pleased through ritual observance. Do not set His grace aside by thinking you can do for Him and achieve for Him.

Rather, let your life now be lived in dependence upon Him, the One who died for you so that, although you know well your human weakness and frailty, yet you do not need to depend upon those human resources. Instead, you rely

The New and Living Way

upon His strength, His life, His love, His power, His Spirit, the work of His cross – all made available to you by His grace.

The answer to the dilemma is not a solution, but a Person – the Lord Jesus Christ. Paul asks "*who* shall deliver me?" It is through what He has done that we are saved from our wretchedness. And it is because He has been glorified that into us comes the Person of the Holy Spirit. Now we can look within to His resources, to His life in us.

The measure of our self-dependence is shown by our imagining that, unless we are active and doing, God will not be at work. It is this attitude that has given rise to the popular saying: "God helps those who help themselves." What a denial of the Good News of Jesus Christ!

The truth is that God helps those who know they cannot help themselves, that all their efforts to help themselves end in futility.

If we could achieve anything for God, we would want some, if not all, of the credit for what *we* have done. We would want the glory, the recognition and the praise – even though we might put on the pious front and say that we wanted nothing for ourselves. God has ordained that *He* shall receive *all* the credit, *all* the glory and *all* the praise, for apart from Him we can do nothing.

And there is always the fear that if we do not initiate action and busy ourselves for God, then our lives will be wasted. That is another indication of the arrogant pride of men! Do you imagine God would waste those who are His, to whom He has given the life of His Son, in whom His Spirit lives for His glory, when His purpose is fruitfulness for His children?

No, God will use effectively all who are His. But His measure of usefulness is very different from our own. To be effectively used by God to further the work of His Kingdom on earth involves living in loving obedience to the initiative of His Spirit, recognising that we have died to self, but live 'in Christ Jesus'.

Your words of faith: "MAY GOD HIMSELF, THE GOD OF PEACE, SANCTIFY YOU THROUGH AND THROUGH." "MAY YOUR WHOLE

SPIRIT, SOUL AND BODY BE KEPT BLAMELESS AT THE COMING OF OUR LORD JESUS CHRIST." "THE ONE WHO CALLS YOU IS FAITHFUL AND HE WILL DO IT."

35

THE JOY THAT IS SET BEFORE US

We have had to speak of many things that appear difficult to us: denying of self, obedience, yielding our independence to God, seeing that the life of the soul and body is submitted to the Spirit – and so on. What we must not lose sight of is the joy that will be ours as more of the Lord Jesus is expressed in our lives.

We imagine that self-expression will make us happy and fulfilled people. Nothing could be further from the truth. The Christian will radiate the true love and joy of Jesus as he seeks to reflect Him rather than the life of self.

Jesus is our joy and, when the Holy Spirit comes upon us, He gives us the anointing of joy that was upon the Lord Himself.

> Therefore God, your God, has set you above your companions by anointing you with the oil of joy (Heb. 1:9).

Joy is one of the characteristics of the Spirit-filled Christian. He rejoices in his Lord and he delights to do His will. The joy goes hand in hand with the peace he knows in his heart because he is accepted and loved by God and is concerned to be obedient to Him.

Along with the joy and the peace goes the love that God has put into his heart and that is to be expressed in his life. The life of the Spirit is a life of love and joy and peace. Living in the power of the new nature enables these qualities to be enjoyed and expressed in the life of the believer.

Together with the love go the faith and hope that come from God. Being at peace with God means that the Christian can live in faith and confidence in the love, the mercy and goodness of God towards him.

> Dear friends, if our hearts do not condemn us, we have confidence before God and receive from him anything we ask, because we obey his commands and do what pleases him (1 John 3:21-22).

That is the reward of faith and obedience: to know that God will give you whatever you ask in fulfilment of His promises. John continues:

> And this is his command: to believe in the name of his Son, Jesus Christ, and to love one another as he commanded us. Those who obey his commands live in him, and he in them. And this is how we know that he lives in us: We know it by the Spirit he gave us (1 John 3:23-24).

And the Christian has the sure hope that God will complete the good work that He has begun in him. He will live and reign with His Saviour and Lord in all eternity.

Let the last word centre upon Him, the one in whom we live by God's own gracious act.

THE SUPREMACY OF CHRIST

> He is the image of the invisible God, the firstborn over all creation. For by him all things were created: things in heaven and on earth, visible and invisible, whether thrones or powers or rulers or authorities; all things were created by him and for him (Col. 1:15-16).

God the Father is revealed through His Son. Jesus shows us the graciousness, the love and the mercy of God as well as His almighty power. It is through Jesus that all things were created: "In the beginning was the Word, and the Word was with God, and the Word was God. He was with God in the beginning. Through him all things were made; without him nothing was made that has been made. In him was life, and that life was the light of men" (John 1:1-4).

Creation exists not only as the work of God, but also for

the glory of God and His Son: "all things were created by him and for him."

He is before all things, and in him all things hold together (Col. 17). God not only created through His Word, Jesus; He sustains His creation by that same Word. "The Son is the radiance of God's glory and the exact representation of his being, sustaining all things by his powerful word. After he had provided purification for sins, he sat down at the right hand of the Majesty in heaven" (Heb. 1:13).

> And he is the head of the body, the church; he is the beginning and the firstborn from among the dead, so that in everything he might have the supremacy (Col. 1:18).

Jesus was the first to be raised from the dead. All those who belong to Him shall be raised with Him. He is the Lord who will always have supremacy, and when He returns everyone and everything that does not acknowledge His authority will pass away. In the new heaven and the new earth that God promises, He will reign without opposition from any spiritual or mortal beings.

Jesus is the head of the body of believers who live in Him, the true and living Church, those who already acknowledge His supremacy and bow to His authority in their lives.

> For God was pleased to have all his fulness dwell in him and through him to reconcile to himself all things, whether things on earth or things in heaven, by making peace through his blood, shed on the cross (Col. 1:19) –20).

Jesus is fully God as well as fully man. In Him, the fulness of God's life exists, and we live in Him and have come to fulness of life in Him once we have put our faith in Him. He died on the cross "to reconcile to himself all things". He made peace between rebellious creation and its Creator, "through his blood, shed on the cross". God's purpose is finally "to bring all things in heaven and on earth together under one head, even Christ" (Eph. 1:10). "God placed all things under his feet and appointed him to be head over everything for the church, which is his body, the fulness of him who fills everything in every way" (Eph. 1:22–23).

The Joy that is set Before Us 301

Jesus reigns supreme for the benefit of the Church, those who live in Him. We can enjoy fulness of life because we have turned our lives over to Him and acknowledge His Lordship.

> Once you were alienated from God and were enemies in your minds because of your evil behaviour. But now he has reconciled you by Christ's physical body through death to present you holy in his sight, without blemish and free from accusation – if you continue in your faith, established and firm, not moved from the hope held out the gospel (Col. 1:21–23).

You are in the midst of God's purpose. He has already reconciled you to Himself "by Christ's physical body through death". You have passed already from death to life. And He will "present you holy in His sight, without blemish and free from accusation".

God will have then perfected us as His holy, set-apart people. Everything about us will reflect His truth and glory. The enemy will not be able to make any accusation against us. He was dismissed from heaven because, when he rebelled against God's authority, he became unholy. He will not be able to claim that justice demands that we too shall be cast from God's presence, because we shall be made perfect in holiness.

Christ is the Head of the body of believers that will be presented to the Father, perfected through His blood. What a mighty privilege to be part of that body, of that purpose that God has! What a joy to know that this 'living hope' will indeed be fulfilled. The body cannot be separated from the head. Because He reigns in glory, God has already "raised us up with Christ and seated us with him in the heavenly realms in Christ Jesus, in order that in the coming ages he might show the incomparable riches of his grace expressed in his kindness to us in Christ Jesus" (Eph. 2:6).

God sees His purpose already fulfilled and we are part of that purpose. For our part, we need to continue in our faith in Jesus, "established and firm, not moved from the hope held out in the gospel" – no matter to what tests of faith we are subjected.

Truth about you: "YOU WERE CREATED BY HIM AND FOR HIM." "YOU HAVE BEEN RECONCILED TO GOD BY CHRIST'S PHYSICAL BODY." "YOU HAVE PEACE WITH GOD THROUGH HIS BLOOD, SHED ON THE CROSS." "YOU WILL BE PRESENTED HOLY IN HIS SIGHT, WITHOUT BLEMISH AND FREE FROM ACCUSATION." "YOU ARE RAISED UP WITH CHRIST AND SEATED WITH HIM IN THE HEAVENLY REALMS IN CHRIST JESUS."

Kingdom Faith Resources Ltd
resourcing revival to the nations through

Teaching Books and Tapes
by Colin Urquhart and others

Live Worship Recordings and Music Books

Way Of The Spirit Bible Study Material
*includes a Bible Reading Course
by John McKay*

Children's Ministry Materials
by Peter & Diane Hellyer

For more information contact
Kingdom Faith Resources Ltd
Foundry Lane, Horsham, West Sussex, RH13 5PX, UK
Tel: 01403 211505 Fax: 01403 218463
E-mail: mailorder@kingdomfaith.org.uk

Friends Of Jesus

"My command is this: Love each other as I have loved you. Greater love has no man than this, that he lay down his life for his friends. You are my friends if you do what I command. I no longer call you servants, because a servant does not know his Master's business. Instead, I have called you friends, for everything I have learned from my Father I have made known to you. You did not choose me, but I chose you and appointed you to go and bear fruit - fruit that will last. Then the Father will give you whatever you ask in my name. This is my command: Love each other." John 15:12-17

Imagine thousands, tens of thousands, millions even, of Christians around the world, linked together in a common bond of love and commitment to Jesus Christ.

Jesus wants you for His friend!

For more information contact
Friends Of Jesus International
PO Box 95, Horsham, West Sussex, RH13 5YA, UK
Tel: 01403 258040 Fax: 01403 258040
E-mail: info@friendsofjesus.net
Web-site: http:\\www.friendsofjesus.net